ISRAEL AT SIXTY

Also by Deborah Hart Strober and Gerald S. Strober

Giuliani: Flawed or Flawless: The Oral Biography

Billy Graham: A Narrative and Oral Biography

His Holiness the Dalai Lama: The Oral Biography

The Monarchy: An Oral Biography of Queen Elizabeth II

Reagan: The Man and His Presidency

Nixon: An Oral History of His Presidency

"Let Us Begin Anew": An Oral History of the Kennedy Presidency

ISRAEL AT SIXTY

A Pictorial and Oral History of a Nation Reborn

DEBORAH HART STROBER AND GERALD S. STROBER

John Wiley & Sons, Inc.

Published by John Wiley & Sons, Inc., Hoboken, New Jersey
Published simultaneously in Canada

Design and composition by Navta Associates, Inc.

For general information about our other products and services, please contact our Customer Care Department within the United States at (800) 762-2974, outside the United States at (317) 572-3993 or fax (317) 572-4002.

Wiley also publishes its books in a variety of electronic formats. Some content that appears in print may not be available in electronic books. For more information about Wiley products, visit our web site at www.wiley.com.

Library of Congress Cataloging-in-Publication Data:

Strober, Deborah H. (Deborah Hart), date.
  Israel at sixty : a pictorial and oral history of a nation reborn
/ Deborah Hart Strober and Gerald S. Strober.
      p. cm.
  Includes index.
  ISBN 978-0-470-05314-0 (cloth)
  1. Israel—History. 2. Arab-Israeli conflict.   I. Strober, Gerald S.   II. Title.
  DS126.5.S77 2007
  956.9405—dc22

                                                    2007026435

Printed in the United States of America

10 9 8 7 6 5 4 3 2 1

In loving memory of our nephews
David Adam Civan and Marc Samuel Hochstein

CONTENTS

PREFACE

Sixty years after Israel's founding, new and ominous challenges loom on the Jewish State's near horizon, not the least of which include renewed fighting with Hezbollah and the threat posed by Iran's nuclear program.

Internally, Israelis' confidence in their political leaders and institutions has been severely shaken by financial and sexual scandals involving the nation's former president, prime minister, former justice minister, tax authorities, and police. Of even graver concern is the sense that the IDF (Israel Defense Forces), the nation's protector since its first hours of statehood, has suffered a crisis of confidence as a result of its encounter with Hezbollah.

For those in the religious camp, comfort can be taken in the promise of the Psalmist that "He who keeps Israel will neither slumber nor sleep." For many of the 80 percent of the population on the other side of the religious-secular divide, there are renewed calls for changes in the country's political system, especially in the institution of a more representative, constituent-responsible legislature.

Taken against the context of more than three millennia of Jewish experience in the Land of Israel, sixty years would seem almost a biblical watch in the night. But what a sixty years they have been!

ACKNOWLEDGMENTS

We could not have embarked on *Israel at Sixty: An Oral History of a Nation Reborn* without the willingness of our interviewees to share their recollections of life before and since May 14, 1948—in many cases, painful memories of persecution in Europe during the Holocaust on their way to redemption in the Jewish state.

Compiling a book that contains many photographs can be daunting. But thanks to the cooperation of the Israel Government Press Office and to individual interviewees who opened their albums to us, we believe that we have been well served. In the latter case, we especially appreciate the efforts of Deborah's brother, Joseph Hochstein, an American-born journalist and émigré to Israel, who assisted us as we made our way through the Press Office's vast visual archive, which contains notations written in Hebrew.

In the United States, we appreciate the assistance of our cousin Scott Strober, who facilitated our interview with his colleague Simcha Waisman.

While we conducted most of our interviews in the English language, in two instances, those of Matityahu "Mati" Drobles and Muki Betser, our interviewees preferred to be questioned and to respond in Hebrew. We wish to thank two Israelis who assisted us: Batia Leshem, translating for Mr. Drobles, and Joseph Hochstein, for Colonel Betser.

At John Wiley & Sons, we wish to express our appreciation to our editor, Hana Lane, who responded to our suggestion that we include *some* photographs in our sixtieth anniversary tribute to the Jewish state, "How about *fifty*?" On the editorial side, we deeply appreciate Hana's excellent suggestions as she patiently guided us in condensing a century of history—pre- and postindependence—into a manageable manuscript. We also appreciate the efforts of assistant editor Camille Acker and production editor Kimberly Monroe-Hill.

We are truly fortunate in having a circle of friends who have supported us in all of our literary undertakings. They include Pauline and Morris Borsuk; Bonnie Cutler and her husband, Mark Heutlinger; Evelyn and Raphael Rothstein; Marcia and Rabbi A. James Rudin; Sarah and the late Ze'ev Shiff; Florence and Harry Taubenfeld; Christine and Eric Valentine; Elaine and Martin Zuckerbrod; and Sheila and Herbert Zweibon.

And how could we have made it through these many months without the devotion of our family? We want to express our deep appreciation to our siblings and their partners, Judith and Dr. Mortimer Civan; Mindy and Myron Strober; Joseph Hochstein; and Ruth Hockstein, all of whom are deeply committed to the survival of the Jewish state.

Through our children, we are privileged to know and to count among our close friends in Israel, Dorrit and Meir Nocham, the parents of Jeremy's wife, Gabi; Daphne and Hummarde Sterling, the parents of Lori's husband, Bryan; and Gene Meyers, the father of Robin's friend Michelle, and Gene's wife, Jan Book.

Finally, we want to pay tribute to our beloved, always supportive children and their partners: Jeremy Benjamin and Gabi, the parents of Eyal Jonathan and Ran Michael; Lori and Bryan Sterling, the parents of Kai Wesley Philip and Marley Grace; Jonathan Strober; and Robin Strober and Michelle Meyers.

CHRONOLOGY OF THE STATE OF ISRAEL

1200 B.C.E. Jews arrive in the Land of Israel.

990 B.C.E. King David captures Jerusalem.

950 B.C.E. King Solomon builds the First Temple.

586 B.C.E. Babylonians destroy the Temple and take Jews into exile.

538 B.C.E. Jews return to Israel.

515 B.C.E. The Second Temple is built.

170–164 B.C.E. The Maccabean Revolt takes place.

63 B.C.E. Pompey, a Roman general, conquers Jerusalem.

4 B.C.E. The birth of Jesus occurs.

66–70 C.E. Jerusalem and the Second Temple are destroyed following a Jewish revolt.

73 C.E. Masada falls.

132–135 C.E. Romans end the Bar Kochba revolt and send most Jews into exile.

1891–1903 The First Aliyah (immigration to Eretz Israel) takes place, following pogroms in Russia.

1896 Theodore Herzl publishes *Der Judenstat*.

1897 The first Zionist Congress meets in Basel, Switzerland.

1904–1926 The Second and Third Aliyahs occur.

1917 The Balfour Declaration calls for the creation of the Jewish national home in Palestine.

1919 Britain is awarded mandate over Palestine.

1929 Arabs riot in Jerusalem and Hebron.

1926–1935 The Fourth Aliyah takes place.

1933 Adolf Hitler comes to power in Germany.

1937 The Peel Commission recommends partitioning Palestine into Jewish and Arab areas.

1939 The British White Paper sharply limits Jewish immigration to Palestine.

1939–1945 In World War II, six million Jews die in the Nazi Holocaust.

1945 Jewish underground groups intensify operations aimed at driving the British from Palestine.

November 29, 1947 The United Nations General Assembly votes to partition Palestine into Jewish and Arab states.

May 14, 1948 As the British withdraw, the State of Israel is established and is immediately attacked by the armies of Egypt, Iraq, Jordan, Lebanon, and Syria.

January 1949 An armistice ends Israel's War of Independence; the Arab world continues to refuse to recognize Israel's existence.

1956 Following the closing of the Suez Canal and the Straits of Tiran to Israeli shipping, French, British, and Israeli forces invade Egypt; later, Israel withdraws from the Sinai.

1964 The Palestine Liberation Organization is founded.

1967 The Six-Day War erupts after Egypt moves troops into the Sinai and closes the Straits of Tiran, and Syria moves along the Golan Heights. Israel launches a preemptive strike, and the war results in Israel's conquest of the Sinai, the Golan Heights, the West Bank, and the Old City of Jerusalem.

1970 In the War of Attrition, Egypt and Israel trade artillery attacks along the Suez Canal.

1973 In the three-week-long Yom Kippur War, Egypt and Syria launch attacks in the Sinai and on the Golan Heights; Israel, after initial reverses, defeats the Arab armies.

May 1977 Menachem Begin's Likud Party wins the election, ending twenty-nine years of Labor Party rule.

November 1977 Egypt's president, Anwar Sadat, visits Jerusalem.

March 1979 Sadat and Begin sign the Camp David Accords, Israel's first peace treaty with an Arab nation.

June 1981 Israel destroys Iraq's nuclear reactor.

June 1982 Israel launches Operation Peace for the Galilee and drives the PLO from Lebanon.

June 1982–1984 The First Lebanon War takes place.

1985 Israel withdraws from most of Lebanon.

1987–1993 The First Palestinian Intifada begins.

1994 Israel and Jordan sign a peace treaty.

November 4, 1995 Prime Minister Yitzhak Rabin is assassinated by a Jewish extremist.

September 2000 The Second Palestinian Intifada begins.

2005 Israeli settlers are removed from Gaza.

2005 Ariel Sharon founds the Kadima Party.

December 2005 Prime Minister Sharon suffers a minor stroke.

January 4, 2006 Prime Minister Sharon suffers an incapacitating stroke and is succeeded by Deputy Prime Minister Ehud Olmert.

January 2006 Hamas, an extremist organization that refuses to recognize Israel's existence, wins a majority of votes in elections held in the Palestinian Authority.

March 2006 The Kadima Party, with Prime Minister Olmert as its leader, wins the parliamentary election.

July–August 2006 The Second Lebanon War takes place.

May 2007 An Israeli government commission releases a report on the conduct of the Lebanon War.

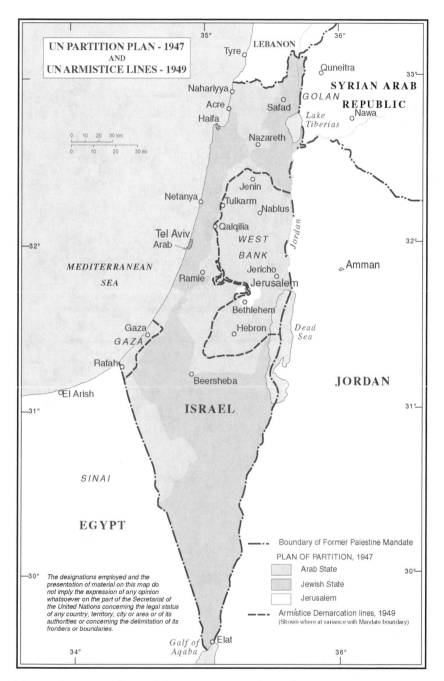

The U.N. Partition Plan and the U.N. Armistice lines of 1949.

THE INTERVIEWEES

Shlomo Ariav was born in Vienna, where he joined Betar, a Zionist youth organization founded by the Revisionist leader Vladimir (Ze'ev) Jabotinsky, at the age of ten. Immediately following his immigration to Palestine in 1939, he joined the Irgun, a right-wing, paramilitary underground organization founded in 1931 and known formally as the pre-state underground Irgun Zvai Leumi ("The National Military Organization"), also called Etzel, the Hebrew language acronym for Irgun Zvai Leumi. In 1946, following his World War II service with the Jewish Brigade, he met and married a young army driver named Tzipora. In April 1948, as head of the Irgun's Medical Corps, he helped to rescue fellow members of the underground wounded in the firing on the Irgun ship the *Altalena*. Following the establishment of the State of Israel, he was sent by Betar in 1950 as its first emissary to South America. In 1979, Mr. Ariav was appointed co-chair of Keren Kayemeth Le Israel (the Jewish National Fund). He was interviewed on February 14, 2007, in Binyamina, Israel.

    Tzipora Ariav left her native Poland in 1938 at the age of ten. A driver during World War II with the Jewish Brigade, she saw service in Egypt. During the battle to oust the British from Palestine, she assisted the Irgun on many occasions, and in 1946, she married Shlomo Ariav. A student of agriculture, she created the lovely tree- and plant-filled compound in Binyamina where the Ariavs have lived since their marriage. She was interviewed on February 14, 2007, in Binyamina, Israel.

    Yehuda Avner was born in Manchester, United Kingdom, and immigrated to Palestine in 1947. Following the establishment of the State of Israel, he served in a variety of governmental positions, including as a political adviser to Prime Minister Menachem Begin, as well as helping to write his speeches, from 1977 to 1981. In 1982, Mr. Avner returned to the

United Kingdom when he was appointed by the prime minister to serve for six years as Israel's ambassador to the Court of St. James's. He was interviewed on February 11, 2007, in Jerusalem, Israel.

Uri Avneri, a German-born immigrant to Palestine in the late 1930s, joined the Irgun as a teenager but later left the movement. A soldier in the War of Independence, following the conflict he wrote two books about his experiences, *On the Heels of the Philistines* and *The Other Side of the Coin*, and in 1949 was an article and editorial writer with *Ha'aretz*. In 1950, Mr. Avneri purchased and revamped a magazine, *Our World*, serving as its editor in chief for forty years, until 1990. The creator and Knesset (parliament) candidate in 1965 of the political party New Force, he was elected to that body, serving for ten years that comprised three periods between 1965 and 1980. He was the founder of the Peace Bloc in 1994. He was interviewed on February 19, 2007, in Tel Aviv, Israel.

Yossi Ben-Aharon was born in Jerusalem but spent much of his childhood living in Port Said, Egypt. A career diplomat since 1956 with Israel's Ministry of Foreign Affairs, he also served as a policy adviser to Foreign Minister Yitzhak Shamir, from 1980 to 1986; as the director general of the Prime Minister's Bureau during the administration of Prime Minister Yitzhak Shamir, from 1986 to 1992; and as the head of Israel's delegation in negotiations with Syria in 1991. Mr. Ben-Aharon is currently a lecturer at the College of Judea and Samaria. He was interviewed on February 18, 2007, in Jerusalem, Israel.

Muki Betser, a colonel, retired, in the Israel Defense Forces, took part in a daring raid in 1973 on Beirut, Lebanon, in which they killed terrorists. He and Ehud Barak dressed up as a "couple" to disguise themselves. He was later the deputy commander of the mission that on July 4, 1976, rescued 105 Jewish hostages, passengers on an Air France Airbus that had been hijacked to Uganda and held by terrorists at the Entebbe Airport. Colonel Betzer currently serves as an educational and social activist. He was interviewed on February 25, 2007, in Herzliya Pituach, Israel.

Bobby Brown, an immigrant to Israel from the United States in 1978, resides with his wife in the West Bank settlement of Tekoah, where both religious and nonreligious Israelis live side by side, and where both he and his wife were elected mayor. Mr. Brown also served as an officer of the Jewish Agency for Israel, as an aide to Prime Minister Benjamin Netanyahu, and most recently with the World Jewish Congress. He is now the adviser to the treasurer of the Jewish Agency for Israel. He was interviewed on February 21, 2007, in Jerusalem, Israel.

Amira Dotan, a career officer in the Israeli Defense Forces, was in

1987 the first woman to be appointed a general officer of that army. Now retired from the military, General Dotan, at the behest of her mentor Prime Minister Ariel Sharon, ran for the Knesset on the Kadima Party slate in 2005 and was elected. She was interviewed on February 25, 2007, in Tel Aviv, Israel.

Matityahu "Mati" Drobles was born in Warsaw, Poland, in 1933. In 1941, at the age of nine, he was forced into the Warsaw Ghetto. He escaped into the woods in 1942 with his older sister and two brothers, and they hid there until the end of World War II. Following his emigration to Argentina in 1946, Mr. Drobles made aliyah to Israel in 1950, where for eighteen years he served as chairman of the Rural Settlements Division of the World Zionist Organization. He is presently the chairman of the Central Zionist Archive. He was interviewed on October 31, 2006, in Jerusalem, Israel.

Rafi Eitan served as an adviser to Prime Minister Yitzhak Rabin on defense and security; in addition, he was a Mossad operative, a member of the Defense Committee of Israel's Ministry of Defense, an adviser to Prime Minister Shimon Peres, and a director of LAKAM (Office of Scientific Liaison). Mr. Eitan, the founder and chairman of Israel's Pensioner's Party, is also an international businessman dealing in agricultural products. He was interviewed on February 13, 2007, in Tel Aviv, Israel.

Akiva Eldar was born in Haifa in 1945. A journalist with *Ha'aretz*, he served as that newspaper's diplomatic correspondent from 1983 to 1993 and as U.S. bureau chief and Washington correspondent from 1993 to 1996; he is currently the chief political columnist and editorial writer. Mr. Eldar also lectures at Tel Aviv University's School of Journalism, is a consultant to CBS News, and is a frequent guest on major networks in the United States, Canada, Europe, and Israel. He was interviewed on February 26, 2007, in Netanya, Israel.

Arie Lova Eliav, an educator, a diplomat, and a politician who at one time was expected to succeed Golda Meir as prime minister, was born in Russia and immigrated to Palestine in 1925, at the age of three. Having joined the Haganah, the pre-state underground Jewish army, in 1936, he served in the British army's Jewish Brigade during World War II and in the Israel Defense Forces during Israel's War of Independence. He was a participant from 1945 to 1947 in the Mossad's illegal immigration operations and served from 1958 to 1960 as first secretary in Israel's embassy in Moscow. From 1949 to 1953, he was the assistant head of the Jewish Agency for Israel's Settlement Department. And for two years, beginning in 1962, he headed Israel's mission to aid earthquake-stricken Iran. He was a member of the Knesset from 1965 to 1979, during which time he broke with Prime Minister Golda Meir over her Palestinian policy and in 1977 founded Sheli, the Israel Peace Party, and again was a member of the Knesset from 1988 to 1992. In 1976 and 1977, he was a participant in early talks with the Palestine Liberation Organization. He later served as a negotiator in the prisoner exchange following the First Lebanon War. As an educator, Mr. Eliav was the founder in 1982 of the Nitzana Negev educational project. In 2000, he became the head of the Labor Party's Ideological Center. He was interviewed on February 15, 2007, in Tel Aviv, Israel.

Reverend Jerry Falwell, a staunch supporter of the State of Israel, was the founder and pastor of the Thomas Road Baptist Church, established in 1956 in Lynchburg, Virginia. Following his establishment in 1967 of the Lynchburg Christian Academy, Dr. Falwell realized a long-held dream when in 1971 he founded Liberty Baptist College, now Liberty University, where he served as chancellor. In 1979, he created and was president of the Moral Majority, which existed until the late 1980s and played a major role in getting out the vote for Ronald Reagan in the 1980 presidential race. Mr. Falwell was interviewed on March 27, 2007, by telephone.

Abraham Foxman was born in Warsaw, Poland, in 1940 and was hidden by his nanny, a Roman Catholic woman. Reunited with his parents after the war and brought to the United States, Mr. Foxman later went to work at the Anti-Defamation League, becoming that organization's associate national director and then succeeding to the position of national director. He was interviewed on March 14, 2007, in New York.

Raanan Gissin, a reserve colonel in the Israel Defense Forces, was responsible for servicing the foreign press during the First Lebanon War, in 1982; in the First Intifada, in the 1980s; and in the First Gulf War, in 1991. A special adviser to the Israeli delegation to the Madrid Peace Conference in 1991, Colonel Gissin served as the senior public affairs adviser and spokesman during the administration of Prime Minister Ariel Sharon. He was interviewed on February 13, 2007, in Tel Aviv, Israel.

Dr. Ronald S. Godwin, a staunch supporter of the State of Israel and a close associate of the Reverend Jerry Falwell, served as the executive vice president of the Moral Majority from its founding by Reverend Falwell in 1979 until that organization's disbanding in the late 1980s. Dr. Godwin left Lynchburg for a time to serve as the senior vice president of the *Washington Times*. On his return, he was appointed president of the Jerry Falwell Ministries and in 2006 was made the executive vice president of Liberty University. He was interviewed on March 27, 2007, by telephone.

Rav (Rabbi) Shalom Gold, an immigrant to Israel in 1982 from the United States, is the founder of Yeshivat Bircas HaTorah, located in Jerusalem. The rabbi emeritus of Kehilat Zichron Yosef, in the Har Nof neighborhood of Jerusalem, Rav Gold was also the Rosh Yeshiva (Head of Yeshiva) of the Rabbi Akiva Yeshiva, in Jerusalem. He is currently the dean of the Jerusalem College for Adults. He was interviewed on February 21, 2007, in Jerusalem, Israel.

Eitan Haber, while serving in the Israel Defense Forces as a military correspondent, was assigned to interview the head of the Northern Command, General Yitzhak Rabin, and remained at the latter's side as an adviser and a friend throughout Rabin's career as defense minister and prime minister. Mr. Haber was at the prime minister's side on the night of his assassination and at his state funeral delivered the emotionally charged recitation of the words of the "Song of Peace," which the prime minister had sung at a peace rally just moments before he was gunned down. Mr. Haber is now an international business consultant. He was interviewed on February 16, 2007, in Herzliya Pituach, Israel.

Joseph M. Hochstein, a writer, an editor, and the brother of Deborah Hart Strober, is a resident of Tel Aviv. He came to Israel on aliyah in 1983 from Washington, D.C., where he published the *Jewish Week*, a newspaper. He was a managing editor of the *Congressional Quarterly* and worked for three newspapers in the United States, as well as being the information chief of a blue-ribbon U.S. government commission. His daughter, Michal, who founded and operates the Lev Ehad Preschool, and his son Tobias, a cinematographer, live with their families in Tel Aviv. Mr. Hochstein's eldest son, Marc, a paratrooper, was killed in 1985 at the age of twenty, while serving in the Israel Defense Forces in Lebanon. Mr. Hochstein was interviewed on March 1, 2007, in Tel Aviv, Israel.

Malcolm Hoenlein is the grandson of Jews murdered during the Holocaust. A fervent Zionist and a frequent visitor to Israel, he was the founding executive director of the Greater New York Conference on Soviet Jewry and the founding executive director of the Jewish Community Relations Council of Greater New York. Since 1986, Mr. Hoenlein has served as the executive vice chairman of the Conference of Presidents of Major American Jewish Organizations. He was interviewed on January 11, 2007, in New York City.

Yehiel Kadishai, born in Israel to immigrant parents from Warsaw, Poland, was a member of the pre-state underground Irgun Zvai Leumi. A participant in the British embassy bombing in Rome, Italy, in 1946 and the commander of the Italian Section of the *Altalena* in 1948, he later served as the long-time personal aide to Menachem Begin. Upon Mr. Begin's election in 1977 as prime minister, Mr. Kadishai was appointed director of the Prime Minister's Bureau. He also served in that capacity during the administration of Prime Minister Yitzhak Shamir. He was interviewed on November 3, 2006, in Tel Aviv, Israel.

Shmuel Katz left South Africa for Palestine in 1936, during the British Mandate. Known in the pre-state underground and later, among friends, as "Meuki," he served as a member of Irgun Zvai Leumi's High Command. Following Israel's declaration of independence in 1948, he was elected as a member of the first Knesset. A founding member of the Land of Israel Movement, he served from 1977 to 1979 as a cabinet member and the adviser to Prime Minister Menachem Begin on overseas information. A publisher and a prolific author, who wrote a biography of Revisionist visionary Ze'ev Jabotinsky, he has also been a columnist with the *Jerusalem Post*.

Joshua Matza, a member of the thirteenth generation of his family to reside in the land of Israel, joined the underground in his early teens, serving with the Stern Group. Elected to the Knesset in 1984 on the Likud ticket, he served for eighteen years, until 2002, and was a close associate of Menachem Begin. In 1996, he was appointed minister of health. Following his distinguished political career in Israel, he was appointed by Prime Minister Ariel Sharon to serve as the president and chief executive officer of the Development Corporation for Israel, known as Israel Bonds, in North and South America, with offices in New York. He was interviewed on May 16, 2006, in New York City.

Dan Pattir, a journalist and a correspondent, served as chief of the Prime Minister's Bureau in the first administration of Yitzhak Rabin and as spokesman in the administration of Menachem Begin. Mr. Pattir currently serves as an official with the Abraham Fund. On February 2, 2007, he was interviewed with his wife since 1956, Professor Yael Pattir, in Ramat Aviv, Israel.

Yael Pattir achieved officer rank in the Israel Defense Forces, where she served in the office of deputy chief of staff Yigael Yadin. A professor of classics in civilian life, Professor Pattir taught at Tel Aviv University for more than thirty years. On February 2, 2007, she was interviewed with her husband since 1956, the journalist Dan Pattir, in Ramat Aviv, Israel.

Natan Sharansky, né Anatoly, the Jewish activist, refusenik, and later prisoner of conscience in the Soviet gulag from 1978 to 1986, was finally freed following a long campaign spearheaded by his wife, Avital, and brought to Israel on February 11, 1986. Entering the political arena, Mr. Sharansky was the founder in 1995 of the Yisrael Be'aliyah Party; he served as a member of the Knesset from 1996 to 2003 and again in 2006 and was minister of industry and trade from 1996 to 1999, internal affairs from 1999 to 2000, and housing and construction from 2001 to 2003; he was deputy prime minister during that period and minister without portfolio from 2003 to 2005. He is currently the head of the Shalem Center's Institute for International and Middle Eastern Studies. He was interviewed on February 18, 2007, in Jerusalem, Israel.

Moshe Sharon is a professor of Islamic and Middle Eastern studies and the chair of Bahá'í studies at the Hebrew University of Jerusalem. The author of numerous articles and scholarly papers on the history of Islam, he has warned of the growing power of Islam for more than thirty years. A retired colonel in the Israel Defense Forces, Dr. Sharon served as the Defense Forces' head of the Department of Arab Affairs, as an adviser to Israel's minister of defense, as a special envoy to Lebanon's Shi'ite community, and as an adviser to Prime Minister Menachem Begin on Arab affairs during Israeli-Egyptian negotiations. He was interviewed on February 11, 2007, in Jerusalem, Israel.

Shabtai Shavit was born in Haifa to Zionist parents who had immigrated to Palestine in 1936, but he was raised in the town of Nesher, which lay between two Arab villages. Following extensive studies of the Arabic language and history, in secondary and high school and at the Hebrew University of Jerusalem, Mr. Shavit joined Israel's famed security service, the Mossad, becoming its head in 1989 and retiring in 1996. He was interviewed on February 27, 2007, in Herzliya Pituach, Israel.

Zalman Shoval, an immigrant to Israel in 1937 from the then Free City of Danzig, East Prussia, was a close associate of Moshe Dayan in the newly formed Rafi Party (the Worker's List of Israel) during the 1960s. He was a member of the Knesset from 1970 to 1981 and again from 1988 to 1990 and served as Israel's ambassador to the United States twice, from 1990 to 1993 and from 1998 to 2000. An international businessman, Ambassador Shoval is currently the president of the Israel Chamber of Commerce. He was interviewed on February 20, 2007, in Tel Aviv, Israel.

Bracha Stock, born to parents who made aliyah from Poland in the 1920s, returned there with them for four years due to harsh economic conditions in Palestine. Following the establishment of the Jewish state, after attending a teacher's college, she worked as an educator, later with Israel's Department of Culture, and for a time for the newspaper of the Mapai Party. Visiting the United States in 1950, she secured a position with the Voice of America. Hoping to study journalism and in search of a scholarship, she met her future husband, Dr. Ernest Stock, when she sought his help in doing so. She was interviewed on February 12, 2007, in Tel Aviv, Israel.

Ernest Stock, Ph.D., a German-born immigrant, first to the United States, where he attended Princeton University, and then to Israel, where he was a journalist with the *Jerusalem Post*, returned to the United States for a time. Deciding to devote his career to serving the Jewish community, he met his future wife while employed in New York as the assistant to the director of the Hillel Foundations. On the newly married Stocks' return to Israel, he began his many years as an official with the Jewish Agency for Israel and became a prolific author. He was interviewed on February 12, 2007, in Tel Aviv, Israel.

Simcha Waisman was born in Palestine in 1945 to immigrants from Europe. Joining the Israeli navy in 1960, at the age of fifteen, he engaged in highly classified intelligence work and served in the Six-Day War in 1967. After his emigration to the United States in 1969, he was the owner of a print shop in the borough of Queens in New York City for thirty-five years. Following his retirement during the summer of 2006, Mr. Waisman became a community activist, serving as a volunteer with the Richmond Hill Block Association. He was interviewed on January 4, 2007, in Queens, New York.

INTRODUCTION:
THE ANCIENT LAND
OF ISRAEL AND THE MODERN
JEWISH STATE

On the afternoon of May 14, 1948, David Ben-Gurion, overcome with emotion in anticipation of what he was about to do, mopped his moist brow and mounted the platform in Tel Aviv's Opera House to read the Proclamation of Independence of the New Jewish State, to be known as Israel. For the leader of the Yishuv, the Jewish community of Palestine, and the people who had more recently made aliyah (to immigrate to Israel), many of them Holocaust survivors, that moment marked the fulfillment of the Jewish people's centuries-long yearning for Zion.

The terms "Zionism" and "Zionist" were coined in 1890 by the Vienna-born Nathan Birnbaum (1864–1937), the first term describing fervor for Eretz Israel, the Land of Israel, and the late-nineteenth-century movement for return to the Jewish homeland, and the latter term, the person expressing that fervor. Both words have ancient roots and modern applications: "Zion," which is mentioned more than seven hundred times in the Hebrew Bible, has for millennia been regarded as being synonymous with Jerusalem, as expressed in the Jewish people's yearning for their homeland through times of exile and repression. This yearning is articulated by Jews throughout the world annually at Passover as they read the passage from the Haggadah "Next year in Jerusalem."

Moshe Sharon, historian of medieval Islam; professor, Islamic and Middle Eastern Studies, and chair, Bahá'í Studies, Hebrew University

of Jerusalem; colonel (retired), Israel Defense Forces, and head, Department of Arab affairs; adviser to Prime Minister Menachem Begin on Arab Affairs during Israeli-Egyptian negotiations This prayer has been said by the same Jew, whether he is in Jerusalem or in Los Angeles. Therefore, the establishment of the State of Israel is, as far as the *Jews* are concerned, definitely as far as many *Christians* are concerned, the fulfillment of a prophecy, the fulfillment of yearning, the fulfillment of the wish that goes throughout history.

Reverend Jerry Falwell, founder and pastor, 1956, Thomas Road Baptist Church, Lynchburg, Virginia; founder of Lynchburg Christian Academy, 1967, Liberty Baptist College, now Liberty University (and chancellor), 1971, and Moral Majority, 1979 (and president, 1979 to late 1980s); visitor to, and staunch supporter of, the State of Israel When our guide told us [in 1970, on Reverend Falwell's first visit to Israel], "We are approaching Jerusalem," I really had goose pimples up and down my spine because I considered Jerusalem—and I do now—the most important city on earth, and the city where my faith was born and established.

PART ONE

From the Rise of Nazism
to Postwar Efforts
to Establish the Modern
Jewish State

Chapter 1

THE PERSECUTION OF EUROPEAN
JEWRY AND FINDING SAFE HAVENS

Adolf Hitler's "Final Solution"—the chilling code words for his hoped-for destruction of European Jewry—would not be felt in its full horror until the 1940s, following the outbreak of World War II, with the full mechanization of his death camps. The Nazi Holocaust was preordained, however, when on January 30, 1933, Adolf Hitler and his murderous minions assumed power in Germany.

The most terrible era in the history of the Jewish people would end only with the unconditional surrender on May 8, 1945, of the remnant of the regime that had for more than twelve years systematically dehumanized, terrorized, ghettoized, and then deported Jews from Nazi-occupied nations, annihilating approximately six million, including more than one million children.

Setting the Stage for the Near-Annihilation
of European Jewry

At twelve thirty a.m. on Friday, September 30, 1938, the British prime minister, Arthur Neville Chamberlain (1869–1940), affixed his signature to the Munich Pact, an act of appeasement toward Hitler, in which the Sudetenland was ceded to Germany, effectively dismembering Czechoslovakia. Hours later, Chamberlain returned to Britain, waving a piece of paper and declaring that his efforts had achieved "Peace for our time."

Shmuel "Meuki" Katz, émigré from South Africa to Eretz Israel, 1936; member, High Command, Irgun Zvai Leumi, 1944–1948; member, first Knesset, 1948–1952; founding member, Land of Israel Movement; cabinet member and adviser to Prime Minister Menachem Begin on overseas information, 1977–1979; publisher; author; columnist, *Jerusalem Post*; biographer of Ze'ev Jabotinsky I arrived in London on the day that Chamberlain arrived from Munich and so I was witness to the euphoria that overtook the public—I don't know *how much* of the public—at Chamberlain's success in staving off war. I was staying at a hotel near Piccadilly Circus. It had been raining, and when it stopped raining, toward evening, I went out for a walk. I came across a crowd of young people. Apparently, they had all been in pubs, or whatever, and were singing, "For He's a Jolly Good Fellow" and "Good Old Neville." I was on one sidewalk, and opposite me, on the other sidewalk, was a dark-haired guy who was dishing out leaflets. So I walked across and took one from him. The heading was "Czechoslovakia Betrayed." The crowd came up around us, and he gave some of them leaflets. They started joking at him; they didn't hit him or anything but were laughing at him, jeering at him, and one of them apparently patted him on the back or perhaps had given him a push. He fell and, as it had been raining, the papers all got wet. His glasses fell off, and he put them back on again. Then he walked away very dejectedly, and I remember thinking to myself, This is the only sane man in the street.

The Situation in Eastern Europe

The Jewish population of Lodz, located in central Poland and the center of the country's textile industry, had grown from 11 people in the late eighteenth century to 233,000 at the outbreak of World War II, comprising a third of the city's population. Following the Nazi Wehrmacht's entry into the city on September 8, 1939, Lodz was annexed by the Reich, its Jewish Community Council was disbanded, and the organization's former vice chairman, Chaim Rumkowsky, was installed as *Judenaltester* (Jewish community "elder"). Within weeks the Nazis had disbanded this new organization, sending its members to a concentration camp. Further acts of terror were carried out against the city's Jewish community, including cruel and murderous ghettoization, vicious pogroms, and deportations to Chelmno, a notorious death camp. By September 1, 1944, most of the ghetto's remaining population of 76,701 had been deported to Auschwitz. When Soviet troops liberated the ghetto on January 19, 1945, only 800 Jews were found there.

Shmuel Katz We [Mr. Katz and his mentor, the Revisionist visionary Ze'ev "Jabo"—a popular nickname for Jabotinsky] came to Lodz [in 1936], where he [Jabotinsky] was staying with a family named Spektor [the family of Jacob Spektor, a wealthy textile merchant and prominent Revisionist, whose son Eryk would one day live in New York and become the head of Herut, "Freedom," U.S.A., the organization established in July 1948 in Israel by the Irgun]. They had an extra room—I think that Eryk was then studying in Jerusalem—and Jabo was to deliver a talk in a cinema in the town, so we all went together with Jabo. They had a car, an unusual thing in Poland, and when we arrived at the cinema, the whole area was full of people protesting against Jabotinsky because he was telling them to get the hell out of Europe. And their argument was: "We're *Polish*; we've been here a thousand years!" We couldn't get into the front entrance of the cinema; the crowd was too thick. So there were police around. A big policeman—I remember him very well—took us around to the back of the cinema. There was a kind of yard behind the cinema, and there was still a crowd back there. It wasn't very thick, and so the policeman told us to wait. He took Mrs. Spektor and led her into the hall through the back entrance. Then he took Jabotinsky and led him into the hall, through the same entrance. Then he came back and took Mr. Spektor. When he didn't come back again, I was left there with the crowd between me and the hall. They wouldn't let me through, so I started pushing my way toward the cinema. The policeman had stationed himself near the hall, and when he saw that somebody was making some kind of disturbance at the back entrance, he came around and saw me pushing through the crowd. He gave me one punch, just one, and I flew across the empty space, onto the sidewalk, and sat there. Then I saw that Jabo, who had already been inside the hall, had come out and was looking for me. Finally, he saw me, and I could see that he wanted to laugh, but he restrained himself. He called the policeman, and the policeman came up to me and led me into the hall like a little boy. And that's the occasion when I heard Jabotinsky speak to a partly unsympathetic audience. They didn't like what he was telling them—some did, some didn't—but it was not the enthusiasm that I had seen at other meetings with Jabotinsky.

Matityahu "Mati" Drobles (with Batia Leshem, interpreter), Polish-born Holocaust survivor; immigrated to Israel, 1950; chairman, Rural Settlements Division, World Zionist Organization; chairman, Central Zionist Archive It was a very, very bad time. When the war began, I was [nearly] seven years old. I came from a good family, of average income. I was in the middle; my sister was two and a half years older, and my brother was two years younger. In 1941, the Germans took us to the ghetto. The whole family—there were 250 people—was killed, but we three children survived.

In the winter of '42, we escaped the ghetto through the garbage, and for three years we wandered through villages and forests—no housing, no place to live. I was nine years old; my sister was nearly twelve years old. We wanted to stay in our Jewish life, but we didn't meet any Jews, and we were convinced that there were no Jews anymore in the world. I was talking with my sister: "What will happen? There are no Jews anywhere in the world." She said, "You know what? I know one place in the world, called *Palestine*. There, I heard that Jews are living. When the war is finished, we are going to Palestine."

The Situation in Germany

Simcha Waisman, born in Palestine to immigrants from Europe in 1945; joined the Israeli navy at the age of fifteen; served in the 1967 Six-Day War; emigrated to the United States two years later; owner of a print shop in New York City for thirty-five years until retiring in mid-2006; currently, community activist, volunteer with the Richmond Hill Block Association, Queens, New York My mother was a registered nurse in Germany. She was one of twelve brothers and sisters, a large family. I met some of my mother's side, her brothers and sisters—they came to Israel later on—and we used to live like a big family. But some of them I never met because they didn't make it; my mother's parents never made it out from the Holocaust.

Shabtai Shavit, Arabic speaker; former head of Mossad Both my mother's and my father's families perished in the Holocaust. My mother was one of eight children, and only one of them survived. In the fifties, he immigrated to Israel. And he succeeded in saving his wife, his daughter, and his wife's sister, and all of them came to Israel.

Malcolm Hoenlein, founding executive director, Greater New York Conference on Soviet Jewry; founding executive director, Jewish Community Relations Council of Greater New York; at present, executive vice chairman, Conference of Presidents of Major American Jewish Organizations My grandparents were all killed. My father came [to the

United States] in June 1940 from Holland. He lost his sister, as well, and a nephew and a brother-in-law. Only one sister survived. My mother was an only child, and her mother and many other relatives were killed. [My family had lived] there for many hundreds of years, much longer than the people who killed them.

Ernest Stock, Ph.D., German-born immigrant to the United States and then to Israel; journalist, *Jerusalem Post*; assistant to the director (United States), Hillel Foundations; official, Jewish Agency for Israel; prolific author; husband of Bracha Stock We got out quite late, after the Crystal Night in Germany in 1938. My father was very hesitant to leave. He was already in his midforties—he was born in 1892—when the Nazis came to power. Now a man in his forties is still considered young, but back then a man at that age would find it quite a difficult move. In fact, I came across something that my father had written, in which he said, "If I had known earlier that it was that easy to become adjusted in America, I would have left Germany earlier." He must have had a mind-set that said, It's going to be terrifically difficult. And another thing, he was a perpetual optimist who felt, This whole business with the Nazis is bound to blow over; the Germans, after all, are not that crazy that they would fall for this guy and let him take over completely. I left Germany at age fourteen with my sister, for France, while my father was in a concentration camp, and my mother was left behind. She let us go to France with the idea that we would somehow all get together and go to America afterward.

Bobby Brown, immigrant to Israel from the United States, 1978; mayor, settlement of Tekoah; aide to Prime Minister Benjamin Netanyahu; currently, adviser to the treasurer, Jewish Agency for Israel My parents came very late, separately. My mother was twelve years old when she came with her mother to the United States. They had the highest numbers on the last legal boat to leave Germany, and they left in April 1940. And there were stories. My grandfather had actually been a leader in a small town called Battenberg, and he had been called in by the Nazis for interrogation. They kept him for a day, and he came home feeling very badly and went to sleep. When he woke up, he died. No one ever knew exactly what happened or found out from the Gestapo. The only doctor in town was a leader in the Nazi Party, so he refused even to come to examine my grandfather's body. And after not seeing my grandfather, the doctor wrote: "Cause of death: heart attack." There was one cemetery for three towns, and on the way, the funeral procession was stoned, and the kids were screaming: "That's the father. When's the *mother* coming?"

When my grandfather died, the request to leave had been submitted in his name. His name was Ludwig, so he was Ludwig I. Neuberger—the "I" was for "Israel," which was the name all Jewish men had to write; Jewish women had to write "Sarah"—so my grandmother all of a sudden realized that she'd have to start the whole process over because *he* had requested it, and now he was dead. She bribed someone to change the "I" to "Inger," which was my mother's name, so that it said, "Ludwig Inger," and then she convinced them that since there was an application from "Inger," she was now the custodian for Inger, so they let her continue in that queue, waiting for numbers to get out. Obviously, had she not done that, and if they hadn't gotten out in April 1940, they wouldn't have gotten out.

After a lot of problems, my grandmother and my mother took a boat from Hamburg to Genoa. There they had to wait three days until another boat took them to the United States. They knew no one in New York; they lived in a public park and ate from garbage cans.

My grandmother's brother lived in Germany with only one desire, and that desire was to get his son out. After working really very hard at it, he got his son on a Kindertransport to England. But that Kindertransport was torpedoed, and all the kids were killed. When my grandmother's brother heard that, he hanged himself. My grandmother knew that her brother had died, but she never knew the reason why—no one ever told her.

My father's mother was a nurse in World War I, and one of her patients was the young prince Haile Selassie [1892–1975, the emperor of Ethiopia from 1930 to 1936 and again from 1941 to 1974. Known as the Lion of Judah, he had close ties with Israel until succumbing at the time of the Yom Kippur War to an Arab inducement to support him in his difficulties with insurgent elements. In 1974, he was deposed by a Marxist council, imprisoned and, reportedly, murdered.]. So when the time came to leave—she was just trying to go *anywhere*—she actually wrote to Haile Selassie and asked whether he would take in the family on my father's side as refugees. He wrote back, "I remember you with great fondness, but it is not a good time to come to Ethiopia." And, of course, a few months later, Ethiopia was invaded by the Italians. He probably knew that that would happen. Otherwise, I might have been the only albino Ethiopian.

My grandparents lived in a small town near Fulda. My grandfather was a big, strapping man—he was a cattleman. When the Nazis came in the early days to his house, he took a chair and broke it and started beating them up. Maybe a couple of years later, that would have been enough to end him, but in the very beginning, the Nazis didn't really know what to do, and they ran away.

They let my grandmother and three children leave the country, but not my father, because he was of military age. And she said, "What do you mean 'military age' for a Jewish boy?" So the Nazis said that "military age" meant that he would have to go into a labor battalion. And those who went into labor battalions usually didn't come out. My grandmother told my grandfather, "You're not leaving; you're staying with Lothar until he gets out." The way the Nazis stopped him from getting out was that they wouldn't give him a passport. So every few weeks, my grandfather would go to the Passport Office, and they would always refuse him, and he'd go back. My grandfather sold cattle, and once, when he was leaving the Passport Office, the head of the Cattlemen's Association saw him and said, "Bernard, what are you doing here?" My grandfather explained the situation, and the head of the Cattlemen's Association said, "I'm also the president of the Passport Office, and if you come tomorrow, I'll give a passport to your son." On Shabbat, the next day, my grandfather asked, "What shall I do?" And my grandmother said, "You get on your bicycle and pedal over to that Passport Office!" Sure enough, there was a passport waiting for him, and my father got out. Who lived and who died was a matter of luck.

Zalman Shoval, immigrant to Israel from the then Free City of Danzig, East Prussia; leader at the age of sixteen, Boy Scouts; close associate of Moshe Dayan in newly formed Rafi Party (the Worker's List of Israel), 1960s; member, Knesset, 1970–1981 and 1988–1990; diplomat, ambassador of Israel to the United States, 1990–1993 and 1998–2000; currently, international businessman; president, Israel Chamber of Commerce I didn't experience the Nazi terror because until 1939 Danzig was under the auspices of the League of Nations, although the population was probably 90 percent German, with Nazi uniforms and everything. But the Jews of Danzig knew what was coming, and most of them got out in time, many of them to Palestine and many of them to America. Some even managed to get their belongings out of Germany. This was after we left. My father was a Zionist and came here first, in 1934, to prepare for our aliyah. But I understand that when the war broke out, it [the Nazi terror] broke out in Danzig. The Nazi *gauleiter* and the Jewish community came to a deal where the Nazis got such and such, and the Jews were able to take many of their own personal belongings and also artifacts from the synagogue.

My parents originally came from Eastern Europe, and all of my mother's family perished in the Holocaust. But some of my father's brothers were in London, and some were here. It's an interesting psychological phenomenon: people didn't want to talk about it. My mother didn't want to talk about her mother and her sister and her brother; it was as if people removed their relatives, at least *outwardly*, from their memories.

Shabtai Shavit   I remember, as a kid, there was not a lot of talk on the topic [of the murder of much of European Jewry during the Holocaust] at all. We carry this burden now because of the silence.

The Situation in Austria

Shlomo Ariav, Viennese-born member of Betar there from the age of ten; immigrated to Palestine in 1939 and joined the Irgun; member, Jewish Brigade; joined the Israel Defense Forces, 1948; sent to South America as first emissary of Betar, 1950; appointed co-chair, Keren Kayemeth Le Israel (Jewish National Fund), 1979; husband of Tzipora Ariav   My life in Vienna was completely Jewish. In our apartment house there were forty Jewish families and two who were non-Jewish, so we were completely surrounded by friends. I used to come together on evenings and weekends with my Betar friends. We were very close; we went to the Jewish theater. I had four sisters—I was in the middle, the "sandwich" of the family—so I was spoiled. I lost my father when I was very young—I was close to thirteen when he died. He was a soldier in the Austro-Hungarian army and was wounded by a sword. Cossacks came down the hill on their horses, he was hit with the sword, and that was it! We grew up not poor— we had enough to eat—but still it was a problem for my mother to raise five children without a man, so my sisters started to work early.

Then, when Hitler came to power, in '38, it was completely different. We were completely shut out—out of school, out of everything—and my family decided to go to Belgium. My mother stayed with me because I was already registered for the Youth Aliyah, to go to Palestine. My mother was there when I left by boat for Italy. Then she left for Belgium to join my four sisters. My four sisters were hidden by Christian families, and not only were they hidden, but the whole community knew that Jews were there.

One of my sisters was hidden by an engineer who worked for the Germans. He had two sisters who were blond, and my sister was blond, too. She heard the German officers who came to the engineer's home say, "One day we will suffer because of what we did to the Jews." She understood

German, but she couldn't say a word. When I came to Belgium, I went to see the family. He was a very, very fine man, and he wanted to teach me about prefabricated buildings, but my head at that time was for girls.

I was a soldier in the Jewish Brigade. After I came back, I went to see them. My mother was taken to Auschwitz a few weeks before the liberation of Belgium, three or four weeks before Belgium was occupied by the British. My four sisters were alive. I asked the people, "Why did you sacrifice yourselves? You could have been killed immediately." They told me, "The Christian Father [the pope] told us to hide the Jewish people."

Zalman Shoval   The closer one came to the end of the war, news of what had happened in Europe became more and more known. But that also was the time of the struggle against the British Mandate to bring the remnants of Jewry in Europe to [what would soon be the State of] Israel, and the complete refusal of the British to let these refugees into the country, which eventually led, of course, to American and U.N. involvement.

One chapter that still has to be written is how, with the fact that Winston Churchill was a Zionist, he, too, averted his eyes from what happened to the Jews in Europe during the war. It wasn't just Roosevelt; it was Churchill, too. From that point of view, there are certainly some black marks against Churchill.

The Jewish Community of Palestine's
Sense of Imperilment

During World War II, there were numerous Allied campaigns against the Wehrmacht in North Africa—notably, in El Alamein, a village on the Mediterranean Sea in northwestern Egypt; and in Tobruk, a port city in the northeastern part of Libya. Both were crucial to the Allies' war against Nazi forces in North Africa. Given that the British had suffered setbacks in their North African campaigns, it was not beyond the realm of possibility that Nazi forces could overrun Palestine, with the resultant peril to the Jews of the Yishuv.

Zalman Shoval   It wouldn't have taken very long for [Field Marshal Erwin Johannes Eugen] Rommel [1891–1944] to get here, and I'm sure that my parents and the older generation were very worried about that. But as kids, we didn't think so much about that. Yes, there was talk about the Haganah organizing a resistance group to fight on the Carmel if the Germans should come, God forbid. But, on the other hand, there were very few real hardships; there was always plenty of food in this country; life went on, the cafés went on. You didn't have the feeling of imminent danger, although Haifa was bombed quite often because of the refineries, and Tel Aviv was bombed several times—never by the Germans; once by the Italians, which created a lot of damage and many people were killed; and the second time by the Vichy French. There was a real war, and we had air raid alarms every night, which was fun for the kids, of course, but there were bombings in Tel Aviv only twice. And Tel Aviv was once shelled by an Italian submarine. But that was it.

Tzipora Ariav, member during World War II, Jewish Brigade; member, Irgun; agriculturist, wife of Shlomo Ariav   I was stationed in Egypt, first in Mena and then between Ismailia and Cairo. I was a driver, and I drove all kinds of cars. In Tel Aviv there was a German settlement so we pushed them out. Sure, we were worried!

Joshua Matza, member, Stern Group until 1948; member, Knesset, 1984–2002; appointed minister of health, 1996; currently, president and chief executive officer, Israel Bonds   There was big tension. There are names that I remember today from the fight in Africa—one is Tobruk. The Germans came to Tobruk. Of course, we were all scared about that, and we knew that if they were coming here, we would have to fight for our lives. And I remember all the names: General Rommel and [Bernard Law] Montgomery [First Viscount Montgomery of El Alamein, 1887–1976]. All of us were tense in those days.

Dan Pattir, journalist; correspondent; chief of the Prime Minister's Bureau, first administration of Yitzhak Rabin; spokesman in the administration of Menachem Begin; official, Abraham Fund; husband since 1956 of Professor Yael Pattir   There was never a question about it. Every day we started to look at the papers—there were three or four Hebrew-language papers a day—and I was taught to look at the maps of the war: Where are the Germans? How far away are they? Where is the British military? Thousands of Jews were volunteers with the British army—in 1939 and 1940, we were about 300,000 or 400,000, and in 1948, we were 600,000—so almost all of us were affected. And our friends would come for holidays in British uniforms. My father was in charge of the security of our area, with the uniform of the voluntary police. We knew that we were involved in a war.

In 1942, we were attacked by the Italian air force, here in Tel Aviv. There was a reality that we were at war. The Jewish contingent in this country was also threatened by the Arabs. In 1939, the riots stopped because the war broke out, but the Arab threat was still there, and they didn't become friends overnight.

At War's End, Finding One's Way Out of the Graveyard of War-Ravaged Europe

Matityahu "Mati" Drobles   If we had a choice where to live, it would be only in Palestine. In 1945, we emigrated from Warsaw. There were refugees from other camps. We went to Italy. There was an official bureau of missing relatives, and there were two uncles—the brothers of my father—who were looking for my father's three children. They found us in Italy, and they took care of us. They wanted to bring us to Argentina.

So I went to Argentina with my brothers and my sister. We thought Argentina was Palestine! I stayed in Argentina for four years. My two uncles supported two private teachers for us to learn. In three and a half years, I matriculated and then had one year in the university. Then I realized that I had come to Argentina and not to *Palestine*! And when I finished my studies, I went to Palestine. At this point, I finished with the Holocaust, and I began to live.

Natan Sharansky, refusenik and prisoner of conscience, 1978–1986; freed, brought to Israel, February 11, 1986; founder, Yisrael Be'aliyah Party, 1995; member of Knesset, 1996–2003, 2006; minister of: industry and trade, 1996–1999, internal affairs, 1999–2000, housing and construction, 2001–2003; deputy prime minister, 2001–2003; minister without portfolio, 2003–2005; head, Shalem Center's Institute for International and Middle Eastern Studies   We had a unique period in our history, after the Holocaust, in which for the first time, after thousands of years of our history, the enlightened part of the world had strong guilt feelings and felt a lot of sympathy for our national group. There was no period in history like this before, and I hope we will never have any period like this in the future because the price of this "love"—six million people—was too high. I don't want to be *loved* again; it's very expensive.

Chapter 2

THE ZIONIST SPIRIT OF SABRAS,
THE INGATHERED EXILES,
AND THE DIASPORA JEWS

Raanan Gissin, colonel (retired), Israel Defense Forces, responsible for foreign press, First Lebanon War, 1982, the First Intifada, 1980s, and the First Gulf War, 1991; special adviser to the Israeli delegation, Madrid Peace Conference, 1991; senior public affairs adviser and spokesman, administration of Prime Minister Ariel Sharon I once took [the late] Lee Atwater, the strategic adviser of President Reagan, on a tour of the West Bank. We got along very well, mainly because he was a folk singer and played the guitar. We played together for hours, and then I took him on the tour. In the evening we had a reception at the Foreign Ministry—and he was really a supporter of Israel; he was a born-again Christian, spoke with a Southern drawl. He said, "Colonel, I have a question on my mind, and if you settle that question, that will help me a lot in defending your position in the United States: There was this decision by the U.N. in '75 equating Zionism with racism; you know, I don't understand 'til this day, could you give me a good answer? What's the difference between a Zionist and a Jew?"

I said, "Lee, there's *no* difference at all." Remember, this is a cocktail party, with all the Foreign Ministry people standing around. I said, "You see me? Five feet, seven inches, that's all. I'm both a Jew and a Zionist. But, anatomically, I have the heart of a Jew, the mind of a Jew. I'm sensitive and compassionate to my enemies; I'm very sensitive to my people. But from my belt down, I'm a *Zionist*. You know why? Anyone who messes with the *Jew* part gets kicked by the *Zionist* part."

16

Now, the Foreign Ministry didn't like that anatomical reference because, to put it mildly, this was not such a diplomatic description. Yes, we *kick*! We kick back. But Bibi Netanyahu, who at the time was the foreign minister, burst out laughing.

Matityahu "Mati" Drobles   Here, I found my real Zionism. I was waiting all my life to come, and I came in 1950. I didn't want a thing from anybody; I only felt now the belonging—I *belonged* to the state; I *belonged* to the earth, to my people, to my nation, to *my* state. I wanted to give to Palestine, to contribute to the state, to give to Israel. Therefore, I went to Mevo Beit Betar. I was already a member of the Betar movement in Argentina, and I was active there, but my dream was to come here and to participate, to realize that my dream was a movement. They wanted to build the settlement [Mevo Beit Betar] and other settlements, and life was very, very hard because six young guys—Betar boys—were killed on the border of Mevo Beit Betar. It was a very hard period of time.

Jewish Palestinians, Sabras

One who is born in the Jewish state is known as a sabra, the Hebrew word for an indestructible desert plant, the cactus, which is prickly on the outside but whose fruit is remarkably sweet.

Moshe Sharon   I am a Palestinian. I was born in 1937, and my family has been in Palestine since the seventeenth century. They came from Poland and the Crimea and lived on a farm in the Jezreel Valley, near Haifa.

Dan Pattir   I am Palestinian because I was born in Palestine [in 1932]. I was born in a rural area called Tel Mond [located on the Sharon Plain], which is not far from Netanya, an area that was bought from the Arabs by a Jewish fellow called Alfred Mond, who later became Lord Melchett [Viscount Melchett], and it was named after him. He planted the first citrus plantations in the Sharon Valley. And my late father was one of those pioneers who in 1929 came to be one of the planters cultivating the land there.

He had fled from the pogroms in Ukraine in 1920, after World War I, and he and a friend of his—they were youngsters, seventeen or eighteen—fled from Ukraine via Warsaw. He got a pioneering document from the Zionist movement to go to Palestine, so he boarded a ship in Trieste and went to Port Said. From there, he came to Jaffa Port. He then went to the agricultural college called Mikveh Israel. ["Hope of Israel." The college was established in 1870, near Jaffa, with a subsidy from a French philanthropic organization, the Alliance Israélite Universelle. This was in keeping with the concept advanced as early as 1843 by Zvi Hirsch Kalisher, an Orthodox rabbi with a pulpit in Thorn, East Prussia, of Jewish salvation through self-help. The concept was to be realized by colonizing Palestine through financing by wealthy Jews and training the colonists in such existential necessities as self-defense and farming. The acquisition of these skills, the rabbi and the concept's other advocates believed, would supplement, rather than detract from, the teachings of the Torah.]

In 1929, the second round of Arab pogroms—what we called "the events"—took place, and he and some others went to help a Jewish settlement in the lower Galilee, in Tiberias, called Khittim. It so happened that in this village was my grandfather from my mother's side, who came from Poland. Orthodox Jews, they were given an order by their rabbi to go to Israel to be Zionists. So they went to Jaffa, and from Jaffa they were sent to Khittim to be agriculturists. My mother was a young girl, and my young father, with his friends, came to help this village survive attacks by the Arabs, and they met.

I still keep my Palestinian ID, and the funny thing is that this terminology of Judea and Samaria didn't start with the Jews but with the British officialdom; my ID is signed by "The Governor of Samaria," and he was the governor of Samaria, of Nablus and Netanya, the Jewish side. He later on became Lord Carrington of Great Britain, the ambassador to the U.N. I once said to Yasser Arafat, "I am as much a Palestinian as *you* are. I have a document that says I am Palestinian. You Arab-Israelis call yourselves 'Palestinians'; you are not Palestinians by *documentation*, only by affiliation."

Rafi Eitan, head, Operations Committee, Mossad, involved in the capture of Nazi war criminal Adolf Eichmann; adviser to Prime Minister Yitzhak Rabin on defense and security; member, Defense Committee, Israeli Ministry of Defense; adviser to Prime Minister Shimon Peres; director of LAKAM (Office of Scientific Liaison); founder and chairman, Pensioner's Party; international businessman dealing in agricultural products   There was Jewish society throughout history, even during Roman times; otherwise, we couldn't have had Jesus. My family was a Zionist family during the time of the revolution in Russia. But, nevertheless, they were divided: some of them went to Zionism; some of them went to communism. And a cousin of my father was Lazar Kaganovich, a deputy of [the Soviet dictator Joseph] Stalin. So it's a good example of how a Jew-ish family behaved. It's the same today.

Muki Betser (with Joseph Hochstein, interpreter), colonel (retired), Israel Defense Forces; participant in a daring raid on Beirut, Lebanon, to kill terrorists; deputy commander, Entebbe rescue mission, July 4, 1976; currently, educational and social activist   My grandfather and grandmother came here a hundred years ago from Russia and were pio-neers and founded Kibbutz Degania ["Cornflower," founded in 1909 at Um Juni, on the shore of Lake Galilee], where they met. Afterward, they moved to Merhavia [a less strictly socialist kibbutz] in the Jezreel Valley, and their first two children, my uncle and my aunt, were born there, and after that, my father.

After that, there was a group at Merhavia that advanced the idea of a moshav, and they established Nahalal, the first workers' settlement, in the Jezreel Valley. Moshe Dayan was born and grew up there, and he and my father were in the same class at school.

An uncle who was born in Merhavia volunteered for the British army. He was on a ship that departed from Alexandria for Italy and was supposed to stop at Malta, but the Germans bombed and sank it, and 140 Israeli fighters drowned, my uncle among them. I am named Moshe for him—Muki is my nickname.

My father fought under [British army captain Charles Orde] Wingate [1903–1944] when he was twenty-one, and he was injured. [Wingate became an ardent Zionist; established contact with the Haganah; trained its Special Night Squads during the Arab riots; in 1939, was banished by the British from Palestine; and died in an airplane crash in Burma.] And my father was in the Palmach, the Haganah, and he was also injured in the War of Independence, so when you talk about Zionism—the whole thing, farming the land—it's part of me.

I have a large family at Kibbutz Ein Harod, and there Haim Shturmann, my grandmother's brother, was killed in 1938. And in 1948, his son Moshe was killed. And in 1969, in Green Island, an operation, his grandson Haim, who was named for his grandfather, was killed. He was my age; we grew up together. We were deep into pioneering and wars. This was understood, not that you talked about it; you just did it.

Amira Dotan, first woman to be appointed general officer, Israel Defense Forces, 1987; now retired; member, Kadima Party; member, Knesset (parliament)   I was born here, and my parents were born here, so I was aware of Eretz Israel from the very, very beginning. For us, it was part of life; you never questioned it. Both of my grandparents were very involved with synagogues and with tradition; my Sephardic grandfather had a synagogue here, in Neve Tzedek, and my Ashkenazi grandfather was the person who was responsible for the charities of the community. It was so much a part of us, we never questioned it, not to mention that my father was in the Haganah. We were brought up knowing who we are; it was part of our education.

Yossi Ben-Aharon, born in Jerusalem but raised in Port Said, Egypt; career diplomat since 1956, Israeli Ministry of Foreign Affairs; policy adviser to Foreign Minister Yitzhak Shamir, 1980–1986; director general, Prime Minister's Bureau, administration of Prime Minister Yitzhak Shamir, 1986–1992; head of Israeli delegation, negotiations with Syria, 1991; currently, lecturer, College of Judea and Samaria We were in Port Said because my father had no work, no means of subsistence, here in Eretz Israel in 1931 or '32, and he had family in Egypt, so that is why we went there. For a period, my mother stayed behind with the children, but finally she realized that that wouldn't work, so we joined him.

I got my whole concept of Eretz Israel from my father and especially from my mother, who spoke Hebrew and taught us the language from discourse, as there was no Jewish school in Port Said. For us, Eretz Israel was the be all and end all, the summit of our aspirations, in prayer and in faith and in belief, to such an extent that we learned from our mother, whose parents and brother and sisters were here, that our stay in Egypt was transitional, that we were aiming toward Eretz Israel, eventually. She even refused to buy new furniture because she said, "Why waste money? Eventually, we have to return."

Yael Pattir, officer, Israel Defense Forces, served in the office of deputy chief of staff Yigael Yadin; professor of classics, Tel Aviv University, for more than thirty years; wife since 1956 of Dan Pattir I was born in Jerusalem, and I'm very patriotic about it. My father came from Germany to this country in the twenties and my mother came from Russia in the twenties. They met in Safed. They were both in the medical field; my father was a medical doctor and my mother was a nurse, and this is how they met, in a hospital, which still exists, and they came to Jerusalem. My father, named Olinsky, was one of the establishers of Hebrew University. He was a professor of bacteriology and received the Israel Prize for Medicine at one point. He was mainly a researcher, a lecturer, and a teacher at the medical school, the Hadassah Hospital [Hadassah Medical Center], Jerusalem. Why do I emphasize "a lecturer and a teacher"? Because he was more of a teacher than a lecturer, and he told me that you can write hundreds of scientific works, but each has an "antithesis." He had hundreds of students to educate, and this was the most important thing, so that they can pass on whatever is known to them.

Shabtai Shavit   I was nourished by my late mother with her breast milk. My parents were very Zionist. They got married in 1936, and the next day they started on their way to Palestine from Ukraine. My father had been a Hebrew teacher in the Jewish community in Ukraine—at the time, it was considered a crime. And my mother as a young girl spoke Hebrew. So from the very beginning, I was brought up based on Jewish history and tradition and Zionism.

Simcha Waisman   My father was born in Kiev [now the capital of Ukraine]; my mother was born in Berlin, Germany. My mother came with the First Aliyah when they made the Shoah [the Hebrew word for Holocaust], and my father ran away after his father got killed—there were pogroms—in Kiev. I was born in Tel Aviv in 1945, and I grew up there. We were busy living, but we had the connection through history to the country, to the land, from what we were taught in school. And you belong to different organizations when you're young—I belonged to two of them, the Sea Scouts and another one, like the Boy Scouts here [in the United States]. The attachment was there; you didn't know then whether it was Zionist or non-Zionist, but that it's *your* country, *your* religion.

Yehiel Kadishai, member, Irgun Zvai Leumi; participant, British embassy bombing, Rome, Italy, 1946; commander, Italian Section, *Altalena*, 1948; longtime personal aide to Menachem Begin; director, Prime Minister's Bureau, beginning in 1977, during the administrations of Menachem Begin and Yitzhak Shamir   I had no problem [in identifying as a Zionist] because, fortunately, my parents left Poland in 1923. They already had six children. I was the youngest, two and a half months old, so I didn't have to be educated on Eretz Israel; I was *born* here. Somebody who was born here was born into the Jewish state; it was taken for granted that there was a Jewish state. I was brought up in an atmosphere, in the surroundings, in the milieu of Jews living in *their* country.

We were a famous family. My grandfather had a printing house in Warsaw printing the Hummashim [Hebrew prayer books] for two or three generations. I actually met one of the daughters of my grandfather in New York. There was an actor, Joseph Buloff; his wife was Luba Kadishman [both Buloff and Kadishman were stars of the Yiddish theater, and he appeared on the English-speaking stage, on radio and television, and in films]; that is the Kadishman/Kadishai [connection], the third branch from my father's side. I met her in New York in 1968.

My father was no Zionist. When he was asked, he would answer, "No, I am a *Jew*, and Jews should live in Eretz Israel." He was religious; he was a Hasid [a term used to describe Jews who adhere to strict religious and moral principles], like the Lubavitchers. [They were Hasidim from the town of Lubavitch, located in Smolensk Oblast of Russia, who were followers of the founder of the Habad movement, Schneur Zalman of Lyady, whose son, Dov Ber, moved to Lubavitch in 1813. The community dwindled from sixteen hundred in 1897 to only seven hundred in 1926. In November 1941, following Nazi Germany's invasion of the Soviet Union, the approximately seven hundred remaining Lubavitcher were massacred. The group's influence would continue to flourish in the United States, however, where Rabbi Menachem Mendel Schneerson, a descendant of Schneur Zalman, established a vibrant community in Brooklyn, New York.] Hasidism is a school of thought, actually. And on this I was brought up, in a home that was saturated with Jewishness—with Jewish spirit, with Jewish radiance, with the Bible, with the Gemara [the part of the Talmud that contains rabbinic commentaries], with the Mishnah [the oral law; the word "Mishnah" was derived first from the Hebrew *shanai*, "to repeat," and later from the Aramaic *tanna*, "to learn"]. And for us it was taken for granted: you're Jewish; you live as a Jew in Eretz Israel, so I had no problem becoming a Zionist.

One of my uncles, my father's brother, Yosef Kadishman, a very nice Jew with a long beard, came here in 1938. In Warsaw he had been very religious, and he said, "I come to Eretz Israel, and they don't keep the Shabbat [Sabbath] here." I remember my father telling him, "What are you complaining about? We, the religious, will be the majority, and we will make laws that people won't drive cars on Shabbat."

Bracha Stock, born in Palestine to Polish immigrants; returned to Poland at the age of two for four years; educator; served in the Israeli army's Department of Culture during the War of Independence; staff member, newspaper of the Mapai Party; staff member in the United States, Voice of America; wife of Dr. Ernest Stock   It [Bracha Stock's Zionist identity] was a natural thing. My parents came here on what we call the Fourth Aliyah [between 1922 and 1928, when seventy thousand Polish Jews fleeing government-inspired xenophobia that resulted in harsh economic conditions, as well as approximately eight thousand Jews from the Caucasus and the Middle Eastern nations, made their way to Palestine] in 1923. They were Zionist idealists. I was born in 1928. Shortly afterward, the Depression had its effect here; there were no jobs for people.

My father worked as a carpenter for the British army in a camp near what is today Rafiah. It was all the way down in Gaza; he came home only once every two weeks. After that job, he couldn't find work here, and he decided to go back to Poland, to Warsaw, and send money home to his family. After he was there for six months, he had enough money to help me and my mother to join him in Warsaw, so we went by ship to Poland in 1930, when I was two years old, and stayed there for four years, until I was six. My brother was born there.

Fortunately, we went back to Palestine from Poland. But many people who went back to Poland decided to stay there because there was no work in Palestine, and you had to be really determined to come back here. They were Zionists and wanted to come back. Many people stayed in Poland and were wiped out, caught by the Germans.

Raanan Gissin   My sense of Zionism came in the least likely of all places, the Diaspora. In 1956, we went abroad and spent two years in Brooklyn. My father was an emissary of Young Judea—they would train and recruit young kids and bring them to Israel. You're never aware of being Jewish or Zionist until you are in an environment where your identity is juxtaposed against a different set-up. Two months after we arrived, I got lost one day in the street. A couple of kids left me out there, and I didn't know the language, and I was roaming around the street, trying to find my way back home. Finally, a policeman saw me, and tried to speak to me, and I couldn't speak the language. He asked me where I was from, and I said, "I'm from Israel." "Ah!" he said, and he took me to a butcher shop. The guy there spoke Yiddish, and I didn't *understand* Yiddish. That was my first trauma, finding out that there are people who are Jewish, but they don't speak the language that I speak—a few words sound familiar, but others were just very strange to me. And the policeman said, "Well, don't you understand?" And I said, "No, it's not my language."

That was my first exposure to the sense of the richness of what being a Jew is. To me, Zionism is the national liberation movement of the Jewish people. When I grew up and studied the essence of Zionism, I understood one important fact: that this is the only *really* successful mass national liberation movement of all the major movements that took place in the nineteenth and twentieth centuries. Communism came and went; socialism failed; Zionism did not fail. And it did not fail because of the richness of its cultural background and heritage and because of its capacity for all kinds of rejuvenation and change and capacity to grow with the changing circumstances.

If I had to summarize it in a sound bite, I'd say, "I was born as a Zionist because I was born an Israeli. I came to *understand* Zionism only when I met other Jews, who did not act like me or who were not dressed like me or did not behave like me." Then I understood what Zionism was all about or the true scope of the Zionist movement, and the reason that it's so successful.

Meanwhile, Young Jews in Europe, America, and Africa Are Aware of Eretz Israel

Yehuda Avner, born in Manchester, United Kingdom; immigrated to Palestine, 1947; political adviser to Prime Minister Menachem Begin, 1977–1981; ambassador of Israel to the Court of St. James's, 1982–1988   Our parents were born in Eastern Europe—I am the eldest of seven. As a kid, I was evacuated at the start of the war [World War II], during the Blitz. I must have awakened to the awareness of Eretz Israel with my mother's milk; she was a Zionist; she may have been more for Jabotinsky. There was more drama in her than in my dad, in that respect, and when as a teenager I discovered B'nai Akiva [a pioneering religious youth group], I became a fervent member, ideologically.

My ideology was reinforced enormously at the immediate end of the war after I learned what had happened in the camps, when child survivors were brought to Manchester and set up in hostels, and we of B'nai Akiva went to play Ping-Pong with them. I decided then: I'm going to throw in my lot against the British because the British were the dealers against Palestine.

I was given a scholarship to the Institute for Youth Leaders from Abroad for a year's study program in Jerusalem. In those days, it was impossible to get into Palestine, so if you got a visa, as I did, the intention was to go and not come back. My passion had been aroused, so in 1947 I set sail for Palestine, having spent a number of months beforehand at the training farm of B'nai Akiva. This was a world of idealism; this was the *new* world. We were all socialists. We were going to change the world! We were going to lead a kibbutz. We were revolutionaries! Here I come from a bourgeois

Anglo-Jewish family, and I'm going to a kibbutz. All these things were real, and you know what? They still linger within me.

Zalman Shoval   I wasn't born here; I came as a boy of seven, and I immediately fell in love with Tel Aviv. It made an impression—the houses in the north of Tel Aviv, and so forth, to the point where I always say that I was born twice: I was born in what was then the Free City of Danzig, which doesn't exist anymore as a free city, and I was born in Tel Aviv. I don't even remember the time in my life when I became a de facto sabra because small children are very quickly absorbed—their surroundings, the language—it was very quick.

And I was very much aware of political goings-on. There was no choice because in the middle of the night we might have an illegal immigrant ship docking right near us because we were living by the seashore, and my late sister, who was older than me, helped these illegal immigrants get to the shore. So you couldn't live a separate life; you were very much part of what was going on.

Uri Avneri, German-born immigrant to Palestine in the late 1930s; joined the Irgun as a teenager; founder in 1946, Young Palestine; soldier in the War of Independence, 1948–1949; author of the war experience books *On the Heels of the Philistines* and *The Other Side of the Coin*; author of articles and editorial writer, *Ha'aretz*, 1949; purchaser and revamper of *Our World* magazine and editor in chief, 1950–1990; creator and Knesset candidate of new party, "New Force," 1965; member, Knesset, for ten years, consisting of three periods between 1965 and 1980; founder, the Peace Bloc, 1994   My father was a Zionist. I don't think he ever came to Palestine, but German Zionists at that time were like American Zionists today. But when Hitler came to power, my father immediately decided to immigrate to Palestine. As a kid, I was very much aware of what was happening around me. It was the last years of the Weimar Republic and the beginning of the Nazi state, so it was impossible to escape what was happening around you, especially if you were Jewish. Practically from the day that I had any understanding at all, I was already very involved with the Zionist youth movement at the age of eight or nine. We read books about Palestine and about Jewish history.

Shmuel Katz   There was a Zionist movement in South Africa. In my family, they were not interested in Zionism. They were religious Jews who knew, This is our country. That was the extent of their Zionism. But at the age of fifteen, I was a rather precocious person—it may not be recognizable—in that I had completed high school at the age of fifteen, and I went to university for one year. Almost a week or two after the school year began, I met a guy on the steps of the main hall of the university; he was a member of Betar—a Lithuanian who had come from France—and he said, "Would you like to go to a meeting, a lecture by Jabotinsky to youths?" I had heard Jabotinsky a few days earlier—it was his first visit to South Africa—and was very, very, very, very impressed. I didn't know that there was any way of joining, but I went along. And that's where I heard Jabotinsky in a small group, where he didn't talk so much about Palestine but about the situation in Europe and how—he didn't put in this way, but that's how it came to me: we're sitting in South Africa, having a lovely time playing tennis, and there are the Jews in Eastern Europe, impoverished and oppressed. That's when I became a member of Betar.

Shlomo Ariav   I was a Betari as a youngster. When I joined, I was about ten years old. Betar was very popular in Vienna; it was the largest Zionist youth organization. And from the beginning, we thought about that one day when we would come to Palestine. Finally, we got certificates, which was very unusual for Betar, but Henrietta Szold [1860–1945, the American Zionist who founded the women's organization Hadassah] arranged for the first time that twenty youngsters of Betar should come to Palestine under Youth Aliyah. So ten came from Germany and ten came from Vienna, and in January 1939, we came directly to Rosh Pina [located in the Galilee, founded by immigrants from Europe, and taken under Baron Edmond de Rothschild's protection]. Rosh Pina at that time—even today—was the main place of settlement of Betar. In Rosh Pina we were fighting the Arabs. Every night we went down. They were in the mountains over there. One of my friends asked me, "Do you remember the first night we came to Rosh Pina?" I said, "I don't remember." He said, "But *I* remember. The Arabs were shooting at us." We came to Rosh Pina for two years, and we had the best teachers—the students were not so good—and from Rosh Pina we were taken immediately to the Irgun.

Yossi Ben-Aharon   Port Said was a kind of international port—it was really under the control, to a large extent, of the British and the Suez Canal Company, which was a foreign company that was running the canal. We lived in the part called the Frankish Quarter, meaning "European." It's no longer there.

We spoke Arabic, but the foreigners spoke mostly "kitchen Arabic," not the real, literary Arabic. They had a law that you had to study Arabic in every school, including in foreign schools. We went to a British school because my father had British nationality. So the Arabic teacher one day asked, "Who has been to Cairo?"—we were studying a text on Egypt—and several of the students raised their hands. "Who has been to Alexandria?" and again, several students raised their hands. He looked at me and said, "Joseph, you haven't been to Cairo?" And I said, "No." "Where have you been?" And I said—this was Egypt before the State of Israel—"Tel Aviv, Haifa, and Jerusalem." And he looked at me because when the Nazi army under Rommel was threatening Egypt in 1942, we escaped by train from Port Said to Jerusalem, and we spent a couple of months there because there was fear that he would capture Egypt. Then when I was bar mitzvahed in 1945, we again came here, and we visited Tel Aviv and Haifa, so that's why I said that. He didn't like it very much.

Ernest Stock   My experience at Princeton University [where there were very few Jewish students at the time] was one of the triggers. But there were other factors as well. I was born in Germany. I went to a Jewish school in Germany for part of the time—I started in a public school in Frankfurt and then transferred to a Jewish school after Hitler came to power, and I remember seeing what we called "Palestine films." They were some propaganda films that were distributed in the Diaspora to make people familiar with what was going on in Israel, which was then Palestine—Jewish Palestine, the kibbutzim, and how life in the Yishuv developed in the thirties. We were shown these films, and there were quite a few of my classmates who emigrated with their parents to Palestine. But in my family, my mother already had several siblings in America who had left Germany in the late 1920s and early thirties, during the time of the Depression. Even before the Depression came to America, there was a Depression in Germany as a result of the inflation after World War I; people found it hard to find work, and they went to America. So it was taken for granted that if we thought of emigrating from Germany, which my parents *didn't* at the beginning of the Hitler period, we would be going to America, not to Palestine. Palestine, I would say, was a very attractive and exciting place for Jews to be, but for us, America was the place to go to because my mother had family there.

Joseph M. Hochstein, writer, editor; immigrated to Israel in 1983 from Washington, D.C.; managing editor, *Congressional Quarterly*, and publisher, *The Jewish Week*; father of two sons, Marc, a paratrooper

*"Our grandfather was a
Zionist, our grand-
mother less so. Their
life in Ukraine had been
marked by the tragedy
of their firstborn, a
daughter named
Rebecca, who had suc-
cumbed to measles. And
their life in Palestine
would also be marked
by the tragedy of the
death in 1906 of their
second-born daughter,
Deborah, who died of a
then-untreatable head
injury, and for whom I
am named."*
—Deborah Hart Strober

Dressed in their European finery, Anna and Samuel Greenhouse sit for a formal photograph in a Jaffa studio in 1908 with their year-old daughter, Leah Herzliya. Born in
Jaffa on April 20, 1907, she was named in honor of Theodor Herzl.

**killed in Lebanon in 1985, and Tobias, a cinematographer, and a
daughter, Michal, founder of a Tel Aviv preschool; brother of Deborah
Hart Strober**   We had some neighbors on the next block [during World
War II, in South Orange, New Jersey] who were from Palestine. They were
a Jewish family; their name was Lieberman, and the sons had Hebrew
names; one of them was Uriel, and they had a daughter named Judith.

I remember in my grandparents' house [in Forest Hills, New York—Mr.
Hochstein's maternal grandparents, Anna and Samuel Greenhouse, had
immigrated to Palestine from Ukraine in 1905 and came to the United
States in 1910], there was a portrait of Herzl done in fine writing [micro-
graphy, a Jewish folk art]. I don't remember what the text was, but it was little, tiny, squiggly pen-and-ink words arranged to make a portrait. And there
were a few statuettes, and there were books with etchings of how the country looked. We didn't talk about it until later.

Bobby Brown   I came from a home of German Jewish refugees from the
Holocaust, and there was always a certain reverence for Israel when we
talked. It always seemed to me that I had the privilege of being born in a

generation of the Land of Israel. And when I was a young man, I joined Betar, which believes that the Land of Israel belongs to the Jewish people and that the place of every Jew is here in Israel.

If I had to summarize what we learned in Betar, it was that everything was bad in Israel; it's run by the Labor Party; it's run by the Histadrut [Israel's labor federation]; it's a terrible place. Yet you have no choice: you have to go there; that's the place you have to be. That kind of steeled us for the worst, so when we came here, it wasn't as bad as we had thought it was! And so if we were waiting half an hour for a bus, and everyone was grumbling, we were saying, "Well, there really is a *bus*." When I came here, I just fell in love with it. I had learned so much about Israel that the reality just filled the picture.

I came here on a college program with a whole bunch of kids, one of whom I eventually married. And we both believed that for our future, we could make the greatest impact on the Jewish people by living *here*. So we came on aliyah in 1978 and never looked back.

Rav (Rabbi) Shalom Gold, immigrated to Israel, 1982; founder in Jerusalem, Yeshivat Bircas HaTorah; Rabbi Emeritus, Kehilat Zichron Yosef, Har Nof, Jerusalem; Rosh Yeshiva (Head of Yeshiva), Rabbi Akiva Yeshiva, Jerusalem; currently, dean, Jerusalem College for Adults
I grew up in the Williamsburg section of Brooklyn [in New York City] with an awareness of Eretz Israel by virtue of the fact that my father, of blessed memory, was a great lover of Eretz Israel; I don't think there was a Friday night at the dinner table when he didn't talk about Eretz Israel. I remember, as a child, seeing my father on the verge of tears or crying, saying, "Poor Moshe [the biblical Moses], poor Moshe, he wanted more than anything else to go to Eretz Israel, and he never got there." After my father died in 1980, the sum total of his estate was not very large—a suitcase, only about a third of it filled. There were only papers, clippings of articles about me and my brothers, and wedding invitations that were already yellowed. Then I found a letter addressed to my father, dated August 8, 1946, that blew my mind:

> Dear Mr. Gold, we have the application for Aliyah for you and your wife and your three children. [Just imagine how many people were applying for Aliyah in 1946.] You have been approved for Aliyah. But, unfortunately, at the present time there are no certificates available. We hope and pray that the day will come when more certificates are available and you will be able to come on Aliyah.

So when Israel was exploding into battles, my father was applying for aliyah. The fellow who signed that letter didn't have a clue that two years later, you wouldn't need any British certificates to get into Eretz Israel because there would then be a sovereign State of Israel.

I knew that sometime in my life I would have to take that step. In fact, I came to study in Eretz Israel from 1955 to 1956, and then I returned to the United States to complete my college education. I planned to return to Israel in 1959, but the head of my yeshiva asked me to go to Toronto to establish a yeshiva there. We stayed there until 1971, when I became a rabbi of a congregation in West Hempstead, New York. We said to ourselves, This is 575 miles closer to Eretz Israel and only twenty minutes away from Kennedy airport, and in 1982, we came on aliyah.

Natan Sharansky   In the Hebrew calendar it's exactly twenty-one years today [February 18, 2007] since I arrived in Israel. When I was released [from the Soviet gulag], it was a very special situation because I was physically taken straight from hell and flown to paradise. That's why the perception of the reality was very holy and unholy at the same time; it was like one big paradise: all the evil is defeated, the aims are reached, a happy end, a big celebration. And when you are in the heavens, there is only one way to go: down, so you start descending. Since then, for these twenty-one years, I am descending all the time; I'm coming closer and closer to earth, to reality.

On the other hand, even with all the difficulties, which are with you every day, you have the point of comparison, which all the time reminds you that it is still paradise. It's very problematic, very difficult, very challenging, and a lot of efforts have to be made. But I will not stop feeling for a moment that we are living in a very democratic, very open, very free, and very Jewish society. People are very disappointed and desperate, so they are inclined sometimes to make awful comparisons—that it's worse than the Soviet Union. My point of comparison is very different. That's why I can say that even today I feel myself in an absolutely unique culture, the only Jewish country for thousands of years, and the only democratic country in this part of the world. To be Jewish and a democratic country at the same time is a challenge!

Chapter 3

LIFE AND POLITICS IN THE YISHUV
DURING THE BRITISH MANDATE

The Jewish community of Palestine, "Yishuv" in Hebrew, was headed by the now-legendary and controversial Laborite David Ben-Gurion (1886–1973), who as a young man had left his native Poland for Eretz Israel. A founder and the head of the Jewish Agency for Israel, he advocated a cooperative relationship with British Mandatory officials. Ben-Gurion would go on to serve the State of Israel as prime minister twice, from 1949 to 1953, and again from 1955 to 1963.

Rafi Eitan   The Jewish Agency was, in practice, the government of Israel before the state was legal. And in the Jewish Agency, you had heads of departments—for example, Moshe Sharett, Shertok at the time, was the secretary of foreign affairs; Moshe Sneh, at the time of the Palmach, was the minister of defense, the head in the Jewish Agency for "self-defense"; and Levi Eshkol, later the prime minister, was the finance minister.

A Competing Ideology: Revisionism

The Revisionist movement was founded by Vladimir Jabotinsky, a Russian-born secular intellectual whose patriotism and love of Russian culture were later shattered by czarist persecution of the empire's Jewish population. Revisionist ideology was based on Theodor Herzl's view of Zionism as a political movement, articulated thus by Jabotinsky: "Ninety percent of

Zionism may consist of tangible settlement work, and only ten percent of politics, but those ten percent are the precondition of success." At the core of Jabotinsky's ideology was his conviction that the continuation of the anti-Zionist British Mandate in Palestine would foreclose the possibility of the establishment of a Jewish state in the entire region, meaning on both sides of the Jordan River.

Jabotinsky founded and was the first commander of the underground Jewish army, the Haganah. Imprisoned by the British for incitement to violence, he was later pardoned, becoming a heroic figure to young Zionists. He became a member of the Zionist Executive but broke with that body because he was opposed to the temperate approach to the British taken by such Zionist personalities as Chaim Weizmann.

Surviving under the British Mandate

The British Mandate had been established in Palestine through a clause in the post–World War I Treaty of Versailles, implementing Article 22 of the Covenant of the League of Nations, in which territories once administered by the defeated Germany and her ally Turkey were to come under the supervision of the victors—namely, Britain and France. In the implementation of the mandate system, Britain was assigned the former Turkish possessions Palestine and Iraq, with Syria coming under French supervision.

Article 22 contains a paragraph that would spur Zionist aspirations for Jewish statehood in Palestine:

> Certain communities formerly belonging to the Turkish Empire have reached a stage of development where their existence as independent nations can be provisionally recognized, subject to the rendering of administrative advice and assistance by a Mandatory until such time as they are able to stand alone. The wishes of these communities must be a principal consideration in the selection of the Mandatory.

Raanan Gissin   Judge [Louis Dembitz] Brandeis [1856–1941; associate Supreme Court Justice 1916–1939] was the one who convinced [Thomas Woodrow] Wilson [1866–1924; twenty-eighth president of the United States, 1913–1921] to accept the Balfour Declaration and integrate it into the League of Nations Mandate to the British; that is, the British got the mandate over Palestine in 1922 only after they accepted the charter of building the homeland for the Jewish people in the Land of Israel. It was very amazing; Brandeis was able to convince President Wilson at the time, who after World War I established the League of Nations and who thought about the moral diplomacy and the importance of correcting all the evils.

But Brandeis was not accepted by the established Jewish community in the United States. They accused him of dual loyalty: this is going to undermine our position. And then he came out with a statement that to this day is the hallmark, in my mind, of the essence of being Jewish and Zionist: "In order to be a good American, you have to be a good Jew. But in order to be a good Jew, you've got to be a good Zionist."

The Atmosphere of Occupation

Dan Pattir   Life was stressful. There were two prongs, so to say, in the way the British conducted themselves: one was separating the Arabs from the Jews. That was the main thing. We saw a lot of British army garrisons here in our area, going down to the western desert, to Libya. And vice versa, we had a good many garrisons of POWs, about three thousand Italians. They were nice people; they taught us how to sing, how to sculpt, how to paint—a good life. But the British were there—they weren't in every village, but it was British rule.

Bracha Stock   We were aware even in school: when anything happened, there was always a discussion in school. I did not belong to the Haganah— I was too young—but when I was about sixteen and a half, I had my first boyfriend, and that's when the British made the curfew. I'll never forget: my boyfriend and I couldn't meet because the streets were closed in different places. I didn't see him for two days, and I couldn't stand it. I had one friend who knew Tel Aviv very well, and he took me all around, underneath yards and into strange corners, until we got to a place where I could talk to my boyfriend from another roof that he came over. That's what the British did to me!

Arie Lova Eliav, Russian-born immigrant to Palestine, 1925; soldier, Haganah, 1936–1940; Jewish Brigade, British army, 1940–1945; Israel Defense Forces, 1948–1949; participant, Mossad's illegal immigration operations, 1945–1947; educator, diplomat, first secretary, Israel embassy, Moscow; 1958–1960; assistant head, Settlement Department, Jewish Agency for Israel, 1949–1953; head, Israeli mis-

sion to aid earthquake-stricken Iran, 1962–1964; member, Knesset, 1965–1979, 1988–1992; participant, early talks with Palestine Liberation Organization, 1976–1977; chair, Israel Peace Party, 1977–1979; negotiator, exchange of Israeli prisoners of war, First Lebanon War, 1982–1984; founder and teacher, Nitzana Negev educational project; head, Ideological Center, Labor Party, 2000   In 1929, there was the first riot in Jaffa and Tel Aviv, and I ran to the emergency room in Hadassah Hospital—it was very close by—and it was the first time I saw wounded people from Jaffa. That was the first time that I understood that it was not a normal place. My older brother was already in the Haganah, guarding the border of Tel Aviv, and at that age I started to understand that this was not a normal life in any way, that my future would not be as a normal child.

Later, around my bar mitzvah, when I was thirteen, there was an event in my life: I met our national poet, [Chaim Nachman] Bialik [1873–1934], and I became very friendly with him—he sort of adopted me—and he started injecting me with the idea that my future was in serving my people. This "love affair" with Bialik had a great impact on my future life.

Zalman Shoval   I didn't have any contact at all with the British, except for trying to throw stones at them. As I look back, compared to some other countries and other police, they were, relatively, quite okay. Because the British did not have enough troops and police to keep the curfew, they brought in troops that were around, Australians. The Australians couldn't care less about the British; they didn't enforce the curfew at all. On the contrary, they cooperated with the Jewish population.

Rafi Eitan   Our daily lives [on a kibbutz] were very quiet. It depended on the mood of the Arabs, with whom we had clashes, in '36 and '39 and in '47. With the British, we had deep friction but not *hatred*. We never—myself, my friends, my parents—hated the British, on the contrary, although we had deep differences.

Simcha Waisman   I remember the British. I was little then, and we were always playing around somewhere, as kids do, and we knew that they were the "bad guys," that this was *our* country, and they were coming and taking *our* country.

Around us then was the headquarters of the Haganah. We have places in Tel Aviv that you don't know about, but the tunnels are still all over town, underground. As kids, we used to play around, and we went there to see people coming out of some places that you didn't think people could come out of! You are a kid; this is a memory. But don't forget, this is also the same time that the British tried to squeeze you, and they gave more freedom to the Arabs than they gave to Israelis—they took sides.

Moshe Sharon   The British were our enemies; they used to come and search the town for guns.

Uri Avneri   I joined the underground, the Irgun, a little before my fifteenth birthday, because I believed we had to kick the British out—it was a foreign occupation, and no one likes a foreign occupation. We thought, It's *our* land, and the British have nothing to do here—and I was an honest-to-goodness terrorist for three or four years. Then I left the Irgun because when I grew up, I had a very profound disagreement with the Irgun on several points. But it was clear to me that we had to kick the British out of the country.

Dan Pattir   The British army started to surround villages in order to find illegal arms. Since we were under eighteen, we were not supposed to be held by the British. But, nevertheless, when we were caught, we were badly beaten by the British and detained overnight. The oppressiveness became all the more obvious in '45, '46, and '47 in the search and arrest. In our village, there was a secret military industry underground, and we were always afraid that the British would come and search. Until the war came to an end, the British rule was not oppressive; they tried to educate us in our daily lives. But they played a divisive game between us and the Arabs.

Yehiel Kadishai   I joined Betar, the movement established by Ze'ev Jabotinsky, almost seventy years ago. I was going on fifteen years old when [Shlomo] Ben-Yosef [born in Poland, né Tabachnik, a Betari, who had immigrated to Palestine in 1937 at the age of twenty-one] was hanged.
[Ben-Yosef was a member of the *plugah* [group] at Rosh Pina. In the early spring of 1938, in an act of protest against continuing Arab violence against Jewish settlements, he and two comrades had shot at an Arab bus. Arrested by the British, Ben-Yosef was hanged two months later, on June 8, despite the fact that no one on the bus had been injured.]
They [the attackers of the Arab bus] belonged to Betar. This, I would say, gave me the push to enter a staunch Zionist movement because there were then two schools of thought on how to deal with the Arab resistance to our existence here. There was a very simple, basic, elementary idea: there were people who said, "You have to behave sharply to those at

fault"—if somebody was caught who had killed a Jew, he should be pun-
ished, but it was not right to punish the general population, in what they
now call "collective punishment." It's an international concept that you
should not commit the government to actual punishment, of course. But
when you fight for the piece of land you want to live on and you are sure is
yours, because it has belonged to you forever, you have to do everything
possible to those who want to prevent you from being independent.

Shmuel Katz   There was an incident in Jerusalem in 1938, just before I
went back to South Africa,. The Irgun had started retaliating to Arab
attacks, and at that time, a guy named Berman, who afterward was a minister in the government here—he's still alive—had returned from England
after studying there. In Jerusalem, I had the use of a car and a driver—
that's how I got to Beirut and Syria a couple of times. I was seen on a street
in Jerusalem with Berman, who was a Revisionist. He had just returned
from England. For some reason, the British already had suspicions of
him—it became clear afterward—and I was seen with him. One day during that period, I got a message that a man named [Binyamin] Lubotsky
[one of the first Revisionists to be jailed by the British, in 1937], one of the
leaders of the Revisionist movement, one of the really brilliant people, was
on the run from the British in Tel Aviv, and he wanted me to help him get
out. So I traveled to Tel Aviv and went to his flat. His wife said that he had
left, but she knew where he was.

I went to this place, but he'd already run from there, and then they told
me that they knew that the police had found out where he was and were
after him *there*. I was staying in a pension, on the ground floor. There was
a flat on the third floor with four rooms; three were rented and two were
empty because people were away for the Shabbat. There was a lawyer
named Goldberg and his daughter, and there were two girls from Tel Aviv,
students who had gone back to Tel Aviv for the Shabbat. I brought Lubotsky to this pension, and he stayed there. The name I gave was Cohen.

Apparently, somebody saw me walking with Berman, and there was a
raid that night—the police raided all kinds of places in the city, and they
reached our pension. How did they get to our pension? I was quite sure
that somebody who was working in the pension was also working for the
police; they'd seen me arriving, perhaps, under suspicious circumstances.
At about nine o'clock in the evening, two detectives came to my room—
they'd already done some searching downstairs—and when they asked me
for identification, I showed them my passport. Legally speaking, they
couldn't do anything.

Then they asked who else was staying there, and I said, "This room is Mr. Goldberg's; he's staying with his sister in Beit HaKerem; that room is a student's room; and there's a man from Tel Aviv who came here to see a doctor named Cohen." And so they went to see the man who came to see a doctor, and, apparently, he broke down and told them who he was. The end of that was that he made a deal with them, and he left the country to go back to Latvia—he came back afterward—but they came back to me and asked me why I'd said his name was Cohen when his name was Lubotsky. So I said, "Because you're arresting people without any trial, and I can't agree with that system"—I was a consular official, after all—"and I can't agree that I have any duty to help you in that."

So they said, "But do you know a man named Raziel?" I said, "Raziel? An Italian? I don't know such a name." They said, "Well, Raziel is a man who throws the bombs, and Lubotsky is the man who writes the articles in the Revisionist paper." I said, "Do you know that there are all kinds of articles of that sort in all the papers? If you don't read them, I'll send you a collection if you like." So the guy said, "Don't you ask for my address!"

He was very annoyed with me because, when he came to the room of Mr. Goldberg, I also said, "I'm not giving you permission to go into his room." He didn't pay any attention; he walked into the room, lifted the pillow, and found a pair of pajamas under the pillow. He said to me, "I thought you said that he'd gone to his sister in Beit HaKerem?" I said, "You know, I've heard of people who have two pairs of pajamas." He got red in the face and very annoyed. At any rate, he left me in a storm; he couldn't do anything to me; he had nothing on me except that I had deceived him, and I didn't admit anything about "Mr. Cohen."

About a week later—I had my spies, as well—the correspondent of the United Press, UPI, a friend of mine named Jack Simon, a good Jewish boy who was friends with all the Arabs, a perfect Arab-speaker (he was born in the Old City of Jerusalem), told me that on that day, the British had added two names to their lists of people whose telephones had to be tapped: one was an official of the Italian Consulate and *me*, so I knew I was in trouble. I assume that's how I got onto their list.

How did I get *off* the list? That's also clear: when the Irgun started operations, while I was in England, they had blown up the police station and the central office of the CID [Criminal Investigation Division]—and had blown up all the records. A neighbor who was in the government told me the story of how the CID documents had been destroyed.

Joshua Matza   I remember very well those days when I was ten or eleven, the British, with the guns and the curfew. I remember when two British policemen with guns were walking in Mahane Yehuda, and a guy—he passed away in Panama six months ago, a guy everyone was afraid of; they called him Small David, but he was a giant—he took the guns from them and ran away. I see this "picture" 'til today. Then I remember the curfew: there was an attack on British soldiers, and one of the guys [one of the attackers] ran to the street where we lived, and we saw the British soldiers running after him and firing with a machine gun, a Bren.

Were There "Good" British Occupiers?

Joshua Matza   Once, when I was a child of eight, in the middle of Jerusalem, at the Circle of Zion, Kikar Zion, there was a patisserie, Kapulsky, a well-known place where the best cakes were sold. One of the cakes caught my attention—I was an eight-year-old boy without a penny in his pocket—so I pushed my face toward the window, just looking and looking and looking at this cake, with all this cream. And, suddenly, a British officer came up to me. He had one of these cakes in his hand, and he gave it to me. So, you see, there were nice people [among the British officers].

I always say that we were lucky that it was not the Germans; we were lucky that it wasn't the regime of the French or even some other European democracy because, really, the British behaved well. But, of course, the consensus was that we had to fight against them in establishing our state. So that's the reason we had the three undergrounds—the Haganah, the Etzel, which is called the Irgun, and the Lehi [Fighters for the Freedom of Israel, per its Hebrew initials], which is the Stern Group.

Shabtai Shavit   I was born in Haifa. My family lived in a small neighborhood called Nesher: the place where the first cement factory was built back in the late 1920s, and the small town was built around this factory. In Nesher there were two British camps where soldiers were deployed. We were teasing the British soldiers and the first English words that I spoke were "Give me chewing gum!"

Eitan Haber, correspondent at the age of fifteen, *Herut*; military correspondent; adviser to Yitzhak Rabin during the latter's tenure as both defense minister, 1984–1990, and prime minister, 1992–1995; deliverer at Rabin's state funeral of the emotionally charged words of the

"Song of Peace," which the prime minister had sung at a peace rally just moments before his assassination; resigned from the Prime Minister's Bureau immediately following the assassination; international business consultant, 1995–present   My father, Yehuda, was a member of Etzel's intelligence group, and my first memory of life is when I was five years old, and I was very, very sick with diphtheria. I was nearly dead. I remember quite vividly—it seems that it happened *yesterday*—that I was surrounded in our one-room apartment on Borochov Street, Number 28, in Tel Aviv, by doctors, my mother, and my father. And suddenly four or five British detectives entered the room and arrested my father. The doctors said, "Don't take him because his son is going to die." But they took him to Latrun, a well-known camp in our history—he was in jail there and in Acre for seven or eight months—and the British detectives promised my father that they would take me to a hospital immediately. I was brought to the British hospital in Pardes Katz, near B'nai Brak today; it was a real *British* hospital—the nurses, the doctors, everything; British and Arabs; no Jews— and I was operated on. You can still see the scar today; in order to save my life, they cut my throat because I needed air. I left the hospital after a few weeks, and there's no doubt that they saved my life.

Arriving in Eretz Israel

Yehuda Avner   You're approaching the shoreline at night [Ambassador Avner was traveling on the *Aegean Star*, a Greek ship], and you see circles of light. Eretz Israel! And we all line the railing of the deck. And then dawn breaks and the mist rises, and what do we see? My first impression was of what the spies reported to Moses about Eretz Israel: they called it "The Land of Giants," and in Haifa these tall, slender buildings cut from the mountainside looked like torsos! This was my first impression; it was only when the sun broke that you saw that these were high buildings, tiered toward these structures.

Down on the dockside, there was a row of six airborne divisions of parachutists and behind them a row of police with truncheons, and it looked as if you were arriving at a penal colony. When we landed, there was an announcement made by an officer, in very ho-hum English: "This is the Immigration Authority speaking. Those with valid passports and certificates please report to the dining room to be processed, and those who do *not*, remain in steerage." When we disembarked and went across the pier to the customs shed, we heard the announcement that the illegals should now disembark. By the customs shed the soldiers had set up concertina

"There was no deep-sea harbor so we were just outside, and passengers boarded small boats."
—Arie Lova Eliav

The scene at the Jaffa Port on November 1, 1933, as arriving immigrants to Palestine transfer from the ship that has brought them from Europe to tenders for the short ride to the shore.

barbed wire, and they [the illegals] were all just shunted into this compound.

There was a Hasid there, constantly carrying around with him a rough, brown-paper parcel—he wouldn't let go of it. He was an illegal. As a Salonikan Jewish porter shuttled my suitcase to the bus to Jerusalem, I saw this Hasid. A British soldier was trying to wrest this parcel from the Hasid's hands, and the Hasid was pulling it back. It eventually split open, and I saw a tefillin bag, an old tallis bag, a Siddur, and a Hummash. This fellow, on his knees, said in Yiddish, "Please, you've already taken my wife, my eight children, *what more* do you want of me?" The soldier was cowed, and he and a sergeant helped the Hasid rewrap the stuff. Immediately after that, as I boarded the bus, two British army trucks passed by, each of them draped in Union Jacks. That was my first sight of Eretz Israel, and it encapsulated the whole tragedy of those times.

Arie Lova Eliav   I and my twin sister were born in Moscow in November 1921. My Russian nanny gave me my second name in Russian, "Lova," a small lion. I didn't see my father for a couple of years. He was chased by the former KGB because he was a Zionist and a bourgeois, so he escaped from Moscow. Later, my mother, my twin sister, my older brother, and I boarded a boat called the *Lenin*, and after a couple of days, we anchored in Jaffa.

When we disembarked, there was at the port a man who spoke Russian, and my mother turned to me and said, "Lova, this is your father." Here stands a man whom I don't know. Then he built this house [on Karl Netter Street in downtown Tel Aviv]—it was only one story, but it would grow—and this is where I live. My awareness of Eretz Israel came to me just playing in the sand a few meters from here. We were happy children, playing in the sand and swimming in the sea. My father was a Zionist—so was my mother—but as children, we felt free and happy.

Uri Avneri   I was a kid, just ten years old, and everything was wonderful, exciting, new, especially coming from *Germany*. Actually, the first impression I always thought was very important because I later read the first impressions of people like Ben-Gurion, who hated the country on sight, not to mention Theodor Herzl, who hated Palestine altogether. We all arrived at the same point, in Jaffa Port. And there's a biography of Ben-Gurion, written by Bracha Habas, the first biography of Ben-Gurion, the very famous one, called *One and His Generation*—generally falsified as *One of His Generation*—and there she describes, obviously from his mouth, his first impressions: how awful everything looked and sounded and smelled to him; how awful Jaffa was. Now my impression was just the opposite: I thought the different language, Arabic, was absolutely wonderful; the smells of Jaffa at that time, the horse-drawn cars with which we went from Jaffa to Tel Aviv; everything was wonderful, new, an adventure. Of course, German children at that time generally had a very romantic perception of the Orient. I came prepared to love the country from the beginning.

The British and the Illegal Jewish Immigration

Arie Lova Eliav   In '46, on one of the boats we took about seven hundred survivors from Sweden, and we were nearly two months at sea. And then we had others, survivors from Italy. The boat was called the *Ulua*. We encountered British destroyers, and we made battle with them and had casualties—dead and wounded—and then they imprisoned us and brought us to detention camps on Cyprus. But then, during this long voyage, I met Tania [Mrs. Eliav], and that was it!

Zalman Shoval   The Colonial Office did everything to prevent Jews from reaching the country before the war, during the war, and after the war. And the feeling in Palestine was—it wasn't just feeling; it was the reality— that the British cooperated almost fully with the Arabs—nobody called them "the Palestinians" at that point—and that we could not expect anything from the British. This sometimes led to extreme, exaggerated expressions here where there were people—and not on the right, interestingly—who unfairly accused Weizmann of being someone who cooperated with the British.

The year 1946 was an important date, when, as a result of the temporary cooperation between the Haganah and the Irgun and the Stern Group, there was an organization called the Hebrew Resistance Movement, where all three cooperated. That ended in 1946 when the British put a great deal of pressure on the majority here, on the Jewish Agency, and put most of the leaders in temporary prison camps like Latrun. Ben-Gurion, to his good fortune, was abroad; otherwise, he would also have been put in a camp. After that, the cooperation broke up among the different organizations, at least *officially*, although, according to rumor, some cooperation went on behind the scenes. At least as far as I was concerned—and I'm sure I speak for many of my age group—we didn't have any doubt whatsoever that we would set up a Jewish state, that this struggle was going to succeed, that this would be it, that we would win. And like many other people, we, almost to the end, did not give enough attention to the Arabs, because most of the focus of our enmity was against the British.

The Peel Commission: A Bad Moment for the Jewish Community

The Peel Commission, known formally as the Royal Commission on Palestine and appointed by the British government on August 7, 1936, was chaired by Earl Peel and included five other members—Sir Morris Carter, Professor Reginald Coupland, Sir Laurie Hammond, Sir Harold Morris, and Sir Horace Rumbold. The commission's brief was to study the root cause of the Arab riots that had convulsed Palestine. The commission's report, issued the following July, recommended the partition of Palestine into an Arab state; a Jewish state, allotted a scant 2,800 square miles, thus causing it to be totally at the mercy of the Arabs; and a British Mandatory enclave, assuring continued British control of Palestine and rendering the Jewish state completely dependent on British protection.

Yehiel Kadishai   In 1937, David Ben-Gurion gave evidence to the Peel Commission after the revolt—the pogroms, actually—on what the Arabs did to us in Shomron, in Safed, in Tiberias, and in Jaffa. I was fourteen years old then—I was bar mitzvahed—and I remember the names of the Jews who were killed in Jaffa, two nurses working in the French Hospital. Two Jewish girls killed, and the Yishuv did not react!

Ben-Gurion gave evidence to this commission, and one of its members, Sir Hammond, asked Mr. Ben-Gurion, "Why do you object to the establishment of the Jewish State? Why are you against it?" In his heart, maybe, he [Ben-Gurion] wanted a Jewish state, but he was afraid to *say* that he wanted it.

Five years earlier, in 1931, at the [Zionist] Congress, Jabotinsky had left the organization [because] the Congress did not want to declare that the aim of Zionism was to build a Jewish state. Do you know what Jabotinsky answered to Mr. Hammond [regarding] why he was against it? "Because if there will be a Jewish government, they will prevent Jews from entering into the country."

There was a student's academic thesis on Jabotinsky's evidence to the Peel Commission. It was a decisive factor—they decided on the partition of Palestine. In 1939, when the White Paper was put into effect, Jabotinsky wrote an article stating that partition would never take place, and he printed it in all the languages of the Jewish world in those years.

Everyday Life in Jerusalem

Joshua Matza   I was born in what in those days was called Montefiore, the first quarter outside the Old City. Yemin Moshe is what, of course, you called it in Hebrew. But the Jews of that time in Jerusalem called it Montefiore, without even mentioning "quarter." "Where are you going?" "I'm going to Montefiore." Today it's called Mishkenot Sha'ananim.

When I was four or five, we left there for a new quarter. But I remember my days in Montefiore, in these stone streets, always going with my father to the synagogue. Then we left Montefiore to live in a new quarter,

"It was a very narrow alley; there was room for only fifty or one hundred at a time, not more."—Dan Pattir, speaking of his visit to the Western Wall in the 1940s, during the British Mandate

Worshippers at Jerusalem's sacred site, known before statehood as the "Wailing Wall" and later as the "Western Wall," on July 1, 1910.

Maskeret Moshe—"the Remembrance of Moses." I remember very well this hall, like a private hall of my grandmother's, with a court inside, and all the homes in a small, private quarter. We lived with her for a while. And then, from Maskeret Moshe, we left for the new neighborhood that was built there, known as Mahane Yehuda. When you say today, "I'm going to Mahane Yehuda," it means you are going to the market, but it wasn't the market then; it was new, three- or four-story homes. We lived in a three-story home, and it was our home for approximately twenty years. And in

A street scene in Jerusalem on New Year's Day, 1921, during the British Mandate, as Emir Abdullah of the Hashemite Kingdom of Jordan, who had conducted secret, pre–Jewish state talks with Golda Meir and whose grandson King Hussein would make peace with Israel, strolls with the legendary Lawrence of Arabia, T. E. Lawrence.

Mahane Yehuda, I attended the well-known school of those days, Alliance Israélite Française.

Zalman Shoval   In Jerusalem and in Haifa, the British Mandatory presence was very marked. When I became older and active in some of our underground activities, when there was much more tension between the British and the

Jewish population here, because of the war and the illegal immigrants and underground activities, I was once briefly arrested by the British, but it was not a very significant development. I was sticking illegal leaflets on the wall.

Shabtai Shavit   When my mother gave birth to me, in '39, there was another period of Intifada—then they didn't call it that; it was "riots." Between Nesher and Haifa, there was an Arab village and in order to go from Nesher to Haifa, we used makeshift armored cars. So when my mother had to give birth, they took her in such a car to the hospital.

On both sides of Nesher, there were Arab villages where now you have Israeli settlements. The overall environment was one of conflict. The fact that you drove to Haifa with armored cars was the best expression of this conflict. Here and there, there were, all of a sudden, exchanges of fire. As kids, we used to sleep on the ground—my mother used to put mattresses on the floor—and outside the house, which was a very simple wooden house, my father had to put a fence up in order to defend us. We were surrounded by conflict and danger.

There is another kind of memory. Nesher was filled with olive trees, and

"Churchill was screaming: 'Either defeat them or get out!'"—Shmuel Katz, speaking of the last months of the British Mandate

Winston Churchill, right, then Britain's home secretary, who would twenty-seven years later preside over the British Mandate's end, confers with High Commissioner Herbert Samuel as they stroll through Jerusalem on March 29, 1921.

once a week, the Arabs from the neighboring villages used to come into Nesher to collect the olives from the trees. These instances were peaceful encounters between the Israelis and the neighboring Palestinians, and that was also the environment where I as a kid started to learn Arabic.

Yael Pattir   As a girl in primary school, I felt okay with the British. For example, there was one wonderful thing: every Friday, before the war, we used to have chocolate crème cake. When the war started, there was no cake anymore on Fridays. There was what we used to call "utility," in other words, the rationing of food and clothes. We had only one blouse and two skirts—one skirt for Saturday and one skirt for school.

Dan Pattir   The British goodies that we really liked—the chocolates, the chewing gum, the Players cigarettes—they always gave us, the good things. And in the British military shops were the good things, the corned beef and whatever, elite food for us natives. That was the good side of the British. The bad thing was their presence in the campaign against the underground.

In Tel Aviv

Zalman Shoval   Tel Aviv was not like the rest of the country; Tel Aviv was an island, from many points of view. Much later, I have sometimes said this to Palestinians, "Maybe I shouldn't say this to you, but you should take an example from us because we already had a state-within-a-state, to a large extent—not *officially*, but we did." And Tel Aviv was an example of that: education was Jewish; we even had Jewish police with a special uniform. So, in fact, I had very little contact with the Mandatory, certainly not as a child. The only thing we knew about the British was that they imposed a curfew on us from time to time and gave us trouble. Besides that, we had a holiday once a year on the king's birthday.

Of course, people who were in business and needed licenses and things like that had to go to the Mandatory authorities. But even there, it was usually Jewish or Arab officials whom they met, not necessarily Englishmen. Only if you went higher when you wanted to see the district commissioner, then they were British.

Bracha Stock   We lived for a time, when I was a teenager, on a street called Lord Byron Street [named after George Gordon, Lord Byron, the British Romantic poet and staunch Zionist, who versified, in "Oh! Weep for

Those": "The wild-dove hath her nest, the fox his cave, / Mankind their country—Israel but the grave!"]. Lord Byron Street was located in a section whose streets were named for famous non-Jews who were good for the Jews or did something for the Jews, such as Gotthold Ephraim Lessing, Émile Zola, and Jean Jaurès. [The three, respectively, were the German philosopher and convert to Lutheranism, 1872–1933, who returned to Judaism, embraced Zionism, and was assassinated by Nazi agents; the French novelist, 1840–1902, a champion in word and deed of Alfred Dreyfus, 1859–1935, the French Jewish army officer who in 1894 had been falsely accused of treason, convicted in 1895, and sent to Devil's Island, the notorious French penal colony in Africa—Zola planned to write a novel about Zionism but never realized this dream due to his untimely death from carbon monoxide poisoning, which resulted from a blocked chimney in his home; and the French socialist politician, 1859–1914, who, along with Zola, spearheaded the fight for the rehabilitation of Dreyfus.] Not one single person on that street knew who Lord Byron was. It was a

"The rooms were along the corridor; and there was another corridor, and at the end was a basin to wash your hands—there was no water in the rooms. And there was no electricity, of course, because electricity was brought to Tel Aviv only in 1927."—Yehiel Kadishai

תל-אביב שכונת רוזנפלד
Tel-Aviv — Rosenfeld's Quarter

A postcard depicting the Hotel Warshavski, located on the almost-empty Tel Aviv seafront, as it looked in the early 1920s.

A now-defunct casino located on the Tel Aviv seafront as it looked in the summer of 1926.

very small street, and for many, many years, until we were married, that street was not paved; it was all *sand*, for many, many years.

On this street lived a microcosm of Israel—Yemenites, Moroccans, Germans, Russians, religious, antireligious. At no other time in my life did I experience such a united community as there was on that street, in which you had people—our next-door neighbors were very, very Orthodox. I loved their Shabbat, when we experienced the joy of their singing. It never occurred to me or to anybody else to turn on the radio [during Shabbat] in this neighborhood; nobody turned on the radio in this neighborhood; nobody disturbed them. They never had any problem with us running around and doing all kinds of things. There was such, not just respect, but *tolerance* between both sides. Today, there is *no* tolerance from their side, even worse.

Yehiel Kadishai   I grew up in Tel Aviv. From Herzliya on the seashore, there was nothing. No street, no number, but it was the only place to live in. The mosque [which still stands and is located just north of the five-star David Intercontinental Hotel] was the last house on the beach before anything on the road.

My father owned a hotel on the beach, in the Rosenfeld Quarter, on the sea. The hotel had been built in 1923 by an American Jew named Rosenfeld. There were two buildings, twelve rooms in each one, tiny rooms to put a bed in and a simple cupboard. Mainly religious people, Hasidim, stayed there. They came by boat to the port of Jaffa. It was a deep-water port, and there was no jetty; the boat was anchored and there were barges.

I asked the three last mayors of Tel Aviv—"Cheech" Shlomo Lahat, Roni Milo, and Ron Huldai—whether they knew where the Rosenfeld Quarter was, and not one of them knew where it was. It was all sand, and a few stones were put there, just so people could walk. Now there is the Promenade here. [It is situated along the South Tel Aviv beachfront and is a popular spot for strolling and people-watching, especially on the weekends. It has shaded benches but also sober reminders of the dangers facing Israel—namely, memorials commemorating acts of terrorism and people killed in such incidents.] Here was a kind of balcony, and this building was the hotel, which was called the Hotel Warshavski because we came from Warsaw. In the wintertime, every one of the children had a room because the hotel was vacant.

My father sold the hotel to a gentleman by the name of Landau, from Poland, who came here and took it over for three or four years. Then it became a car park. My father left it because of religious reasons: ladies were going there to swim—not wearing bikinis, but still it was no good for the religious who came from Poland. They stopped coming there because my father had no *heksher* [a Hebrew word commonly used to denote a stamp of approval], no certificate of kashrut [Hebrew for "the state of being kosher"].

I wouldn't say the twenties were years of real *hunger*, but people didn't have what to eat. We were living on bread and oranges, and the oranges were not bought; they were taken by sea on rafts from the *pardesim* [orchards]. They loaded the oranges in wooden boxes on camels. This was the normal way of exporting citrus—grapefruits and Jaffa oranges—to Europe. They were coming from Jaffa harbor; there is no harbor anymore, just a marina there. Ramat HaSharon, north of Tel Aviv, was all *pardesim*; the land has changed; there are now no *pardesim* anymore in this area because the land is like gold in comparison with *pardesim*.

There [at Jaffa harbor] they were landing people as well. A few weeks after my father came and started the hotel, he wrote to my mother to come, and she left [Poland] with the children on a Turkish boat. She caught a train from Warsaw to Constanta [a port city on the Black Sea] in Romania, because Poland didn't have a port; they had only Gdansk, Danzig, and they were fighting with Germany. Then she traveled by boat to Jaffa, and when she arrived, my father was standing there, waiting for her. He always knew when the boats were coming, and he would have a car and a driver with a sign to bring tourists. He almost went bankrupt because the driver, a Russian guy, wanted more money, and my father couldn't pay him, so the guy took out the engine from the Rolls-Royce. As my father waited for my mother to get off the boat, she saw that the people were being carried by Arabs on their shoulders, on a rope ladder, to the raft, so she said, "No! No man will touch me! I'm going back to Warsaw!"

On the Kibbutzim

Simcha Waisman   On the kibbutzim, you don't have to worry about where your next meal is coming from; in the city, you do have to worry where your next meal is coming from. On the kibbutzim, you don't have to worry in the morning that you have to prepare breakfast—you have a meal, and that's the end of the story. Come lunchtime, you have *lunch*; come dinnertime, you have *dinner*.

My parents came to Kibbutz Ein Harod, and from there, they and other members put together a branch, Kibbutz Adonim, for what reason, I don't know. It was probably politics inside the kibbutz, you know: what to do, which direction to go; which direction *not* to go; what is what and who is who. And my parents were no longer interested in it so they packed up and left. The kibbutz was a great place for a while. But that's reality for the kibbutz; that's not reality for the *city*.

On the Moshavim

Muki Betser   I was born in October 1945 at Nahalal. My first recollection is that when I was three, I got kicked in the stomach by a colt. But what I remember is work on the farm, which I loved very much. I don't speak English well because I didn't study; I *worked*. My grandparents milked the cows by hand— I'm talking about the mid-1950s; there were no machines.

There were five of us, four boys and a girl, and my father and my oldest brother would go outside in the dark to turn off the water at around eleven in the evening. But when I was nine, when my sister was born, my father, thinking of me as bigger, sent me to do it. When I went out into the darkness and crossed the yard, the jackals were howling and I was afraid. Instinct tells you to go back, but I couldn't go back because that would have been a disgrace, so I had to go forward and complete the mission. As I got closer, the howling got louder, and I ran and turned off the water valve as quickly as I could and ran back. In the yard, I calmed down and went inside; everybody was doing what they were doing—my father was writing and my mother was working—and in a little while everyone would go to bed and nobody knew what happened to *me*.

At school the next day, that was the only thing I could think about. Why was I scared? It was only a yard. So when I got home from school, I ran straight to the water valve, and I told myself, Tonight I'll turn off the water again; I'll walk slowly and return slowly, and I won't be afraid. That night, I volunteer, "Father, father, I'll go out to turn off the water." I go out and the jackals are howling, but I just walk slowly. I close the faucet, walk back slowly, turning my back on the jackal, and stand there in the yard. I have conquered my fear.

I didn't realize it at the time, but years later this incident would be reflected in the operations and wars I would go through. Actually, when we charge against the enemy and they are firing at us, one's instinct is to run away. But you understand that you must carry out the mission, and you go forward.

Chapter 4

THE UNDERGROUND AND THE
BATTLE TO OUST THE BRITISH

Those who waged the long battle for independence ranged from Laborite political and military activists to Revisionists, the latter the Irgun and the Stern Group, known as the Etzel, a Hebrew acronym for Fighters for the Freedom of Israel, and the Lehi, respectively.

An Underground Foot Soldier's Ideology
versus Ben-Gurion's Policy

Joshua Matza All my life I have believed that Jordan belongs to us. When I was at school—when you listen to the lectures, you draw something—my group was always drawing the *Shtei Gadot la-Yarden* [the symbol depicting Eretz Israel as Greater Israel, encompassing Palestine and Jordan]. That's what I did all the time.

I was thrown out of secondary school—this was a school that belonged to the Labor Party—after Ben-Gurion called on the teachers to throw out members of the Stern Group; I finished secondary school though external exams because they drove me away when they knew that I was a member of the underground.

When the British Mandate was terminated, in 1947, I also participated in operations in Jerusalem against a command car of the British, throwing grenades on them and operating a bomb against this car. Today, when I'm in a car with my wife or my children, I explain to them, "That is the place where

"Always it was the Shtei Gadot la-Yarden [the symbol of Greater Israel] and then came the rifle."—Joshua Matza

Joshua Matza, then a fourteen-year-old foot soldier of the underground, poses with his weapon in the spring of 1948, on the eve of the War of Independence.

the car was driving." In those days, cars didn't have the power of cars of today, of course; when you came to the top of the hill, you had to change drives [gears] there. When you changed the drive, you stopped for a second, so that was the time when you operated the bomb, and you threw the grenades.

The Palmach, the Commando Unit of the Haganah

Rafi Eitan   The Palmach was never an organization in itself; it was always under the commander of the Haganah and the jurisdiction of the Jewish Agency.

Arie Lova Eliav   In '45, when the Second World War was won, *our* war was not won yet, so, by orders of the Haganah, a number of us stayed on in Europe, and we became very much involved in the so-called illegal immigration project. The Haganah was a much bigger, armed organization, and in this "illegal boat" period, the Haganah manned about sixty boats, and the Etzel had one or two boats. We didn't fight them, but we were much, much bigger in numbers. I was with the "illegal immigration" because inside Eretz Israel, sure there were frictions and in some periods they cooperated and sometimes they fought each other, but *not* on the boats.

We said, "One day we'll achieve a state of our own." But we had no time to think about it because we were very involved in helping Jews to board the "illegal" boats and come ashore. That's what I did with Tania and many, many, many thousands of others. I commanded a boat from Sweden in this "illegal immigration," a former American warship that we turned into an "illegal" boat. So from 1945 to '47, we were fighting to achieve a state of our own one day. But we didn't have time to think about it too much; we were very busy in our activities.

The Irgun

Shmuel Katz   The Irgun regarded Jabotinsky as the leader—actually, he had never been appointed leader, but they were working in his spirit, and he accepted the situation. So how did we keep in touch? The British had a very severe censorship of letters and telegrams. I was a consular official, and I could travel around; several times I traveled to Lebanon to send letters or telegrams to Jabotinsky. I also sat in on meetings when they decided on what to do with Raziel and [Avraham "Yair"] Stern [1907–1942, the founder in 1931 of Lehi, also known as the Stern Group and, pejoratively, as the Stern Gang, which broke away from the Irgun in 1937].

Shlomo Ariav   My contact with Begin from 1939 to '40 was through Chaim Landau and through David Israeli. They were very close. He was one of the members of the Irgun at that time, in Tel Aviv, and he had contact with Begin. I met Begin as head of the Irgun for the first time in Tel Aviv, at one of our camps that prepared soldiers before we started the Battle of Jaffa. At that time, I was in charge of the Medical Corps of the Irgun. Afterward, I was in his home many, many times for tea, with his wife.

Yehuda Avner   [On Ambassador Avner's first day in Eretz Israel, in 1947] we had come down Jaffa Road, and we had come to the crossing of Jaffa Road, and there was an Arab policeman standing on a pedestal, directing traffic. As the bus was approaching, this Arab policeman suddenly starts rolling his hands around to indicate there's a pest over there, and the driver leans over and says, "They're chasing an Irgunist." There was a kid who had evidently been putting up fliers, and the road was full of fliers. And they beat him down—I didn't see that part; all I saw was as he was being shoved into a Black Maria [a sinister-looking car used by security police].

My second view of Jerusalem was the next morning. I went to see the King David Hotel [which had been bombed by the Irgun the previous July], and out of the YMCA [on St. Julian's Way, as King David Street was called in those days, located directly opposite the hotel] came a red MG [a dashing British sports car]. In it was a fellow named Jock MacAdam. I was carrying a *Palestine Post* in my hand. I was just by the driveway, looking up into the south wing, where there was rubble, and he called over to me and asked whether I could lend him the paper, that he wanted to check the rugby scores. I saw this MG—it was a dream, an MG in Jerusalem? But he's checking the rugby scores, and I'm looking at his MG, and he asks me how long I've been here. I say, "One day." And he says, "Oh! Would you like me to give you a spin around Jerusalem?" And he gave me a spin around Jerusalem! It transpired that he was from the Shetland Islands, that he was a sheep farmer who had come into big money and he was on a tour—he had driven his MG across Europe, through the Dardanelles. I later bumped into him again, during the siege of Jerusalem.

Shlomo Ariav   I came back to Palestine and immediately rejoined the Irgun. And I found my wife in '46. We married in front of this house [now part of a lushly planted family compound, but then consisting of a single one-room house, in the wine-growing town of Binyamina, located thirty-five miles north of Tel Aviv].

Tzipora Ariav   I helped a lot. When they attacked the train station—they wanted to take ammunition from the British—two boys got killed and one was wounded. They brought a doctor, but the doctor refused to look at them, and they asked me to take him to Hadera.

Uri Avneri   At that time, in 1938 or '39, Etzel was the only organization fighting against the British. The Haganah was not fighting at all; they had a policy of not reacting. I'm talking about 1936, at the time of the Arab rebellion, the so-called riots, disturbances, and the official policy at the time was not to retaliate. I, at the age of fifteen, thought that was completely wrong, that we should retaliate, and one of the groups that was doing it was the Irgun. The Stern Group was formed later, in 1940. Actually, as an Irgun member, I was in the middle of the controversy with the people who created the Stern Group and those who remained in the Irgun. I would probably have joined the Stern Group except that they were advocating an alliance with the Nazis against the British, and I could not, under any circumstances, agree to that. So I remained in the Irgun until I left.

I left because, first of all, I thought that the whole idea of terrorism was basically flawed. Not morally flawed—at the time I was not interested in moralizing. I thought that the right way to conduct the fight against the British was mass mobilization—rather like what Gandhi did. The "terrorist" organizations, by their very nature, believed in action by the few, who drag the masses behind them. Second, I was very much against the Irgun's anti-Arab actions. I was for the anti-British actions, but not for the anti-Arab ones, so I left. In 1945, I wrote a brochure—my first publication ever—called "Terrorism, the Infantile Disease of the Hebrew Revolution." That was the end of my chapter with the Irgun.

What I brought from that chapter is that I understand how such organizations work. Even ex-"terrorists," like Yitzhak Shamir, are quite unable to translate their own experiences into others' experiences—they all think that they are unique—so I understand the workings of organizations like Fatah and Hamas and so on, much better than most because I just translate my own experiences to theirs.

Leaving the Underground and
Making a 180-Degree Turn

Uri Avneri   In 1946, I created a new organization that we called Young Palestine. We published a periodical called *In the Struggle*, and people generally knew us as the "In the Struggle Group"—the official name was quite forgotten. This created a huge outcry in the Yishuv because it was a totally heretical organization in practically everything, our main thesis being that we are a new Hebrew nation that belongs to the country and to the region and to the continent. The Canaanites said two things that we totally rejected: that we are not Jewish, that we have nothing to do with the Jewish people, with Jewish history, or that anything that happened to the Jews outside of this country is irrelevant and we are a new nation only of people born in the country. The second point was that they thought that there is no Arab nation—that there are no Arab nations, there is no Arab people, that they are really disguised Hebrews who cannot find their way to coming back to being Hebrew, and we shall create a big empire from the Mediterranean to Iraq, and everybody in it is really Hebrew.

I rejected this totally, and we said, "We are a new Hebrew nation, and, as a Hebrew nation, we are *part* of the Jewish people, much as Canada or Australia are part of the Anglo-Saxon people, a new nation but part of the bigger commonwealth. And, second, there *is* an Arab nation, there *is* an Arab national movement, and as a people belonging to this country, we are the national allies of Arab nationalism. We have a part to play in this, and we, together with the Hebrew national movement and the Arab national movement as allies, must join in the fight against colonialism and imperialism because the Middle East at that time was still under colonial rule. I wrote a pamphlet in September 1947 and delivered it to an Arab newspaper in Jaffa. Then the war started, and everything became obsolete overnight.

Personalities of the Underground

Vladimir Jabotinsky

Shmuel Katz I had, by chance, been given a copy of the Yiddish translation of Jabotinsky's book on the Jewish Legion [Jewish volunteers who had fought in World War I in the British army for the liberation of Eretz Israel from Ottoman rule]. I decided, This book must appear in English. So I translated it into English. I didn't know anything about how one published a book, but I had the manuscript typed, and I got Jabotinsky's address and sent it to him in Paris or London or wherever he was.

I had a reply from Jabotinsky in which he told me that there was somebody else translating the book and that he had to decide between us. I decided I'd go and see him when I was on my way to Palestine [to take up the cover position as "South African consul"] and ask him, "What's happening to my book?" He was in Paris at the time, and so, instead of going the cheaper way to Palestine, up the east coast of Africa, I went the other way, through Europe. He sent me a telegram to come to see him in Paris. On Christmas Day 1935, when he came to the door, he gave me the biggest compliment I have ever received: he looked at me and said, "I thought I would meet an *older* man."

The conversation I had with him was quite short—he was a busy man—and he told me that he hadn't any news for me, but that he did have messages that he would like me to take to Palestine for him. That's when I met his son, Eri [the head of Betar in Palestine], who had immigrated to Palestine. And so I went off to Palestine. A few months later, he [Jabo] told me that the other guy had dropped it and that he was taking my translation. And that's how the book came out finally. It didn't come out in his lifetime because he himself didn't find a publisher, and he was too busy, probably. It came out in America in 1945, twelve years after I had translated it. That was my first contact, personally, with Jabotinsky.

At the beginning of October 1937, I went off to meet Jabo in Warsaw. He said to me, "You've obviously come to see me, and I'm about to tour for a few days, so you'd better come with me." On the train, he had opened a small suitcase, a kind of "James Bond" case, with books in it. I saw that he had four books, and I said, "Mr. Jabotinsky, you're going away for three days; what do you need *four* books for?" He said, "I dip into each one of them from time to time." The book on the top was a detective story by Dorothy [Leigh] Sayers [1893–1957, a British writer of mystery novels whose works reached new audiences through their dramatization on television]. From then on, the conversation on the train was about Dorothy Sayers and [Dame] Agatha Christie [1890–1976, a contemporary of Sayers]. We agreed that Dorothy Sayers was a much better writer than Agatha Christie. We sit there as though we had been to school together, and we're discussing detective stories! Later, people who knew him for years in Europe told me he also liked Wild West films; whenever he came to a new place, he would find out if there were new Wild West films.

Jabotinsky died in August [1940, of a heart attack, during a visit to a Betar camp near New York City]. There was a letter from him that he had written from the boat—he had already gone to America—twelve pages long, giving me directions on how one could mount a propaganda campaign. Some of it was a little outdated because he was relating to the propaganda campaign he had conducted in 1916–1917. However, there were some important principles there. For example: always reply; don't let anything go by without replying.

After he died, a quarrel broke out between the Londoners and the Americans who had been with him in America. [The Americans] said that they were the leaders of the movement, and the people in London, the old Londoners, at any rate, said that they had remained on the spot and that's why *they* were appointed. But the whole movement started collapsing. And then, of course, the contact with the main part of the movement in Eastern Europe disappeared—Poland was the mainstay of the Revisionist movement, or had been—and that's how the Revisionist movement, as we had known it, collapsed. [While] it still remained and continued operating for several years afterward, until the state was established, it had no influence anymore.

Menachem Begin

Uri Avneri He was a Johnny-come-lately; he joined the Irgun and became the commander only after he came to Palestine with the Polish exile army of General [Wladislaw] Anders. He did not desert the Polish army here as everybody else did—all the other Jews who came with the Polish army deserted immediately when they came to Palestine. Begin was an honorable Pole, and Polish honor was more important to him than anything else, so he waited until he was regularly discharged. *Then*, in 1943, he joined the Irgun, when the Irgun was starting to degenerate. The great achievement of Begin was that he took all these people and practically created a new Irgun. The morale changed completely, and it became an active organization again.

Shmuel Katz   Jabotinsky was sitting with Begin, whom I didn't know, really—I had met him in the street with other people one day, but I didn't know him. I had never spoken to him, but I knew he was one of the leaders of Betar. I sat in the corner while they finished their talk, and then I talked with Jabotinsky. He pulled out a small typewriter and was about to start typing, but it was in Latin characters. So I just reached across the table and said, "Look, I'll do it for you." And he said, "You give that typewriter back; you're my guest!" He typed it. I don't remember what other conversation we had, but when I was leaving, he took me out to the corridor and said that the party was in very bad financial straits—as it always was—and he said to me, "Instead of opening new branches, we have to close them." But, he said, "Even if I have to work from a hotel room, I'll continue working." That was the last I heard from Jabotinsky.

In 1946, I again met Begin, who was in temporary residence under his home [hiding under the floorboards]—he stayed most of the time at home, but there were times he stayed with some of the Irgun members. It was nine years since the first time I had seen him with Jabotinsky in 1937. After we had said hello to each other, Begin said to me, "Do you remember the last time we met?" I said, "Yes." He said, "What you don't know is that while you were trying to retreat—you wanted to come in; you had been asked to come in and saw me and were trying to retreat—Jabotinsky whispered to me, 'Don't worry; I have no secrets from him.'"

Now, the remarkable thing is that nine years later, Begin, who after that meeting in '37 went through all his troubles in Siberia—a terrible time—remembered this little incident of my coming into Jabotinsky's room. I think that is one of the reasons why I finally was pushed out by Begin: somebody from whom Jabotinsky had no secrets must be a very important guy—which Jabotinsky had said, obviously, as a matter of politeness. It occurred to me later that Begin had taken it seriously; he remembered it all these years—possible rivalry, you see. But I had no such intentions. I didn't even want to go into the Knesset.

Shlomo Ariav   Begin was sitting here [in the Ariavs' dining nook]. I first met Begin in '42 or '43 in Shuni [near Binyamina, the headquarters of Betar]. I was a soldier in the Jewish Brigade, and he came as a soldier to see the members of the Irgun and the members of Betar. I was in uniform, and Begin was in uniform [of Anders's Polish exile army]. I could not at that time imagine what he would become. I was in the army, and our minds were occupied with different things. At that time, he was not famous; he came as simply *Begin*.

Going Underground

Shmuel Katz I arrived [in Palestine] in January '36. [Jan Christiaan] Smuts [1850–1950, the prime minister of South Africa, 1919–1924 and 1939–1948] had been defeated by the Nationalists, and the Nationalist government was much more friendly to the Revisionists than to the other kind of Zionists. They were all friendly to Zionism, as it happens.

In April '36, the so-called [Arab] riots started, and that dominated life for the next three years. My life wasn't typical because throughout that period that I stayed in Jerusalem, until October '38, I continued the same kind of life. And so, in the morning, I was a vice consul—I used to issue visas for South Africa and so on—and in the evening, I went to meetings of the Irgun.

Eitan Haber Immediately after the war—I was eleven years old—I joined the Betar movement. But you have to understand, then to be in Betar was like being today in the jihadist army. All of us in Tel Aviv–Ramat Gan were there in the best times of Betar. We were 120 youngsters— HaShomer HaZair, for example, was 4,000. My father didn't know that I had joined Betar. He said, "I don't want you to join Betar because I suffered too much, and I don't want *you* to suffer like I have suffered until today. If you want to join a youth movement, go to the Boy Scouts or other organizations. Don't go to Betar." But I did it.

Betar then had its own uniform, a dark blue one, and I put mine in the house of my best friend, Shlomo, with whom I had joined Betar. Every Saturday I would go to Shlomo's apartment, which was far away from Metzudat Zev, and then I would have to go back to Metzudat Zev. My father understood after some time that something was happening—maybe somebody saw me wearing the uniform—and he came to Metzudat Zev and gave me such a *potch* [Yiddish for slap] that I'll never forget! And he shouted, in front of all of my young friends, "I ordered you not to do it! Why did you *do* it?"

So I left Betar and joined the Religious Boy Scouts. Many years later, when I asked my father why we were not religious people, he said that he wanted, immediately after the Shoah, that I would be a good Jew, so I had to learn Bible, Torah, Talmud, and so I joined the Religious Boy Scouts and the Bilu School. But I didn't like school and, after a few months, I came back to Metzudat Zev. And since then, fortunately or unfortunately, I have been well known in the Betar movement because of everything I wrote—placards, everything.

Later on, when I was fifteen, I joined the election campaign of the Herut movement. I was responsible for propaganda in the Tel Aviv area; I was responsible for the loudspeakers at all of Begin's gatherings with the famous speeches.

The Lives of the Foot Soldiers of the Underground

Joshua Matza   I was a member of the extremist underground, the Stern Group. I was recruited at the age of fourteen. A woman who spoke well came to my school on behalf of the underground. She called to me, we walked a little bit, and she suggested to me that I join the underground. I looked at it as being an honor, and I agreed and joined that day. Of course, this was a very, very secret underground because nobody could know more than five people there.

In my first years, I went at night to post notices on the walls—every morning at two o'clock, three o'clock, four o'clock, going out and putting up these papers. They called us the "journalists"—and then the British were there, with their small tanks, and were after us all the time. One day, one of the youngest people of Lehi—they called him the "youngest soldier," a Lubavitcher—disappeared. He was a young man, my age. They had caught him putting these papers on the walls, and they took him. And from that day until today the Lehi didn't know what had happened to him. He was buried, they say, somewhere in the Arava, near the Dead Sea, in the desert. One day, the Stern Gang revealed who the person was who had kidnapped him. The man had returned to Britain after the Mandate, and he received a letter bomb one day. He opened it, and he died. It's a well-known story in Israel about this Lubavitch, this soldier, the youngest man.

We, the underground, were not many, a few hundred, and were very, very much ideological—no one could be in the Lehi if he wasn't also ideological. It wasn't a mass of groups they recruited; they chose one by one. When we were in the Lehi, we had to deliver this small booklet that we published, named "Growing: A Judea That Is Rising." I was still doing the work on walls and giving the booklet at homes, and they sent me to give it to a well-known one of us, [Dr. Joseph] Klausner. [Klausner was a major Zionist personality, who, along with Eliezer Ben-Yehuda and David Yellin, was invited in 1922 by Ronald Storrs, the military governor of Jerusalem, to be in charge of the Hebrew Department of the Council for the Establishment of a Palestinian University. Storrs had formed the council as an alternative to the proposed Hebrew University of Jerusalem. Six years later, on August 24, 1928, in a precursor to the Arab riots of 1929, after an attack by Arabs on sixteen Jewish homes in Talpiot, where the council was lodged, and their evacuation by the British police, the houses were immediately looted, resulting in the destruction of the libraries of Klausner and of the famed writer S. J. Agnon. By then, Klausner had become a professor of Hebrew literature at the Hebrew University of Jerusalem. This was a harbinger of the massive Arab rioting of the following year.] So I went with my friends to see Klausner. I knocked on the door, he opened it, and I gave the booklet to him. He looked at it and embraced us, then took us into his home, gave us some candies, and sent us away.

Surviving in the Underground

Joshua Matza   I didn't know any of the leadership; they were *underground*. We always listened to their speeches, and, of course, we knew them by their voices, with the radio of the underground giving the messages. And then we knew them through the papers, where twice a week they presented their ideas to the public. That's how we were acquainted with them.

My family was a very nationalistic one: my family is thirteen generations in Israel, and their ancestors lived all the time in the Old City, so it's obvious that such a family would have nationalist ideas. And the family members from my mother's side were called *parnass*—civil servants. We were four brothers, and three of us were in the underground—one was in the underground of the Haganah; one was in the underground of the Irgun Zvai Leumi, Begin; and I was in the Stern, so [there were] three different undergrounds in our home.

One of my brothers was put in prison by the British, in the Russian Compound. Those of the Irgun Zvai Leumi were put in prison in the Russian Compound, most of the time for two or three years, near what is today called Latrun. They detained my brother there because they couldn't charge him with anything, legally. They detained all these people there whom they thought, or whom they knew, were members of undergrounds, but they couldn't charge them in the courts.

I was the youngest son, and then the second and third were each four years older. There were a lot of discussions at home between father and sons; they weren't disagreements, but discussions about how to get rid of the British and how to establish the state, how to conduct the fight.

Our fathers and mothers were against our being in the underground because, of course, they were afraid. I remember when it was revealed that I was in the underground, there was a fight at home, and I left for a few nights. I didn't come back because it was really a very severe fight, like throwing me out of the house, and for a few days I lived in the streets. The people who took care of me were members of the underground, giving me a few cents to buy falafel during the day so that I could eat something. Then, on the third day, they took me someplace to be able to sleep—they had a few rooms in Jerusalem. Of course, my parents were worried! They looked for me, and they tried to ask people, but nobody could tell them where I was 'til one day—it was four or five days—they reached me and begged me to come back home. Then I returned home.

Notable Underground Actions

Barclays Bank

Barclays Bank was the target of several attacks by the Jewish underground, including actions on November 15, 1945, and on February 28, 1947.

Joshua Matza   We [the Stern Group] attacked, with the Lehi, in the well-known operation of trying to break the walls in front of Barclays Bank, where the Jerusalem Municipality is, near the New Gate. We tried to enter the Old City by exploding the walls near the New Gate, and we created a new, very special big bomb—it took more than ten people to carry it to the walls. We put it into the walls, and *nothing happened*! We had wanted to enter into the Old City to rescue people who were in the Jewish Quarter. The Jordanians on the wall were firing and firing on us from all sides.

The Bombing of the King David Hotel

Just before noon on July 22, 1946, the south wing of the elegant Byzantine-style King David Hotel in central Jerusalem, which housed British government, military offices, and the Criminal Investigation Division, was blown up by the Irgun following the issuance of a warning twenty-five minutes earlier to evacuate. Ignoring the Irgun's warning, Sir John Shaw, the British chief secretary of administration, forbade anyone to leave the building. It would later be reported that in dismissing the warning, Sir John had barked, "I give orders; I don't *take* orders from *Jews*." Eighty people were killed in the blast, including high-ranking Britons, Jewish officials, and visitors to the administrative offices housed in the hotel. Arab workers in the kitchen, however, did heed the warning and escaped.

Yehiel Kadishai I was not there when the King David was blown up; I was in Italy. All these events took place because we wanted to get rid of the British in Palestine. There was what we call common sense about the timing of an action, and not just the timing but also the way it was done—not to hurt people.

The Attack on the British Embassy in Rome

On October 29, 1946, a contingent of Irgun operatives blew up the British embassy in Rome.

Shmuel Katz I brought the instructions to Eli [Tavin] to get permission to blow up the British embassy in Rome, which he did. The British were running Italy then, and Eli went to Rome and organized the operation. The Italian police got on his track. I went off to Rome to look for him, to see whether he needed any help—somehow we had heard that he was in trouble. But there was no help that we could actually give him. He thought that he would get out of it. He still had to maintain contact with the people who had actually done the operation; he had to get them out of Italy. As a matter of fact, two of them had gotten out of Italy.

Yehiel Kadishai What has Rome, Italy, got to do with *our fight*? Where's the wisdom? We had to explain it, and we did explain it in Italy: we like the Italian people, they are friends of ours, and we know that they support our fight against the British who don't let the survivors come into their own country. We had quite a network of publicity, of advertising, of information, and the press was for us there, all the papers. A new paper, *La Repubblica*, was established at the end of 1946—it exists there to this day—and in the first issues, on the first, second, and third day, they had the story, with the front-page headline, "What Is the Irgun Zvai Leumi?"

Yaakov Levin and I gave interviews to a journalist, in the garden of the Villa Borghese, by night, on a bench that faces two ways. People sit on opposite sides, so the journalist faced one side and we sat facing the other way, speaking to him so that he shouldn't see us. He was using a kind of small battery wire [recorder]; they didn't have these [indicating the Strobers' tape recorder] in 1946. All of them who participated in the blowing up of the embassy in Rome are no more; the only one left is myself.

The Acre Prison Break

During the Mandate, the British established a prison in the ancient, northern coastal city of Acre at the Fortress of al Jazzar, named for Ahmad al Jazzar, who had held off Napoleon during the siege of 1799. Among the noted Jewish opponents of the continued British occupation of Palestine who were imprisoned there were Vladimir Jabotinsky in 1920 and Moshe Dayan, from 1939 to 1941, as well as many foot soldiers of the Haganah and other underground organizations, including Betar activist Shlomo Ben-Yosef, the first Jew to be executed by the British in Palestine. He was hanged there in 1938.

By the 1940s, increasing numbers of underground activists were being held at Acre, under extremely harsh conditions. On May 4, 1947, in a major and daring action, Irgun operatives attacked the prison, resulting in the escape of twenty of their fellow resisters.

Tzipora Ariav   The men who went to Acre to open the prison lived here [in Binyamina]. One of them left in the morning from a few houses down the street from here. I saw him on a motorbike, and I didn't know where he was going. After the bombing, at three o'clock in the morning, they knocked on the door and asked for Bubie [Mr. Ariav's nickname] to go and to show the prisoners, who had run away, the way and to hide them somewhere because the British were looking for them. At three o'clock he went into the fields to look for the men who had escaped. I was pregnant, and it was scary.

The Run-up to Partition

Shmuel Katz   In February 1947, nine months, approximately, before the Partition scheme was propounded, and before the Jewish Agency accepted the Partition scheme, Ben-Gurion was telling the British minister in London—it's all documented; they had the so-called Roundtable Conference in London; the "Roundtable" was *two* tables; the Jews sat *here* and the British *there*—that we suggested that the British should accept a hundred thousand refugees from the DP [displaced persons] camps [in Europe, where Jewish survivors of the Holocaust were subsisting] and then reinstate their rights under the Mandate as they had been in 1937. Nothing about a Jewish state; not *at all*. Ben-Gurion at some stage decided that that was the only solution for us.

Somewhere between February and September, he decided on the Jewish state, so he became the "father of the Jewish state." He became the father and the essential prime minister, but he knew the truth. It's true, once he decided, he was very effective, very fixed about it; he didn't withdraw at any stage. But he knew who had brought about this situation.

Yossi Ben-Aharon   My parents didn't want my two older sisters to get married in Egypt because they might remain there, so [my mother] sent them when they were of age to Jerusalem, in the care of her sister. Eventually, the older one, Yona, met an Israeli. They were going to get married on the twentieth of November, 1947, nine days before [the United Nations vote on Partition Resolution]. After some difficulty, the consul in Port Said gave visas for a short stay, and we came by train to participate in their marriage. We left my older brother there.

Sure enough, after a few days, there was the Partition Resolution, and immediately, the Arabs started attacking us. In Jerusalem, they set fire to the central business section, close to the Jaffa Gate. It became worse and worse, and after a few days we realized that there was no return. We also heard that there were pogroms in Egypt, so we telegraphed my brother: "Leave everything. Sell whatever you can sell, and come immediately." He came, but by then we were already cut off—it was the siege of Jerusalem. He came to Haifa, but he was taken to the army, and we never knew. Only after the cease-fire in July we heard that he was alive!

What Role Did the Underground Groups Have in the Achievement of Independence?

Shmuel Katz   I used to send material to the newspapers and to the local authorities in England, asking, "Why do you want to risk your sons' lives in a country that doesn't belong to you at all?"

Dan Pattir   I believe that we exaggerate when saying that we—whether it's Etzel or Irgun or Lehi or the Haganah—drove them out. I think it would have happened anyhow. Remember what happened around us: the Indian subcontinent had been divided—the British pulled out. The trend was to abandon, to retreat to the homeland. And Palestine was one of those things. They stayed here [as long as they did] only because of the riots, mainly because of the strategic position of Palestine vis-à-vis the Suez Canal and the eastern Mediterranean. It would have happened anyhow. But maybe we *accelerated* it.

Yehiel Kadishai   Dr. Abba Hillel Silver [1893–1963, the eminent, Lithuanian-born American Reform rabbi and Zionist leader who, from the age of twenty-four, presided over Congregation Tifereth Israel, in Cleveland, Ohio] said, "The Irgun will go down in the annals of history as the body that without its activities, the Jewish state would not have come into being." He doesn't say that the Irgun brought about the state, but that *without it*, it might have come into being ten or a hundred years later, but not at *this* moment or, maybe, *never*.

In Jabotinsky's poems, published in 1930, in one of his greatest works is the motto "There is the gold and there is the goldsmith, to melt the coins for the freedom of Israel . . . and in fire and in blood, from the teeth of the Egyptians to the teeth of Islam." This was written in 1929.

Shmuel Katz   When the Irgun was dissolved in 1948, it didn't go out of existence in Jerusalem because the Jewish Agency had agreed to the Partition scheme, and Jerusalem was left as an international city. And so Haganah and the Irgun and the Lehi continued to operate independently in Jerusalem. We worked together, actually; there was an agreement for the division of labor, so to speak.

Joshua Matza   In 2002, the special public body for commemorating the heritage of Herut issued these commemorative plaques and [former prime minister Yitzhak] Shamir [known as Michael Collins in the underground] signed it. A group came, and they presented it. "Yossi Avishai"—my underground names were Yossi and Avishai—"an anonymous soldier in the ranks of the Fighters for the Freedom of Israel, who was recruited for all of his life in all the days, the red days and the black nights, for the establishment of his country."

Shmuel Katz   Churchill's attitude at the end was not because of pro-Jewishness, but because he had a hundred thousand soldiers in the country, and they were costing millions. Britain was in a terrible state economically after the war, and so he said they couldn't afford it, apart from anything else, and he called it "this sordid war." I don't remember his objecting to hanging us, but that was another matter. Maybe, if he had been asked, he would have agreed to hang us.

PART TWO

The Proclamation of the Jewish State and Its Upbuilding

Chapter 5

MAY 14, 1948: DECLARATIONS
OF INDEPENDENCE AND WAR

Lest the concept of Jewish statehood be considered—as enemies of Israel are wont to suggest—a response to the twentieth-century Nazi Holocaust, the expression "Eretz Israel" ("Land of Israel"), meaning the nation of the Jewish people, was first found in the ancient Mishnah (oral law).

Joshua Matza   There are people who will say to me, "Look, Mr. Matza, if not for the Holocaust you couldn't have established the State of Israel." This is a wrong idea because the underground fought the British Mandate, and the British didn't have any other choice but to leave Eretz Israel. They brought it to the United Nations, and the United Nations made the resolution to end the Mandate in May '48. That is how we established the State of Israel. It had nothing to do with the Holocaust.

The Run-up to Independence Day: November 29, 1947

On November 29, 1947, the United Nations General Assembly, meeting at Lake Success, New York, approved Resolution 181 by a thirty-three to thirteen vote, with ten abstentions, providing for the partition of Palestine into Jewish and Arab states, with Jerusalem becoming an international city. The Jewish Agency—the organization responsible for Jewish affairs in pre-state Palestine—welcomed the plan, despite the fact that the territory allotted to the Jewish state would be quite small, while the Etzel and Lehi underground organizations rejected the Partition Plan, as did the Arab nations, albeit for different reasons.

On the day following the General Assembly vote, the Arabs of Palestine launched murderous attacks on the Jewish community of the Yishuv.

Arie Lova Eliav   The U.N. decision was important; it was the first time that an international body said that there should be a Jewish state. But the sword decided the borders; the borders of '48 were decided by battle, and they were somewhat larger than [those of] the U.N. resolution. As far as I am concerned, these borders, which are Israel *proper*, without the West Bank and Gaza, were the borders that I thought should complete all our Zionist moves.

Rav Shalom Gold   I remember being in the house where my parents were sitting in front of one of those big wooden radios. As the vote was taken, someone in the house was marking off the names, and when there was a majority, I was elated.

Dan Pattir   I had left my village in 1947, and I was in Tel Aviv. We didn't have the communications we do today; we had a big box radio—Marconi's old-fashioned World War II kind of thing—and we said to each other, "Shhh! Let's listen!"

Rafi Eitan   I was a soldier in the Palmach at the time. We were all beside the radio: "Venezuela? Yes! Saudi Arabia? No," and things like that. And we celebrated. We in the Palmach knew that the Arabs would start something very quickly. We heard it at night, maybe it was nearly midnight when it was announced, and immediately I knew as a commander in the Palmach at the time, I immediately started to gather my equipment. What should I do? What should I prepare for the next few months? We *knew*, and it happened very quickly. The announcement was in November, and the first riots started in December and January, and in February, I was already fighting the [Fawzi el] Kaukji soldiers who came from Syria.

Simcha Waisman   Where we lived, at the back, was the antenna for the Haganah transmission. Everything came to us firsthand, since all around, between us and the water and the Haganah headquarters and the underground, we were constantly exposed to the news. I remember when the U.N. voted, the music, the singing, the dancing, the loud relief for a lot of the people who came out of concentration camps. It was like somebody took a stone out of your chest, and you could breathe easily.

But by the morning, we already knew that we were in trouble. As a kid, I didn't know about it, but I remember people talking about what was going on now—the Arabs firing and killing. It was not only a joyous celebration, but we were starting to get independence and freedom, and nobody could persecute us. Nobody could chase the Jews away from their own land. It's not only okay; the United Nations has voted for it. The people can live independently from somebody who constantly tried to chase them and kill them. So it's not only joy, but a big relief. If you saw some of the people there, they hardly could walk because of where they came from. It was like a pressure cooker being exploded all of a sudden. I was too small, really, to appreciate it, but as you grow older, you start putting the pictures together.

Yossi Ben-Aharon   We were living in Jerusalem with my aunt and my grandparents. I was already sixteen years old. I wasn't working yet, but we already considered that we were staying because the idea of going back to Egypt was not so attractive. When the news came, we were all sitting there, and my aunt had the radio on, and we listened. I understood English, and I understood what was happening, that this was an earthshaking event, and then I went out to Jaffa Street and I saw something that I couldn't believe. Jerusalem was then divided—there were barbed-wire fences throughout the city; the British had taken hold of certain parts of the city, and they closed them because there was fear of the Stern and the Etzel groups—and when you saw British soldiers or police, you kept your distance. We saw these bulletproof cars that the police and the army used; we saw Jewish kids, together with the [British] soldiers, pounding on them and shouting, "Hooray! Hooray!" This was it; we thought that this was a day of celebration! There was dancing in the streets! I didn't join the dancing. But then the next day, we heard that there were killings of Jews.

Bracha Stock   We met at a very famous coffee shop where all the very big writers met. On Dizengoff, there were a lot of people, and they climbed up on top of the cars and went from car to car because the streets were so full that you couldn't get through. We were standing and yelling and shouting and singing, and he says, "*Wait*, tomorrow we are all going to war." I'll never forget that. Nobody listened to him, but that was exactly so. All the boys disappeared. My boyfriend was killed in the War of Independence.

Dan Pattir   We saw these lines of division [based on the Partition Plan] and said, "If we can divide the Galilee and the Negev, how can we survive that?" But the main idea was: it's very temporary; there's a starting point, and we are not going to stay in these lines. There was also the realization that you could not defend yourself in these kinds of lines. We started to mobilize more people into defense, and the country was cut off. We say in Hebrew, "The whole country is the front, and the whole nation is the army." I realized that this Partition Plan was very temporary, that we could not sustain these lines. These were bad times; we didn't know whether we could survive.

Shmuel Katz   After the Partition decision, the local Arabs started terror, and among the things that they did—strategically speaking, it was good that they did it—was to start shooting into Tel Aviv from Jaffa. You couldn't walk down Allenby Road without the danger of being hit by a bullet. A lot of kids were evacuated from the border area and brought into North Tel Aviv. We kept a little kid at home for a few weeks.

And so the Irgun decided that they were going to take Jaffa. While we were fighting—I say *we*; I wasn't here in those days, I was still in Europe—and had not succeeded on the first or second day, the whole world's press and everybody in public life was jeering at the Irgun, which had failed to take Jaffa.

Begin wasn't quite sure what was going to happen. Gidi [Amihai Paglin, the Irgun's chief of operations] came to him and told him that Jaffa could be taken, so he gave permission to Gidi to do it. We had quite a few losses—a number of our people were killed. The British intervened—they took part in the battle. They couldn't actually proclaim to the world that that was what they were doing, but that's what they *did*; it's all recorded.

And so, at the end, Jaffa had been captured. The British wouldn't sign a document with the Irgun; they had to sign another one, with the Haganah, so the Haganah is part of the peace. But as far as public opinion was concerned, people knew who had done this, and Begin was the most popular man in the country. One couldn't tell then exactly what the percentage of power was, but he certainly was very popular.

Joshua Matza   I remember that night very well because I was one of the thousands of people dancing in the streets. Then I and a group of friends decided to go to Tel Aviv to celebrate. We went that night, after dancing, straight to Tel Aviv with cars and trams. And we danced there, we celebrated then, and in the evening we came back. Then attacks on the buses started; the first attacks started on the bus from Tel Aviv to Jerusalem, passing through the village of Ramle. In those days, if you had to go to Jerusalem, you had to go through Ramle.

We didn't think about a war or starting a war, *nothing*, because we were so concentrated on dancing, and then it started with the attack of the Arabs on the buses. There, I can say, "There started the War of Independence." There were some people killed or injured. It is well known that this was the first attack after the announcement in the United Nations about the establishment of the rights of the State of Israel.

Shlomo Ariav   We knew that there was going to be war, and we were prepared for it. I wouldn't say we were afraid, but we had the feeling that we were very strong. We had prepared our people for it, and we were waiting for the moment when it would start. We were at that time sixty thousand soldiers. More than six thousand were killed at that time, a little bit more than 1 percent [of the total Jewish population of 650,000]. In my group we were eighteen boys, and four were killed.

Choosing a Name for the Reborn Jewish State

The decision by the leaders of the Yishuv to call their hard-won nation the "State of Israel" was inspired by the biblical patriarch Jacob. Following his struggle with the angel, Jacob had been granted the name Israel, a designation of honor, "for thou hast striven with God and with men and hast prevailed." Thus when Jacob's offspring, "the children of Israel," became a people, they were designated "the people of the children of Israel."

Independence Day

Yossi Ben-Aharon   I heard the ceremony at the museum in Tel Aviv; it was replayed so many times. The only newspaper that we could read then, that was available in Jerusalem, was the *Jerusalem Post*—the others were not available because Jerusalem was immediately under siege, even before May 14, at Passover of '48. I remember it was the first time we thought that we wouldn't have matzoth, or anything kosher for Passover. Then, due to the building of the "Burma Road" [a makeshift conduit for supplies named

"I remember the day of the establishment of the state very vividly, and I get choked up when I think of it."—Rav Shalom Gold

David Ben-Gurion, overcome with emotion in contemplation of what he is about to do, wipes his brow seconds before ascending the dais at the Tel Aviv Museum, on Rothschild Boulevard, on May 14, 1948, to read the new Jewish state's declaration of independence.

Moments later, a composed Ben Gurion, flanked by his provisional government, begins to read the declaration.

for the famous road built by the Allies in Asia during World War II], the first convoy came just a few days before Passover. I remember, I was standing in Mahane Yehuda on Jaffa Street, and I saw that some of the Palmachniks were there, with their wool caps. They were sitting on top of stacks of cartons and boxes of matzoth, wine, and all kinds of things. By that time, the only food we could get was rationed: we used to get several slices of bread with the ration book that was issued, and no water. You could only get water from pumps, from rainwater. There was no kerosene. Once in a while, there was a truck with kerosene; we used to stand in line, and if you were not lucky, there was a shell launched from the hilltop where the Jordanian Legion was deployed with British officers. They were shelling Jerusalem, and I used to listen to the shelling—the artillery would go off, you'd hear a boom from afar, and then you'd count: one, two, three, and then *swish!* And it would explode. If you were in the queue waiting for some kerosene, you'd have had it.

Much later, we heard that there was a big pogrom in Aden—my father came from Aden—a day or two after. That was the first big pogrom in any Arab country: they attacked the Jewish Quarter, burned the synagogue and shops belonging to Jews, and killed eighty-seven Jews. This was the worst pogrom. And, subsequently, we heard that the British police were there and didn't get involved. Some of the police officers had served in Palestine, and some of their friends had been killed by the Etzel and the Lehi so they felt, Let the Jews learn a lesson from that experience.

Simcha Waisman The apartment building where we lived was at the big circle—if you remember the pictures from Independence Day, there was a big celebration. The day of the independence celebration, I remember, we were sitting down around an old, brown radio that was so dead—the tubes were so old—that we had to hold the tubes down.

Rav Shalom Gold It was erev Shabbos [Shabbat], at Minhah [afternoon prayer time]. As I came into shul [synagogue]—Yeshiva Torah Das, at 207 Wilson Street in Brooklyn—I saw that about five hundred people were present. I recall someone running in and saying that President Truman had just recognized the State of Israel. The week before, there had been five hundred people for Minhah, but on May 14 five hundred *giants* were there. Anyone who didn't experience that feeling lacked *Yiddishkeit* [Jewishness]. I sometimes get impatient with young people who have no idea of the significance of the State of Israel. They take it for granted.

A Critical Moment for the New State:
Would Israel Be Recognized by the United States?

Abraham Foxman, born in Warsaw, Poland, during the Holocaust and hidden by Gentiles; post–World War II immigrant to the United States; associate national director and currently national director, Anti-Defamation League   Even though we have now learned that Truman was blemished by anti-Semitism, it was a courageous step for him to recognize Israel when he did. Imagine if he hadn't: the State Department said no. How do you measure that one dramatic, courageous step, which gave Israel legitimacy? Once the United States did it, that was it!

Raanan Gissin   The question of whether Israel would survive was on Harry Truman's mind right after he recognized the right of the State of Israel to exist. In late 1948, he commissioned a secret White Paper from a group of Harvard economists and strategists, and said, "Look, keep all the data that you have about the Jewish community in the Land of Israel, and tell me how long will that community survive now that it has been invaded by seven Arab armies?" They crunched all the numbers and all the facts, and they said, "Six months." Why? They said,

> In six months, the new state is going to run out of ammunition; in six months, it's going to run out of fuel; in six months, since the country does not have any natural resources, it's going to run out of the ability to buy things from other countries; and in six months, it will run out of heavy weapons and airplanes and artillery. And, worst of all, in six months, if the war continues, it's going to run out of manpower—the Jewish community there was only 650,000.

Six months passed, and that prediction did not come true! And another six months, and now we're standing here sixty years later, and Israel is a leading military force in the world. As an economic force, tied to the network of globalization when it comes to economic capabilities, it's one of the leading countries in high tech and biotechnology. And you think back and you ask, "What was missing in the equation that these Harvard economists put in 'six months'"? The Jewish nation and the Land of Israel, which is the essence of Zionism, never ran out of Jewish love and commitment—every place in the world, Jews supported this land because it's part of their vision, of who they *are*.

Chapter 6

AFTER THE CELEBRATION, WAR

On May 15, 1948, one day after Israel's declaration of independence, the new Jewish state was invaded by the armies of Egypt, Syria, Jordan, Iraq, Saudi Arabia, and Lebanon. In addition, several other Arab nations sent troops and supplies to the invaders. Upon the cessation of hostilities in January 1949, Israel had significantly increased its allocated territorial base under the terms of the Partition Plan, gains achieved at great cost: approximately six thousand dead, or 1 percent of the Jewish population. And while Israel signed armistice agreements with Egypt, Lebanon, Jordan, and Syria, the entire Arab world would refuse to recognize the Jewish state's existence.

Yehuda Avner   The siege was well underway by then. When independence was declared, the IDF was established everywhere except for Jerusalem because Jerusalem was meant to be an international enclave, and so Ben-Gurion, in his declaration of independence, excluded Jerusalem. Therefore, the Haganah, the Irgun, and the Lehi continued in Jerusalem.

Now, you have to imagine the scene: I am part of a group of thirty-odd people and we're desperately building fortifications, and we are on the eve of that Friday, May the fourteenth. We are where Yad Vashem [the Holocaust Memorial] is now, and we are digging a trench, snaking toward Ein Karem below, and the paramilitary assaulted Ein Karem. It was a rumor because everything was rumors; we had no communications of any sort, we didn't have a radio with us. A fellow by the name of Elisha Linder—he subsequently became well known here in Israel because he was the founder of the science of marine archaeology in this country; he's in the Marine Archaeology Department at Haifa University, and he was a professor there. But then he was a youngster in Jerusalem, and he was a driver of our commander. This was Friday, and there were no communications.

I met Jock MacAdam again during the siege because Esther [Cailingold, the sister of Ambassador Avner's future wife, Mimi] called and said that I should meet her at the Atara Café. Ben Yehuda Street had been blown up, the Atara Café's windows had been blown out, and they didn't have a menu. They had something called *kubeiza*, which was a plentiful weed that, when boiled, tasted like stringy spinach, and they had some powdered eggs, and that was it, and some smear on some kind of bread that tasted like sawdust.

She said, "I have a surprise for you!" What was the surprise? There she is with Jock MacAdam! Jock MacAdam had decided to volunteer, and he handed over his MG to the Haganah for the war effort. He had come to where Esther was—one of Esther's jobs was to vet volunteers, and she had asked, "Who do you know who can vet for you?" And he said, "There's this guy . . . " And this was the surprise: Esther said I should take him to our outfit, the bucket-digging brigade, so that's how I met him again. It was there that Esther told me that she had volunteered for the Old City.

So there we are now, on the fourteenth, and I'm on water duty with Jock MacAdam, shuttling jerry cans of water. They're digging the trenches, and there was a well about half a kilometer away. To get to this well, there was a zigzag part of a hillside, and they were exposed to sniper fire. There was a Jordanian brigade that was moving up to Jericho, toward Ein Karem, and it was going to meet with an Iraqi brigade. They're going to be attacking Jerusalem from Ein Karem, from the west, and *we* were supposed to stop them. We had a few Enfield rifles, World War I rifles, so Elisha Linder asked Jock MacAdam, "Go into town and find out what's happening"—we were *blind* up there.

It was Kabbalat Shabbat [the welcoming of Shabbat], and there was one other fellow with me, a Hasid from Mea She'arim ["Hundred Gates" in Hebrew; the ultra-Orthodox Jewish Quarter of Jerusalem], called Mendele der Hasid. Jock MacAdam eventually turned up—and he was wearing his raincoat even though it was May—and out of it he brought Cadbury's real chocolate and Kraft cheese. It blew me away! What happened, he said, was that the British left by the Jaffa Road, through all the Old City. Jock said, "I found these in the mess; I just *took* 'em!"

Then he brought out a bottle of wine. A celebration of the British having left, he told us; Ben-Gurion had declared the state. So here was a bottle of wine, and he said, "Let's drink *l'chaim* ["To life," a traditional toast]!" And the Hasid said, "Let's make kiddush [say the blessing over wine]." I'll never forget *that* kiddush! And after we made kiddush, we all drank a *l'chaim* and Elisha Linder asked, "What's the name of our state?" There was silence; Jock MacAdam hadn't thought to ask! So somebody called out, "Its name is probably 'Yehuda'—'Judea.'" And another one said, "Maybe it's 'Yisrael.'" It wasn't until the next day that we found out what the name of the country was!

Dan Pattir   We were in the last class of high school, in Tel Aviv, and the building was actually very exposed to fire from snipers from Jaffa. I remember lying on the floor so as not to get shot when they started in the middle of a Bible lesson. We sat on the floor because of the guns. Then we were sent out for about three months for military service. The change was very abrupt, from a placid way of life into war.

Yossi Ben-Aharon   I had taken a course in Morse code—the Haganah had a special course at a school in Jerusalem—and I was then sixteen and the Labor Exchange sent me. They said, "Go to the school." It was run by the Jewish Agency, to prepare for the bureaucracy of the state-to-be. They also prepared the people who worked in the ministry of communications, as well as Haganah. So some of us who finished the course came to the Army Signal Corps, where I subsequently went, and some of them went to the dead center of Jerusalem, which was under constant shelling. And I had to do it; I was working already. I had to walk from where we lived to the Central Post Office, under shelling, and work there. The Post Office was not a post office; it was the only means of communication for the army between Jerusalem under siege and the rest of the world.

When I was eighteen, I went to the army and became a Signal Corps officer. I taught Morse code in the training center of the Signal Corps and served for almost three years. It was very important before we had the kind of communications we have today.

Malcolm Hoenlein   I was four years old, but I do remember certain things. I remember my parents showing us images from *Life* magazine at the time of the gun-running. I clearly remember pictures of people dancing at a port here in New York where they were sending off weapons.

Joshua Matza   The first thing I did was sign up to train to be an officer. After the first training, I took a course of nine months; it was then somewhere around one year for becoming an officer in the field artillery. I served in the Israeli army in the artillery division, and it was fascinating for me. But after getting the rank of captain, I didn't want to continue because I wanted to begin my civilian work, to continue my studies and my career, and that's what I did.

Simcha Waisman   My father used to drive one of those motorcycles that had the sidecar, and they used to go from place to place, in the Galil, in Haifa. He and my mother, who was a nurse, had to go to Arab villages and treat the families and the soldiers. Everything was so old, and one time or another, the sidecar broke off from the motorcycle, and my father kept going. All of a sudden, he looked around and said, "Oops!" And my mother's sitting there on the side of the road, so he turns around and goes to get her.

Dan Pattir   We felt that we were very unsafe, and the future was very gloomy. Everybody felt that we were with our backs to the wall and had nowhere to fight back, that nobody would do it for us. We lost about 1 percent in dead, about 3 percent in wounded; it was a big toll. Everybody knew everybody, and there was no family that was spared from grief. My first cousin, a student like myself—we were in Herzliya High School—he was killed on the last day of the cease-fire. So it affected many other people in many ways.

Yossi Ben-Aharon   We were renting an apartment close to where the greatest shelling was taking place, Or Yehuda, and we escaped to the western side of the city. I remember my mother standing with her hand on the mezuzah, praying for my brother. [A mezuzah is a parchment scroll that is blessed and affixed to the door lintels of Jewish homes and that contains in miniature the biblical texts Deuteronomy 6:4–9 and 11:13–21 and, on the scroll's back, the words "Almighty" and "Guardian of the Doors of Israel." Usage of the scroll dates from the period of the Second Temple.] My mother didn't know whether he was alive or where he was. We had no communication. And then, in August or September of '48, he came back, wearing some kind of military uniform.

The Siege of Jerusalem

In the period following passage of the U.N. Partition Plan, the Arab community sought to isolate Jerusalem's hundred thousand Jewish inhabitants, achieving considerable success by placing the city under siege. After weeks of privation, the Jerusalemites were resupplied when a new road was cut through the mountains. It bypassed the main Tel Aviv–Jerusalem highway and was named the Burma Road for the road the Allies had built during World War II linking Burma with China.

Yael Pattir   We were teenagers. I was wounded by Arab shrapnel. We were living in Rehavia [a lovely, tree-lined district of one-family houses, now home to some of Jerusalem's wealthier citizens]; it was so beautiful. It was not rich because no one was rich. It was middle class—academicians, university people. Very close to us there was a small landing pad for light aircraft—not a real airport; just an airstrip. And every few days, we waited for the plane to come and bring something. All the children in the neighborhood used to run to the so-called Valley of the Cross and wait for the plane. Usually, it brought bread. During the siege, there was no bread, nothing! We would cut leaves from red grapes—my mother used to make a salad out of it—because this was in the garden, so it was very easy. Or they sent us to the fields, and we used to look for a kind of green with a taste that was very sour, and we used it to make a salad.

Dan Pattir   There was one bus per day, and the bus was sheltered against stones by netting. We got stoned and we got glass broken; it was a daily occurrence. Did we get used to it? Yes, we got used to it. We didn't *like* it. To tell our grandchildren that that's the way we lived, they can't visualize it.

Yehuda Avner   Life during the siege certainly got worse eventually, but one became conditioned to it, and it was gradual. It wasn't thrust upon you. Gradually, Mahane Yehuda [Jerusalem's large open-air market] shut down; gradually, the buses stopped running and the streets were empty; gradually, the shelling began.

Yael Pattir   We all went out to the fields. We were a youth regiment, and we had little jobs. The British were still here, so we were like information messengers. I remember putting a note in my shoe and bringing it from one place to the other. So we had the feeling that we were also part of the Haganah.

One day I was washing dishes in our kitchen—today, you would call our apartment a penthouse, but it wasn't. It was just a roof, and across the road from it we could see the village called Beit Jallah, from where they would shoot all over. And all of a sudden, there was a boom, and I nearly fell. I went out and saw that on the side of the door there were two bullets. They are there to this day.

Dan Pattir   As we were eighteen, we thought we were immune from arrest. I was also carrying secret caches in a sack, and we were ordered to go from one place to another and do it secretly. We definitely felt part of the process. Looking back, it was participating in the cause itself. We went to the beaches to help to get newcomers off the illegal ships. All the time; there was no limitation of assignments: carrying food, carrying secret messages, carrying some guns illegally, *everything*.

Yael Pattir   It's an age where you look for adventure, and we were part of the adventure. Sometimes it was a game; when we, after doing a job, met with our friends, we talked about it as if we were "Secret Service."

Dan Pattir   The difference was that we didn't create the adventure; the adventure was there. We were *a part* of it, and we participated in it. Reminiscing later about it, there also was a sense of pride.

Yael Pattir   But there were also losses. For example, a classmate of mine, the best student in the class, went on an ordinary bus when the British were coming out of their base in Jerusalem. They were shooting all over, and she was shot, while sitting on a bus, going home. Things like that made us feel very strongly, The British must leave!

Yehuda Avner   I was in a support unit of the Haganah. I knew one person in Jerusalem, Esther Cailingold, from B'nai Akiva in England. She was older than me, and she was a teacher. When the siege began, she volunteered full-time for the Haganah. I was living in Beit HaKerem, and she was also in Beit HaKerem—that's where they had their training base. She used to tell me about her younger sister, Mimi, in London. Their father was a very well known dealer in and publisher of Judaica.

Well, to get to the heart of the matter, Esther volunteered for the battle for the Jewish Quarter in the Old City. It was impossible to get into the Jewish Quarter. The status of the British was amazing; after the Partition Resolution, the British had declared that they would leave on May 15 and that until then, they would adopt "passive neutrality" in the fight. In that "passive neutrality," they controlled the gates into the Old City, and you had a situation in which there was fighting inside the Old City, against the Jewish Quarter. That was possible because the British controlled the gates and let reinforcements in. Esther got in as a teacher, and she went straight into battle.

Three days before the Old City surrendered, she was mortally wounded. She died on the day [May 28, 1948] that the Old City fell. She was twenty-two years old. She is buried on Mt. Herzl. After the war, I went to England to finish my studies and, having been one of the last to see Esther alive, I paid my respects to the family. Mimi opened the door. She never closed it; we have now been married for fifty-one years.

Esther wrote a remarkable letter—her last one to her family—which was discovered in the ruins of a bombed-out building in the Old City. It's her farewell to her family. To those who question whether Trumpeldor really said, "It is good to die for our country," he *did* say it. And this was

Esther's saying it in a letter to her family. She's asking for forgiveness, and her last line is: "Remember me in happiness."

The Sinking of the Altalena

On June 11, 1948, the Irgun ship *Altalena*, an American LST [landing ship-tank] purchased by the Etzel and named in memory of Ze'ev Jabotinsky, who had died in 1940—"Altalena" was his nom de plume—left Port de Bouc, France, for Israel. The *Altalena* carried nine hundred fighters, including Holocaust survivors, who were to join in the struggle for Jerusalem, as well as a large cargo of arms and ammunition.

The *Altalena* had sailed to France in early May 1948, anchored near Marseille, and loaded with French-made weaponry, including 5,000 rifles, 450 machine guns, and millions of rounds of ammunition donated at the behest of the French prime minister, Georges Bidault (1899–1983). At first, the Irgun and representatives of Israel's Defense Ministry negotiated the disposition of the weapons with roughly 20 percent to remain in the Irgun's hands. Then, on the late afternoon of June 20, as the vessel dropped anchor off Kfar Vitkin, a communal seaside settlement north of Tel Aviv populated by Mapainiks, David Ben-Gurion persuaded his cabinet to demand that all arms and ammunition be turned over to the fledgling Israel Defense Forces [IDF].

At Kfar Vitkin, the Irgun commander, Menachem Begin, boarded the ship. That evening, a furious firefight broke out on the beach between IDF forces and members of the Irgun. The *Altalena* then made its way to Tel Aviv, weighing anchor off Tiger Cat Beach, at the foot of Frishman Street. Ben-Gurion, likely worried that the Irgun planned to use the arms to launch an uprising—a claim vigorously denied by Begin—ordered the ground forces to shell the ship, despite the fact that a white flag had been raised from its deck. As the *Altalena* began to sink, frantic efforts were undertaken to evacuate the wounded.

Many of those on the left who defend Ben-Gurion's action in ordering the firing on the *Altalena* cite his assumption that weapons were being smuggled into the new Jewish state to be used by the Irgun to foment civil war.

The Run-up to the Operation

Shmuel Katz   In October, the man you might call Begin's chief of staff, Haim Landau, asked me to go to Europe. A Zionist Congress was going to take place in December, and there was a problem with the man who ultimately got the arms for the *Altalena*, [Shmuel Elhanan] Ariel—the man we called "the Irgun ambassador in France." He was a very good guy, but there were a number of Betar people in Europe who were wary of the Irgun. They hadn't joined the Irgun, but they had the stamp of the Betar on their reputation so there were always quarrels between them. They reported to Landau, and I brought the instructions to have him replaced.

Ariel was a unique character, a Romanian with a very, very sound French education—his flat was littered with French literature; he spoke French like a Frenchman; and he behaved like a Frenchman. You'd find him at one of the famous cafés in Paris practically every night, and his best friends were some of the girls in those cafés. He had made friends with a woman called Vayda [Madame Claire Vayda], one of the Jewish leaders of the Resistance [during World War II, who also ran an organization that helped Jewish refugees], and she had all kinds of contacts in the government. That's how Ariel made his contacts in the government, which finally led to them giving us arms for the *Altalena*. He was a great man in this respect.

He apparently was a good diplomat—he knew his stuff—and was very well educated, very intelligent. But he liked women—a lot of people like women. The day I met him, I came with written instructions, which I carried in the sole of my boot, that he was to be dismissed from the work he was doing. He wasn't a representative of the organization; he just was a kind of "ambassador." The man who ran the Irgun in Paris was Eli Tavin.

When I came to see Ariel, he invited me to lunch. He was staying at not a top hotel, but a good hotel. He had champagne on the table, and I said to him, "What do you have champagne for?" He said, "Look, I have lunch or dinner with people from the Foreign Office, with ambassadors, with other officials, and they drink champagne. I've got to live in a way that doesn't seem strange to them. They have to feel at home when they talk to me." So I said, "But *I* don't need champagne." He said, "Alright, so don't drink it!"

Ariel maintained his contacts with Mme. Vayda and with the official designate for about a year, and then he was sort of reinstated because a number of us—Eli and others—thought it was nonsense to tell a man like that it was our business whether he lives a loose life or not. He does what he has to do.

So it came about that he was the man who sent the memorandum at the beginning of '48 to Bidault, who was prime minister, explaining the importance to France of the Irgun and the need to supply arms because of the embargo. Without him, I don't think that anything like that would have happened. We didn't have anybody else who had such contacts in Paris. So he played an important role.

The Actual Attack: The Situation at Kfar Vitkin

Shlomo Ariav   At that time I was in charge of the Medical Corps of the Irgun; I took care of too many wounded. I came to the *Altalena* to help our people to come home. We were down on the sea. I took nothing with me; I didn't come as a medical officer. I was on the ship, too. When they landed, we went there to take some things off. I took some valises. It was nighttime—the moon was full, and you could read a book under it—and we were standing in line. Begin spoke to us and explained that he had an agreement—he had promised that we should be able to take part of the arms to the Irgun in Jerusalem; at the time, the Irgun in Jerusalem was still active—but that Ben-Gurion had failed to keep this agreement.

While we were standing in the line that evening, they started to shoot at us, and some people were wounded very badly. I had nothing with me, no bandages, nothing to help them. One man was dying in my arms; he was talking to me and showing me his pictures.

Finally, I went over to Ya'akov Meridor [an Irgun colleague who would one day become a government minister] and told him, "Ya'akov, I have to go up and help to take out the wounded." So he said, "Okay, take my car." I went up, but I couldn't do anything so I sent the driver back. Finally, it became a little bit light, and I said, "I can't stand it; I'm going back up," because they were dying for nothing; I couldn't help them. So I went up slowly. But one of the officers pulled me aside, and at that time I met with Moshe Dayan and told him that I would try to take off the wounded and that I would like to take them to Tel Aviv and to take the girls off. He told me, "You can take out the wounded; you can take out the dead. But the girls are soldiers; you can't take them out."

I looked up and saw what they were preparing to do there. They had no tanks, but heavy cars and mortars, and they were ready to destroy every-thing down there. So I asked, "What are you doing? There will be an explosion any minute because you're shooting at material that's already taken off the boat." But he said, "Who cares? Let them explode."

I went back. I saw that in these units, there were many people from the Lehi, and I saw some of the people I knew from Rosh Pina, from Betar. There were two brothers, and one of them remembered me. And finally he gave me a car to go down to try to take people out. I went to Meridor and told him, "Ya'akov, they're going to kill everybody. We must stop the fight-ing. Give me the right to tell them that it has to be stopped." And he gave me the right to tell them that. I went up and told them, "Meridor is ready to sign a treaty," and I left with the wounded for the hospital in Tel Aviv.

Nobody had taken care of them. A doctor had taken care of the wounded in the beginning, only dressings. I only heard afterward that Meridor had signed a treaty, but that some of them were taken to prison. They sent an officer with me, that I shouldn't escape.

When I came to Beilinson [a hospital in Tel Aviv], they didn't want to accept the wounded. Among them was a person who was wounded in his eyes so they took him in. But I was told afterward that he escaped the same night. Then I went to our base to tell Haim Landau what had happened and that I had to go back to Kfar Vitkin to tell Meridor. He said, "Everything is okay. Meridor has signed an agreement." And then I left.

Why Was the Ship Fired Upon?

Shlomo Ariav   After Begin spoke, they started to shoot. At night you could see the tracer bullets, and they were shooting not at the people on the beach, but at the people on the boat. This was nine o'clock at night. And then the ship left for the beach of Tel Aviv.

Yehiel Kadishai   Ben-Gurion was the leader of a party, not a leader of a nation, and he was concerned that *his* party and no other should rule. On the fifteenth of June his men came to him, [Israel] Galili [the Haganah leader] and others, and told him that the boat was on its way and that the Irgun wanted to get more people in—the survivors who were in France then, in camps, waiting for a boat to go to Israel. There was a state already so there was no problem with certificates. But they didn't want to let them go on *our* boat, the *Altalena*. We are going to make a coup d'état here!

Shmuel Katz   In my opinion, there was nothing else on the *Altalena* that could deserve being blown up by the government, except *Begin*. This was an attempt to murder Begin; I said so in my book [*Days of Fire: The Secret Story of the Making of Israel*]. I thought that the day after the book came out, I would have the police on my tail for slandering Ben-Gurion. There was an underground sort of campaign against what I had written, but nobody came out to charge me with it.

Joshua Matza   Begin was on the *Altalena*, and Ben-Gurion tried to kill him with his order to sink this boat.

Shmuel Katz   When the government was formed, they refused to have an inquiry as to why it happened. Now, why was Ben-Gurion so serious about it?

On June 22, the *Altalena* lies at anchor off the Tel Aviv coast, afire as the result of shelling by Palmach troops commanded by Yitzhak Rabin.

I wrote a long article on the *Altalena* in the *Jerusalem Post* some months ago, but it was a long article, and they cut out the last part, which gave the answer to this question: that Begin seemed to Ben-Gurion to be a serious threat. There were going to be elections, and the only man entitled to be prime minister, according to Ben-Gurion, was *Mr. Ben-Gurion*, first, because he had not fought the British at all; he had been the head of the Jewish Agency; and, as the man in charge of the Haganah, he was the defense man responsible.

They were still negotiating with the British in February 1947. All these years, they had fought Jabotinsky; they had fought the Revisionists; and in 1935 they had proposed plans for what they called "parity"—that the British should remain here at the top and that the Jews and the Arabs would each have a share in the government. And then came the White Paper of 1939, which turned a Jewish state into an Arab state. And *still* they were not prepared to fight the British!

Yehiel Kadishai   I was one of the two commanders, actually, of the Italian group on the boat. Eliahu Lankin was the commander of the boat; he passed away a couple of years ago. No one who knew what was going on could think that this group of people came to commit a *putsch*, a coup d'état, to overturn the government.

"I ran from one to another to try to help them."—Shlomo Ariav, speaking of the chaos that followed the attack on the *Altalena*

There were about 930—790 boys and 140 girls on the boat. I was the one who was writing their names in a book, but it was burned, so we don't even know all the names. We left on the tenth of June from Port de Bouc [near] Marseille, and we actually reached Tel Aviv on the twentieth. In accordance with the government's orders, we moved to Kfar Vitkin, and there we moved back to the sea.

It was a crime committed by a person who was full of wickedness and paranoia. In later years, Ben-Gurion said that if he had known Begin in those times, he would have not considered him an enemy. Ben-Gurion was evil.

The great revolutionaries, the wise men who opposed the British and fought against them and put bombs under the houses and did all those "dirty" things? We killed them with *sechl*, with common sense; we revolted against David Ben-Gurion. We are going to fight with weapons against the government? This man was just meshuga [nutty]! And he was wicked; he didn't like opposition; he was *kleine, kleine kepele* [small-minded].

Yossi Ben-Aharon   We knew very little about it because we were cut off. The *Jerusalem Post* was run by [Gershon] Agronsky [Agron, 1894–1959, the Ukrainian-born founder in 1930 of the *Palestine Post*; from 1950 on, the *Jerusalem Post*], who was a Mapainik, and of course, they took only that which the government gave them. Only later, I began hearing the actual story. Much of this, by the way, was not known by the public until much, much later, when people belonging to the Herut Party told of what had really happened. All we heard was just that there was fighting.

Eitan Haber   On the Saturday immediately after they bombed the *Altalena*, my father took me down to the cellar of Metzudat Zev [the Herut headquarters] and showed me parts of clothing and a bench [retrieved from the ship], and he said, "Look, my son, here Jews killed *Jews*," and he started to cry.

Shmuel Katz   After the *Altalena* business, the head of the Irgun in Jerusalem, who had been the district head before, got in touch with the High Command, which theoretically had been dissolved but was still meeting. He asked Begin to come to Jerusalem to take over the branch, because Ben-Gurion was due to visit Jerusalem and the Irgun people here—some people suspected the Irgun people here of planning to do something to Ben-Gurion that would not be *nice*; some people tell me now that they had heard about it. But Begin's colleagues, members of the High Command, persuaded, and Begin agreed, that as there would soon be elections to the Parliament, he had better stay in Tel Aviv and concentrate on that.

The result was that I came to be the last head of the Irgun in Jerusalem. But after all the fighting was over, or when the fighting was nearing the end, Begin came on a visit to Jerusalem, sort of to review the troops.

Shlomo Ariav   In '69, I was in New York, at a camp of Habonim [a Jewish youth group], in Ellenville one night. We were sitting, and someone starts to speak about the *Altalena*—he didn't know that I was involved—and he says, "I was an officer in Shin Bet, and at a certain time, we got the order to start the shooting." So I told him, "We heard that *we* had started the shooting." He said, "What are you *talking* about? I'm proud of it. I did it because this was my job."

Postwar Realities

Arie Lova Eliav   We knew that the War of Independence was the cause of an Arab refugee problem. But that's the way wars go, not only here but everywhere. If we had lost the war, no doubt, the Arabs would have made us refugees or would have thrown us back into the sea. We won the war, at a very great cost, and out of this zero-sum war, the Palestinian Arab refugee was created. I, for one, thought from the very beginning that Israel should help Palestinian Arab refugees to resettle in the West Bank, Gaza, Jordan, wherever, but *not* bring refugees back into Israel *proper*.

Actually, my view to this very day is that in what was Mandatory Palestine, two refugee states were created: Israel, which is a state of refugees or sons of refugees—my wife is a refugee, in a way *I* am a refugee, my parents ran away from the Soviet Union—so Israel is properly a state of refugees; so should the future Palestinian state, which I called for, in the West Bank and Gaza, maybe one day federated with Jordan, also be a state of refugees. They can rehabilitate themselves where they live. But I'm dead set against bringing back Palestinian refugees from 1948 into Israel's borders today because it's a recipe for the destruction of Israel. I'm all for helping, through international bodies and Arab states, to settle Palestinian Arab refugees in the future Palestine and Jordan and other Arab states.

The Assassination of Count Bernadotte

On September 17, 1948, the United Nations mediator and Swedish diplomat Count Folke Bernadotte, accompanied by four associates, was en route from the former British Government House to Rehavia, where he was to have had tea with Sir Bernard Joseph, the Jewish military governor. A jeep carrying four men swerved in front of his car and shots rang out, killing the count and one of his associates. While his assassins have never been apprehended, various groups claimed to have been responsible, among them Hazit Hamoledet, "Fatherland Front," a group falsely accused of being associated with Lehi. And to complicate matters, a drunken member of Lehi even boasted that members of his group had done the deed.

Joshua Matza I was in a camp of the Stern Gang. It wasn't a shock for us because the underground of the Stern Gang always used to execute people when they thought that they were against the purposes of Israel, or the State of Israel. Just hearing about Bernadotte's announcement to establish an international city in Jerusalem really disturbed me.

The leadership of Lehi was in prison because of the murder of Bernadotte. Shamir was sent by the British to Eritrea, and he escaped, but ["Rabbi" Yisrael] Scheib and [Nathan] Yellin-Mor remained in prison. If you were elected [to a political office], you got out of prison, so I participated in Knesset elections on Lehi's list, *Ha Lohamim*, "the fighters," just to liberate Yellin-Mor, and he gained a seat in the Knesset. I didn't remain with them; my purpose was to release Yellin-Mor from prison.

"We knew the day that Bernadotte was murdered that now they were going to arrest the entire underground, so they released us, and I went home."—Joshua Matza

Count Folke Bernadotte visits with Foreign Minister Moshe Sharett in Tel Aviv on September 9, 1948, only days before his assassination.

Chapter 7

THE INGATHERING OF THE EXILES AND THE CREATION OF POLITICAL AND SOCIAL INSTITUTIONS

The major initial challenge facing the new Jewish state was the absorption of Jews from the Diaspora, ranging from tens of thousands of traumatized Holocaust survivors to the more than one million who were summarily expelled from neighboring Arab nations following Israel's Declaration of Independence.

Later, Israel would absorb several million additional immigrants, endangered Jews from Yemen, Ethiopia, and the Soviet Union, despite the new state's severely limited resources and little planning.

Natan Sharansky   On the positive side it is a very deep, very vibrant, very strong Jewish and democratic society, which also has a unique capability to absorb millions of new immigrants in such a way that all of society is always enriched. And, in fact, in the third generation, the immigrants are at least as successful as the veteran immigrants. Even in times of war, our economy is so strong that they prosper. So we have unique talents built into this country and the society.

Now, on the negative side, when it comes to the reality, there are so many groups that belong to different worlds that religion becomes not something that unites us with the generations before and with our future, but a political tool that divides people, a lack of tolerance among different groups, and the feeling that, in fact, there is no way that we can be at peace with one another as long as there are those who will not accept *my* position. All these things are very upsetting and very difficult to accept.

Ernest Stock   I don't think that there was any real plan, except for what they called then "Population Dispersion and Housing." Ben-Gurion was more or less the initiator and the ideologist when it came to immigration. His vision was, We need many more Jews here, and we are able to absorb them. Let's get them here; we'll find a way to absorb them.

The British had used this slogan of "Absorption Capacity"; they wouldn't let Jews in. There was a strict quota system during the British Mandate, which was based on one of two principles. One, if a person was a so-called capitalist, which means they had to show that they disposed of a capital of a thousand British pounds, which was then quite a lot of money—the rate of exchange before the war was $4.20 to one British pound; a thousand British pounds was $4,200—you had to show that you had that money in the bank. The dollar in those days—the 1920s and '30s—was a lot of money.

Ben-Gurion said, "I don't believe in this business of 'Absorption Capacity'"; it was just a British excuse for keeping Jews out. So the British said, "Either you have this money and you can start a new business, or you can live for a while on your own," or the second category that they would let in was called "Pioneers," *Halutzim*. That means if you were going to a kibbutz, then the kibbutz would take care of you and you were not going to be a burden. And the third category, which is talked about much less, was the so-called Youth Aliyah—they were youngsters who would come here with a youth group and usually would also go to a kibbutz. Quite a few German Jewish kids, aged, say, from fourteen to eighteen, would come under this system.

But Ben-Gurion was not much of an economist. There was no plan for industry. In those days, the most productive thing was considered becoming a farmer, so they would use a lot of the money that had come in from UJA [United Jewish Appeal] and similar types of fund-raising abroad to found new agricultural settlements—moshavim or kibbutzim—and to buy cows, to teach people how to become farmers. And there were a lot of mistakes made.

Some of the early sociology at the Hebrew University dealt with the principles of how to settle the new immigrants. For instance, I found out that if you took the Yemenites and you put them in a village together with Romanians, it just wouldn't work out. And it took them a long time to come to the conclusion that these villages should be homogeneous—you'd have a village of Hungarians here and a village of Moroccans there—and you're much better off than mixing them in one community because even their religious services were of a different kind, and certainly their courting habits and educating the children and that sort of thing.

So I would say that there was not enough planning, and there was not enough social work. When I came here for the second time, in 1952, there was no real social work training here. The first School of Social Work at the Hebrew University was put in as late as 1960, and there was an American, a Gentile woman, a social worker who was training the people who would later run the School of Social Work. The whole thing was very amateurish.

I was in Dimona, and I observed the Jewish Agency procedure there. The so-called social workers—the Jewish Agency called them social workers—were just housewives who were drafted to go around and help the immigrants get settled here. They were not professionally trained, and the social work was considered showing the people where the grocery store was and where the children would go to school and where the clinic was and how to sign up for welfare benefits. It was all very matter-of-fact and concrete, and nobody asked the women, Do you have any problem adjusting to your new environment? Do you need any kind of support? That was completely unknown here. That kind of psychology came much, much later; there was no psychology involved at all here.

For instance, I took a trip, as the Jewish Agency's observer, from Venice to Haifa on an immigrant ship to see how they were handling the immigrants. All they were asking them were matter-of-fact questions: Where were you born? How old are you? How many children do you have? What kind of training do you have? Do you have relatives in the country? That played a role in where they were sent; if they didn't have any relatives who could help them out, they'd be sent to outlying areas where it took them years to move away from. You'd see the same people in Dimona, like the guy who says, "I'm a butcher." And they say, "Never mind, here you're going to do building work." He would still want to find a job as a butcher, and he would do all in his power to find a flat, let's say in Jaffa, where he could move his family, but the Jewish Agency would say, "Okay, if you move away from here, you're not getting any support from us." So he was on his own, but he would get a job as a butcher somewhere else, so the planning was *very* poor for these immigrants. And the main thing was housing: we've got to find housing for these people; we can't keep them in the tents until when the rains start again because in 1952 or '53, there was a terrible, rainy winter, and the floods and water were flooding these temporary camps. They had a campaign to help people take in the children—older populations would take in the children till the rains stopped because there was no way of keeping them dry. So the planning was poor. And if you look back on it, you wonder why the Jews of America, who already then had fairly well-developed communal agencies, took so little interest—they were just raising the money. The slogan was: "Israel Needs Your Support" and you contributed to the UJA, and the UJA sent it to the Jewish Agency. But nobody said, "Why don't you have an American adviser tell you how to handle these children?" It's true they had the Joint [the American Jewish Joint Distribution Committee]. Now the Joint was setting up an organization here, the Institution for Handling Handicapped Immigrants. They had specialized care for people, let's say, who came with tuberculosis or the blind—they had a village for the blind that they had set up that handled the very difficult cases. And they also took care of the aged. They set up relatively comfortable homes for the aged population who needed institutional care. There was an agreement between the Jewish Agency and the Joint that said, "You handle the people who are old, who are handicapped, and who are blind." Israel had no institutions. The basic population here—the six hundred thousand Jews who had been here in 1948—were a relatively healthy population and had very few cases of the handicapped. So the Joint set up these old age homes. I was working for the Jewish Agency at the time.

Arie Lova Eliav   I was very deeply involved—I was the right-hand man of Levi Eshkol—in bringing a million Jewish refugees, especially in the fifties. I was deeply involved in bringing as many Jewish refugees, Holocaust survivors and others, from the East and from the West, from Yemen, Syria, Lebanon, Iraq, and Libya, all in all, about a million Jewish refugees.

Dan Pattir   For me, the big change came with the influx of newcomers, with temporary tents, the *ma'abarot*, in the transition camps. It was dramatic but not easy. For youngsters born into the Israel independence, I imagine it was different, more gradual.

Yael Pattir   For us in Jerusalem, it was different from Tel Aviv because we had the feeling that *we* were the center, so when the war ended, there was a certain feeling that we had shared it, that we had been a part of it, and that we knew that we were part of the establishment of the state.

Moshe Sharon   When the State of Israel was established, it was clear to every youngster that what you have to do is build more, establish more; nobody cared about Arab lands, even *the leftists*. Most of the kibbutzim that were created were created on what used to be called "Arab land," which was taken after the war. The whole idea was to strengthen the borders, to establish more towns and villages and more agriculture.

The dream of a young man in my time was called [in English-language translation] "the fulfillment." And what was the personal fulfillment? You create another kibbutz on the border. That was what a Shomer HaZair used to do. The most important thing was fulfillment—to create a strong state, well-defended, a wonderful army; that was the dream.

Akiva Eldar, born in Haifa in 1945; author; journalist with *Ha'aretz*: diplomatic correspondent, 1983–1993, U.S. bureau chief and Washington correspondent, 1993–1996; currently, chief political columnist and editorial writer; lecturer, Tel Aviv University's School of Journalism; consultant, CBS News; frequent guest on major networks in the United States, Canada, Europe, and Israel My parents came here, and they built the state. I personally feel that my generation has betrayed our parents. What we are going to transfer to our children is not something that my parents built. My generation has destroyed the country by our lack of ability to make peace. The easiest way is to blame it on someone else—the Palestinians, the Americans. But it is my generation that failed. I feel very bitter about this. I can say that since I am not able to guarantee my children a safe future, I wouldn't blame them if they would leave.

Everyday Life in the New State

Tel Aviv

Simcha Waisman We lived in an apartment building, Allenby 19, with something like ten boys and five girls from different families. The thing that struck me the most was the diversity among all the people living under the same roof. And it didn't matter where they came from or what language they were speaking; eventually, all the neighbors understood one another and always lived in harmony. The whole family got together. It didn't matter which house; it didn't matter how much food you had. There was always food on the table for the Friday night meal. It was quite an experience, you know. My parents always kept us together.

It was a very, very upbeat city, every day new. You could walk in the streets. Besides bicycles and buses, we didn't have cars; you could take a bus at midnight and sit in the station and wait, and nobody bothered you. I used to travel all over—a very friendly, very warm city.

A lot of people were going to work very early in the morning and finishing work and still at night going out to the cafés, which were full. And the beaches were full. The Tayelet [seafront promenade]—that was not this

Tayelet now [the current, extensive promenade is landscaped and includes benches and, sadly, memorial plaques for Israelis killed in military actions or terrorist attacks]—was full. We felt so safe and secure that my parents didn't even wonder when I was not home at night. We didn't roam too far away since we lived at Allenby 19—you were by [where] the Dan Hotel, the Sheraton, [and] the Hilton [are now]. And Sderot Rothschild [the street in downtown Tel Aviv named for Baron Edmond de Rothschild, a scion of the French branch of the famed European banking family, whose philanthropy to the Yishuv, and later to the Jewish state, was legendary] was down the block. If you wanted to go to the movie theater, we had five in a matter of six blocks from us.

I had a lot of friends. Sometimes my best friend was a Muslim, sometimes a Christian. Sometimes I didn't know what they were, even, and it didn't matter. I grew up with a lot of good kids, maybe not with money and clothing, but whatever you had, whatever you wore, you *cherished*; that would be your clothing for the next year. We were rich with love from our parents, and that's sometimes more important than anything else.

I stay in touch with two of them. One of them—my best friend, actually—is in real estate; buys, sells. He escaped from Lebanon in 1957 in a rowboat. And my other friend is working as a technologist in a place that fixes planes. None of them are in the military. Some of them retired because you get bored after a while with what you do. Some of them are running hotels; some of them are working in a big insurance company as investigators.

During the crises, during the wars, everybody lived together. Crisis was every day there because Allenby comes from Jaffa. We used to go to the roof, and the sharpshooters from Jaffa, the snipers, used to shoot. If you go to the house, you can still see the bullet holes. But we always pulled together.

Jerusalem

Akiva Eldar We were very poor and were very concerned with how to make a living, but everybody was poor, so it was okay. Both of my parents worked so I had to take care of myself. I went to the very prestigious, private Reale School, which included a military academy, and even then I had to work. Many people who later became generals—Amnon Mitzna, for one—attended the school. If you made it there, the sky was the limit for you.

Rav Shalom Gold When I came to yeshiva in B'nai Brak [in 1955], there may have been twenty American students in all of Israel. Today there are thousands and thousands of American students. It was a poor but growing

A scene of contentment: Ein Hanatziv, the kibbutz where Ernest Stock worked for a time in the early 1950s.

country, and there was a tremendous sense of being involved in a great undertaking, of building a country.

It was the end of the period of rationing, which means there were three eggs a week, two or three ounces of meat, and lots of tomatoes. I can't forget the tomatoes. I was eating one, and an Israeli student came over to me and said, "This is not the way to eat a tomato." He puts a tomato on a plate, takes out a knife and a fork, and cuts the tomato in half with real fancy wrist action. He says, "You see these two lines? These are the bones. You see this part . . . ?" It was as if he were describing a *sirloin steak*! That "steak" was just a tomato, but a tomato wasn't a *plain* tomato. It was a staple of food.

"My grandfather and grandmother made aliyah from Russia. They were pioneers and founded Kibbutz Degania."—Muki Betser

Abraham Foxman In 1958, it was still close to the pioneering days. There was the absorption of immigrants, and everybody was a lot closer, a lot warmer, reaching out. Wherever you went, there was a very, very comfortable feeling. Jerusalem was divided then, and so it was a little bit tense. I remember going to Ramat Rachel to really see the border—I climbed up one night to see the other side of Jerusalem. But it was just very, very small and comfortable.

On the Kibbutzim

The Reverend Jerry Falwell   On my first trip to Israel [in 1970], I stayed on a kibbutz up near the Galilee, and I got to know some of the people there, and I fell in love with them immediately. I was so impressed at how everyone on that kibbutz had assigned responsibilities. Young and old, they all did what needed to be done; they were able to teach their children the chores that they had to do. While the kibbutz is not typical of Israel, it gave me a week to be around salt-of-the-earth people there.

Knesset Elections

Shmuel Katz   I proposed, when the Knesset elections were about to take place, that I didn't want to stand for election; I preferred very much to take over the paper that they were starting. But [Yohanan] Bader insisted that I go into the Knesset. I never quarreled with Begin. I *disagreed* with him very often, in the Irgun. He was 100 percent in the Irgun, but when he became a politician it was impossible.

I always tell people that Begin had three personalities—we all probably have more than one personality. In Poland, he told me, in that first conversation, how he became the new leader of the Irgun after Raziel had died. He said that in Poland, when he wrote what he called "The Declaration of War against the British," his people who knew him in Poland said, "Oh, that's nonsense; this is all just talk." He said that about himself, and I gathered that in Poland he had that reputation of being a big talker. What else could you do in Poland except talk and write? You couldn't kill anybody.

But when he came to Palestine, he became a new man: he didn't talk to anybody, and he ran the Irgun. He was the best man as a leader of an underground movement. He was very brave and very democratic. In the Irgun, no decision was made unilaterally; everything was decided after discussion, as far as I know. Usually, the initiative came from [Amihai] Paglin, "Gidi," as he was known then, and it would be discussed. And one of the questions always asked was, Could this possibly kill civilians? If the answer was yes, we didn't do it. It was absolutely banned. And when it had to be done where there were civilians, they were warned, as they did in the King David [Hotel].

Joshua Matza   I was very close to the Herut Party but not a member of the Herut Party. When the demonstrations began against German reparations, the demonstrations of Begin, I decided to officially join the party because I was really so against it. But I couldn't make speeches against it in the street, speaking against it without doing something more official, so in 1952, I joined the Herut Party. This Herut Party has disappeared.

Confronting the Painful and Divisive Issue of Reparations

In September 1952, Konrad Adenauer, the chancellor of the Federal Republic of Germany, signed an agreement to provide hundreds of millions of dollars in goods and services to Israel, as well as allocating additional funds for rehabilitation and resettlement and direct payments to 275,000 Holocaust survivors.

The reparations issue was fiercely debated in the Knesset, with the opposition leader, Menachem Begin, characterizing the funds as "blood money."

Joshua Matza   Germany! That was the first reaction when I saw what happened there. Thank God that my family wasn't involved—we are thirteen generations in Israel—but, look, it was Germany, of course, the Holocaust. When we are speaking about politics, those were the years where I found myself really involved in politics with the Herut Party, mostly involving Germany in those days. I wasn't in those demonstrations of throwing stones at the Knesset; I wasn't then a member of the Herut Party, but after the Reparations Agreement, I joined them because I felt that I had to help them.

I can tell you, until 1999 I didn't even dare to own something produced in Germany—not a car, not a pin—nothing at all! I was against it, and I demonstrated against people buying from Germany. And I can tell you that even today, I am against the German people and against all that is connected to Germany.

It was too early to start with them in the lifetime of Ben-Gurion. We should be compensated, of course. Millions of dollars is not enough— whatever you sign with them, it's not enough; nothing can compensate us. But '52 was too early; it was seven years after the end of World War II, too early to legitimize the Germans, to say to them, "Okay, you are welcome to the family of the democratic world."

Begin demonstrated against it. We could find other ways to be compensated, even in those days, but not by shaking hands with Adenauer in the

Waldorf-Astoria Hotel. [On March 14, 1960, Ben-Gurion shook hands with Konrad Adenauer (1876–1967), the chancellor of Germany (1949–1963)].

We could find another way, not giving them the "certificate" to cleanse them; we cleansed them seven years after they destroyed our people. And I always mention in my speeches that if it hadn't been for the Holocaust, there could be fifty to sixty million Jews in the world today—*fifty to sixty million Jews!* We had to demonstrate against them; it was too early. One day, of course, we had to finish all this settlement, to be compensated, because they owe it to the Jews and to the people.

After many years in the Knesset, I was heading the interparliamentarian committee and we had to go from place to place, throughout the world. I headed it for ten years, participating with one of my friends from the Labor Party, and one day we had to go to Berlin. This was my first time being there, and I am sure it will be the last time, because I don't believe that they can change. I still have hate against the Germans even if I shake their hands in Parliament, even though I visited Berlin, even though I know that they're a great help to Israel, and not only with money, but by helping us in the world—with Europe, with the United Nations—being our friends. So I shake their hands. But can I *love* them? Never! They killed us like *animals*.

Despite Israel's Acknowledgment of the Value of
Reparations, Calling the Nazi Regime to Account:
The Capture of War Criminal Adolf Eichmann

On May 11, 1960, little more than seventeen years after the end of World War II in Europe, Mossad agents, in a daring action that took place many thousands of miles from Israel, captured SS officer Adolf Eichmann in Buenos Aires, Argentina. During the Holocaust, this Nazi functionary had, with startling efficiency, implemented Hitler's "Final Solution."

Eichmann was spirited to Israel on a special El Al flight that had brought Israeli foreign minister Abba Eban to Argentina for ceremonies marking that nation's 150th anniversary. In Israel, Eichmann was tried, convicted of crimes against humanity, and sentenced to death. He was hanged at Ramle Prison, outside Tel Aviv, shortly after midnight on June 1, 1962. This was twenty years, four months, and twelve days after he and his colleagues had decided during a conference held on January 20, 1942, at a villa in the Berlin suburb of Wannsee, to launch the Nazi regime's annihilation of European Jewry.

Rafi Eitan At the time, the Mossad and Shabak were under one commander, Issar Harel; he was called the man in charge of the secret services. Both the Mossad and Shabak had only one Operations Division; I was the head of this Operations Division so I was aware of the contact with the unit that searched for Eichmann. I'm talking up to '57, '58—the Mossad and Shabak purposely did not look for ex-Nazis because we were too busy. We had a lot of other targets, and only after '56 Issar Harel started thinking about it, and in '56 or '57 he put together a special unit to try to find ex-Nazis. Now we were looking for ex-Nazis, but especially, we were looking for four people: [Martin] Bormann, the deputy of Eichmann; [Heinrich] Muller, the commander of the SS and the Gestapo; Dr. [Josef] Mengele, who was very well known; and Eichmann, the one responsible for the "Jewish Department" of the Gestapo. Then we were looking, and we were sending people to look according to information. And I, as head of the Operations Division, supplied them with equipment, sometimes with operatives to help them. So I was aware, since '58, '59, '60, about all these small operations of looking for ex-Nazis.

When Zvi Aharoni sent his message that he was sure that he had found Eichmann—Zvi Aharoni was also in the rank of head of a division in the services at the time, and he was a very serious man—we were sure that he was right. When Zvi Aharoni sent the message, Issar Harel called me, and before Issar Harel told me, Amos Manor warned me that Issar Harel was going to ask me to help the unit take Eichmann from Argentina to Tel Aviv. Issar Harel called me and very simply told me, "Here are the facts." I asked for the files, and he told me, "Look, I order you to do the whole operation, to choose the people, and to coordinate the time with me. The target is to capture Eichmann and bring him into Israel and to trial." Immediately, I understood the historic effect of an operation like that. We were talking about it with Issar Harel, but both of them were very cool and analyzed it as we analyzed any other operation. Then I told him, "Look, I need a day or two to study all the facts." And I also told him, "Zvi Aharoni is on the way from Argentina to Israel, so I shall study it and give you my plan." Then I started, as usual, to sit with my people, to choose the people, to choose the equipment. And when Zvi Aharoni arrived, I analyzed the maps—remember, none of us had been in Buenos Aires before that. We took the maps, studied the city. We already had a method of how to study a foreign city and know that city before we arrived, by buying some books on this city to study the roads. That's very easy, by the way; you need about ten hours to study a city, and then you can feel quite safe when you drive on foreign streets. And we did it. I prepared all the equipment; I prepared the people.

Then Zvi Aharoni arrived, and he was a partner in all we did. That was at the beginning of April 1960, and on the twenty-fourth of April, I was already in Buenos Aires. Issar Harel went to Buenos Aires before me, and we divided the work between us. He took on some of the logistics and also coordinating with El Al about the plan. I took on details of the plan physically—we prepared some elements inside the airplane—and I also took on finding alternatives, meaning by ship if we were not able to do it by air. Then I went to Argentina and met Harel every day, sometimes three times a day, and that's now part of history.

Coming Face-to-Face with the Personification of the "Banality of Evil"

Rafi Eitan   His [Eichmann's] head was on my knees. You know, all of us during World War II had a song in Israel, the "Partisan's Song," and it says, "Don't say this is my last time. We shall come again and everyone will say, 'We are here.'" And that's what I thought at the time.

Could the Team Have Captured Dr. Mengele?

Rafi Eitan   There was a discussion. At the time, we had information that Mengele was living in Buenos Aires, and Issar Harel brought a few people, besides my team, to look for Mengele. He came to me and said, "Rafi, we know where Mengele is. Let's prepare an operation." And I refused. I said, "Issar, no way!" Why? That was after Eichmann was already in our hands, and we had a very good chance of bringing him to Israel with no problems. Everything was already prepared, and we already knew that we could smuggle him to the airport. "If I go and capture Mengele now, I'm risking the first operation. Now my opinion is that the first operation is so important that it would be a crime"—I didn't say "crime," but I meant it—"to risk it with another operation."

Fortunately—because otherwise I would have gone with Issar—when our people arrived at the house of Mengele, the neighbors said, "He left a month ago." They didn't know where to, but he had left. Probably he left because of the news in the newspapers in 1959 and 1960 that Nazis, including Mengele, living in Argentina were many. Therefore, he felt he was not safe and he left Argentina before he knew that Eichmann had been captured.

Eichmann's Reaction on Being Captured

Rafi Eitan   He had fear, no doubt; his body was trembling. He was very afraid that we were going to kill him immediately or maybe torture him. But we calmed him down with a few words, and later, in the house, he was quite calm. He understood that he was going to be brought to Israel and to face trial. We told him, "We're going to bring you to Israel; you are going to face trial in a democratic country. You could have a lawyer, anything." And he told me, "I knew that you would come after me."

Chapter 8

IDENTIFICATION IN THE DIASPORA WITH THE NEW JEWISH STATE

Malcolm Hoenlein   I grew up in a religious Zionist home where Israel was always important. My parents were active in a religious Zionist organization, and we had ties to people in Israel. Even before that, both of them, in Germany, had been in programs to go on aliyah. But, obviously, the war interceded and they ended up in America.

But things from Israel, things about Israel, were always very important from as early as I can remember. In the early '50s, they went out of their way to get Israeli products, and that was always something very special. I remember their sending packages to survivors who had come to Israel, coffee and other things. I grew up in schools where all of this was taught. So Israel was always central, a natural part of everything. I don't know that there was one point where, all of a sudden, somebody said, "There's a place called Israel." It's something we grew up with and were surrounded with.

Combined with that was the Holocaust, also an important theme, though never focused on by my parents so much as [being] something that affected *me*. I knew that the answer to the Holocaust was two things: Israel and Jews empowering themselves. And I got involved from the time I was, literally, ten years old. I got involved in political campaigns: when I was eleven, I snuck into Adlai Stevenson's hotel room when he was running for president [for the second time, in 1956], and he took me around with him for two days on his campaign appearances. I would go to school and come right afterward, and we talked about a lot of issues. I once met Abba

Eban—he came to Philadelphia to speak and I went; I just recently found a note he gave me at that time.

Then I was teaching at Penn and doing my doctorate, and before the '67 War, I literally went speaking everywhere, for every cause, and for everybody, raising money for the families, and [later] for people suffering from the War of Attrition. Then I went to work for the JCRC [Jewish Community Relations Council] in Philadelphia because the Israeli consul general, Issachar Ben-Ya'akov, called me and said, "Listen, we need you to do this; you've got to do it." That's how I got on this slippery slope that led me here [to his current position at the Conference of Presidents].

My whole life was geared in that way. I can't say when I first thought of it, but I have a predilection toward politics anyway, or an interest, and had one from a very young age, although I liked baseball, too. But the Holocaust and its aftermath were motivating factors—that Jews can never be put in that position again. America is unique in that respect, in giving us the opportunity to really have a voice, and a voice in the one superpower in the world, and to have a disproportionate voice, because most people don't care. So those who care get hurt, and, over time, it's the credibility of the arguments you're making, the legitimacy of the case you're making. It's not just something you can impose, which is why this whole argument about "the Lobby" is so pernicious, for many reasons, but also that it's not because 2 percent of the population advocates something; it's because the cause is a just one.

Rav Shalom Gold   I came by boat from Venice with a group of five other yeshiva students; we were going to be counselors at a summer camp for children from Morocco. Also on the boat, with about fifty of his Hasidim, was the Satmar Rebbe. It was a five-day trip, and on the last night we stopped at Limasol, Cyprus. We knew that whoever remained on the boat was bound for Eretz Israel. There were religious and nonreligious people aboard, and there were arguments during the night. I don't think anybody slept. Then, at about five a.m.—it was June 27, 1955—all the arguments ended. People lined up on the deck to catch the first glimpse of Haifa, and at about six-thirty, we were close. You couldn't buy the experience of the emotion of our first glimpse for a million dollars. As we came into the harbor, we noticed that three or four little tugboats, each with a band on board, had surrounded our ship. They had come to greet the Satmar Rebbe.

Abraham Foxman   I went in '58, when I was eighteen, and I went by boat because it was too much of a dream, and I wasn't ready to be here on

Monday and be in Israel on Tuesday. I had been taught, and it was part of my upbringing, and so I went by boat. Every day, we got closer and closer to Israel, and the night before, we all stayed up to wait to see Haifa. I felt very comfortable. I'd come from having been born in Poland, and then coming to America, I really wasn't sure where my home was. I knew it wasn't *Poland*. America became my home, and then Israel became my other home, a very comfortable feeling.

My dream and the reality of Israel matched. I was eighteen, and I traveled with a student Zionist organization—there were several hundred Jewish students, from the United States and from around the world, with whom we interacted. We traveled across the land—it took three and a half hours to get from Tel Aviv to Jerusalem. I worked for two weeks on a kibbutz. To hear Hebrew spoken, to see Jews in the streets, all these things were magnificent; everything was wonderful. Every moment was exciting and new. I was raised traditionally—I went to yeshiva—and so to see the Bible alive, to visit these places, there were no disappointments, no disillusionments. Later, I began to see some of the realities versus my hopes and expectations and the fantasy of this perfect Jewish existence.

Joseph Hochstein   I became interested in coming to live here in the early seventies, but knowing about Israel as a place, some time in the fifties. But in terms of actually living in Israel, I can date that to when I was here in 1972 on a visit. For a lot of American Jews who used to come here, the first trip to Israel, in one way or another, exceeds your expectations. I've talked to any number of people who have had some extreme reaction—that there was something about it that really grabbed them, and they really loved it.

On my first time here, I remember riding in from the airport at night with a group of American Jewish journalists. Dick Yaffe [a colleague based at the New York *Jewish Week*] and I were talking—this was not *his* first visit—and as we rode through the night and you could see the lights of villages, he was calling out the names of places we were passing. These were all places I had read about in history books or the Bible, and that was really exciting. Then the whole experience here was just so different from what I knew in the States or what I had seen elsewhere. I'd traveled a bit by then in Europe, and I had been in South America for a while, and I just found this whole thing very different and very exciting.

I went one evening alone to sit in Dizengoff Circle [where Mr. Hochstein would be wounded some years later in a terrorist attack], before they built the overpass in the 1980s—this was in 1972—and I was sitting there. Some families were walking around, with children, and this was a time when families like ours, with little children—our youngest was two years old—didn't walk around downtown [in Washington, D.C.] in the evening with their little kids. Only a few blocks away was a little school that I walked by one day and saw the kids, and I wondered how it would be if my kids went to that school, or if we lived in Tel Aviv what life would be like. So at that point, I started to think about it [making aliyah].

We sent our son Marc here in the summer of 1979, when he was fifteen. He had wanted to do some kind of summer trip, and he had thought about trying to go to California or Europe. He was going to McLean [Virginia] High School—kids were doing trips of one kind or another—and we suggested to him that he go to Israel on a trip with a group that was organized through the Jewish Community Center of Greater Washington. They had a program that had recently begun with Kibbutz Beit Hashita [in the north of Israel], and he was in the first group of U.S. teenagers who went there for the summer. They had a program worked out for them where they worked on the kibbutz and also did some touring around the country.

The decision for aliyah was made in September 1974, when I was here with my late wife, Anne. It was her first trip. She was quite struck by Israel, and we talked about it. Then she died unexpectedly in March 1981. I remarried in 1983 and sold the *Jewish Week*. My wife and I arrived in Israel on September 12, 1983.

Dr. Ronald S. Godwin, executive vice president, the Moral Majority, 1979–late 1980s; senior vice president, the *Washington Times*; president, Jerry Falwell Ministries; appointed executive vice president, Liberty University, Lynchburg, Virginia, 2006; staunch supporter of Israel   Having been raised as an evangelical Christian from birth and having grown up on Sunday school and Bible stories about the Holy Land, all of these early childhood stories and images and impressions were stored tightly packed in my mind when I arrived, as a young adult, in Israel. And so it was a very spiritual and thrilling experience to finally land on that soil. Now, when I got there, the reality didn't disappoint me. The fact that I was looking at a modern country and all the accoutrements of a modern country and a very sophisticated, modern airport, for some reason, in no way struck me as being discordant or different. I, of course, knew that the other half of my brain had all that information tucked away, so I just neatly mixed my anticipation of arriving in the biblical land with arriving in modern Israel and accommodated both of them. And it was a very exciting moment.

But I was sobered by the heavy military presence; the military shot up somebody's luggage just outside the terminal because they didn't know who had identified it, and that was a sobering moment when I looked up and saw somebody's luggage that had been aerated by an Uzi out there.

Joesph Hochstein   Israel was different from what I had planned and expected. I thought I would take some time off and gradually establish myself here. Instead, I wound up being sucked into work early on, establishing a small business. We went to an ulpan in Tel Aviv. It was pretty intensive and took a lot of time and energy. It might not have been a typical aliyah. I wasn't under pressure immediately to go out and get a job, so we weren't starting life from ground zero. We rented a furnished apartment and spent time at the beach.

At the beginning I was elated at certain elements of feeling connected. I used to take the bus frequently. I would look at the people on the bus, and two things, particularly, got to me. One was that on the bus or on the street I'd see older people who were obviously survivors of the Holocaust or people who had come from countries of the Middle East. To me, the idea that this was some kind of victory over the Holocaust was very exciting.

The other thing, which was nonideological, was that I discovered as I looked at the peoples' faces that some of them could have been the faces of people I knew in the States. I worked with someone in Washington who was of Dutch Jewish extraction. I swear I saw him one day on a bus in Jerusalem. It *wasn't* him, of course, but someone who looked just like him. Something else that struck me was that Jews here don't all look alike. In the United States they may look more or less alike, members of the same family or clan. Here you have all these different facial and body types. It's a mixed population.

Ronald Godwin   I didn't find the Israelis particularly prickly; I just found them to be very intelligent. I felt like, Now here's a nation of people, no wonder they're achieving, no wonder they're accomplishing, because this is an intelligent and highly creative people. I like these people. And I never will forget my arrival at the Hilton. The gentleman behind the desk looked me right in the eye and said, "Welcome home!" I was just very captivated by the warmth and friendliness of the hotel people, and even the airport people and the bus people.

Chapter 9

ISRAEL'S POLITICAL LEADERSHIP, PAST AND PRESENT

Since Israel's establishment on May 14, 1948, the Jewish state has had twelve prime ministers. The first five were from the Labor Party. Following the election of Menachem Begin in 1977, the next three were from Likud. The Labor Party returned to power in 1984 on the accession of Shimon Peres, according to the terms of a unity government. In 1996, the Likud candidate, Benjamin Netanyahu, was elected, followed in 1999 by Ehud Barak, who established the One Israel Party. In 2001, Likud returned to power on the election of Ariel Sharon, and in 2005 the prime minister created the Kadima Party, under whose banner he was expected to be reelected in March 2006. In January 2006, following Mr. Sharon's stroke, he was succeeded by his deputy prime minister, Ehud Olmert.

David Ben-Gurion (May 14, 1948–December 7, 1953; November 2, 1955–June 21, 1963)

Born in Poland in 1886, Mr. Ben-Gurion made aliyah in 1906. After serving in the Jewish Legion during World War I, he was a founder of Histadrut. Leader of the Jewish Agency during the pre-state era, as Israel's first prime minister, he was the new state's architect, establishing its institutions and increasing its population. He retired in 1953, only to return as prime minister two years later. After leaving office for the second time, he retired from politics in 1970, returning to his home on Kibbutz Sde Boker. He died there in 1973.

Joshua Matza   It isn't easy for me to say that Ben-Gurion was a great leader because there are some chapters in his life with which I wouldn't agree. But I have to look at the establishment of Israel—creating the Haganah and the kibbutzim—all these helped us to gain and to establish the state. There was a saying in those days: "Another *dunam*, another *dunam* [a unit of land area, about one quarter of an acre]." I look at all these kibbutzim that were established, places where we could stand and expand.

Zalman Shoval   Ben-Gurion was probably the greatest leader the Jewish people have had for many years: he combined leadership capability and the capability of a politician—it's not always the same—and being a strategist. And Ben-Gurion knew how to exploit that very well from his political point of view. He sometimes created antagonism with Begin because he thought that it was politically helpful to him to create an enemy, even when the enemy wasn't so terrible.

"Ben-Gurion's mind was probably more attuned to strategic realities and necessities than many of the professional military men. Without him, there wouldn't have been a State of Israel."—Zalman Shoval

Former prime minister David Ben-Gurion, who is about to begin his second term, converses with outgoing prime minister Moshe Sharett on August 15, 1955, during the official Knesset ceremony marking the change of administrations.

Joshua Matza   Ben-Gurion and Begin, and Begin spoke, of course, of the Kingdom of Israel. Begin's vision was of the bigger Eretz Israel. We had in Israel two giants: Ben-Gurion and Begin. And they were rivals—oh, what rivals!

Moshe Sharett, né Shertok
(December 7, 1953–November 2, 1955)

Born in Kherson, Ukraine, in 1894, Mr. Sharett arrived in Palestine with his family in 1906. He settled first in Ayn Siniya, an Arab village in Samaria, where he became familiar with the Arabic language and culture. Two years later he moved to Jaffa, where his father, Yaakov, was a founder of the Ahuzat Bayit Quarter, from which Tel Aviv developed. After leaving for Turkey to study law and on the outbreak of World War I volunteering for the Turkish army, Mr. Shertok returned to Palestine. There he served first as secretary of the Jewish Agency's Political Department and later as its head, playing a key role during the British Mandate in establishing the Jewish Brigade.

He later served as the State of Israel's first foreign minister, at which time he changed his surname. He succeeded David Ben-Gurion as prime minister, but his tenure was marked by many difficulties. On the overturning of Mr. Sharett's cabinet in June 1955, Mr. Ben-Gurion once again became prime minister. Mr. Sharett resumed his position as foreign minister but soon resigned. He died in Jerusalem in 1965.

Levi Eshkol (June 21, 1963–February 26, 1969)

Born in Ukraine in 1895, Mr. Eshkol made aliyah in 1914. A founder of Kibbutz Degania Bet, he later served in the Haganah. He was a cabinet minister during the Ben-Gurion era and served as prime minister during the Six-Day War. He died while in office.

Arie Lova Eliav   I was the right-hand man of Eshkol, and to my mind he was the best prime minister we've had. Ben-Gurion was the father, and it's hard to compare them—it's like comparing an American president with [George] Washington. But otherwise, Eshkol was the wisest, cleverest prime minister we have had.

"Levi Eshkol took a very poor Israel and in a very few years, Israel emerged as self-dependent in economy."
—Rafi Eitan

Prime Minister Levi Eshkol discusses the situation in Israel with President Lyndon Johnson at the latter's Texas ranch on January 6, 1968, almost seven months to the day after the beginning of the Six-Day War.

Yehuda Avner   Levi Eshkol is emerging as the Harry Truman of the State of Israel—the fact that he held the army back the way he did [before the outbreak of the Six-Day War], subject to abuse of the military command, until he had exhausted the diplomatic opportunities. Only then did he give the permission to go.

Zalman Shoval   Levi Eshkol was very far from being the Harry Truman of Israel! I'll tell you why. Much less at the time, but now, in retrospect, I have a great deal of admiration for Levi Eshkol. He was a very pragmatic man; he was a patriot; he certainly played a very important role in building up Israel because he was very practical: we have to do this, we have to do that. And he had a good sense of humor, which politicians don't always have—but he was much less confrontational than Truman. Truman was confrontational, and he was not. I think he [Eshkol] did not understand well enough the bigger political issues of Israel. There was a great deal of hesitancy on foreign policy issues. And he didn't really understand sufficiently well the issues that came up on the eve of the Six-Day War. So was he a good leader? He was. But he was not a *great* leader.

Rafi Eitan   No doubt, Levi Eshkol was one of the best prime ministers of Israel, although he emerged at the time as a rival to Ben-Gurion. And that was because of Ben-Gurion, not because of *Eshkol*. Eshkol was a practical man, very wise, and he was a master of money. Israel needed that at the time, and, therefore, he was a great prime minister.

Yossi Ben-Aharon   In my mind, he was not a towering figure, nothing to compare with Ben-Gurion. Levi Eshkol's biggest problem was that he was constantly being compared with his predecessors, and the difference was very clear: Eshkol was a Yiddishist. If you pushed him, he would react in Yiddish rather than in Hebrew, which was not the case with Ben-Gurion, who became a modern Israeli in that sense. But Eshkol was also considered to be kind of a bridge between the founder, Ben-Gurion, and subsequent ones, like Rabin. And Golda was also considered something akin to Levi Eshkol—the immigrant who came because of a Zionist vocation and laid the foundation for the state.

Golda Meir (March 17, 1969–June 3, 1974)

Born in Kiev, Ukraine, in 1898, Golda Meir immigrated to the United States in 1906 and made aliyah in 1921. One of the two female signers of Israel's declaration of independence, she served as Israel's ambassador to the Soviet Union and as foreign minister. She became the prime minister following the death of Levi Eshkol. Unbeknownst to the public, she had been diagnosed with lymphoma. She left office in April 1974, in the wake of the Yom Kippur War. She died in Jerusalem on December 8, 1978.

Akiva Eldar   Golda is the one who missed the greatest opportunity when she refused to negotiate with Egypt. She ignored the Palestinian problem and the existence of the Palestinian people. On the other hand, it is not fair to judge her, knowing what we know today. After the Six-Day War, we believed we were a superpower. The man in the street didn't see peace or coexistence as something practical. Knowing what we know today, it is easy to say, "She made those mistakes, and we are now stuck with the Palestinian problem."

Yossi Ben-Aharon   She was my boss. I admired her very much. She was a proud Jewish lady. The picture in the American media of her as a grandmother pushing a baby carriage, of course, endeared her to the public, and the way she spoke—straight—because what she had to say was coming from the heart. She was an asset.

I served in Washington when she was already prime minister, in '69, when Eshkol died. We hosted her at the embassy for meetings with Richard Nixon in 1969 and 1970. And the down-to-earth terminology that she used in explaining our situation and our problem with the Arabs was very close to what I believed was the right way to present it.

Arie Lova Eliav   Golda Meir was a very good ambassador [in the 1940s to the Soviet Union], was an excellent Labor minister, and was a very good foreign minister. But she was a very bad *prime minister*. I was at the time very high up in the Labor hierarchy—I was the general secretary when she was prime minister—and we had a head-on collision because I thought she was very, very wrong and that she was an obstacle to future development, especially when she said, "There is no Palestinian problem; there is no Palestinian *people*; I am a Palestinian." And I said, "It is *the* problem that we have to face." No doubt, if we hadn't clashed, I would have succeeded her. I have a book of hers in which she writes to me—I was at that time the head of a big Israeli mission to Iran—that I was to be her heir.

"Golda was not religious, but it was clear that from her childhood she has an affinity with the Jewish peoplehood and to the connection between Am Yisrael, the People of Israel, and Eretz Israel, the Land of Israel."—Yossi Ben-Aharon

On February 27, 1973, eight months before the Yom Kippur War, Prime Minister Golda Meir poses with the visiting Dr. Henry Kissinger and her ambassador to the United States, Yitzhak Rabin, and his wife, Leah.

Simcha Waisman   In my book, Golda Meir and Ben-Gurion were two of the strongest prime ministers we've ever had because they had the roughest time in keeping the country united. At the same time, Golda didn't get accepted by the Arab League as a prime minister because she was a woman. And she showed everybody: you're *wrong*! I can do better. They realized very fast: don't fool around with this lady; she'll take you for a ride.

Yitzhak Rabin (June 3, 1974–April 22, 1977; July 13, 1992–November 4, 1995)

Born in Jerusalem in 1922, Mr. Rabin joined the Palmach and served in the IDF, becoming the chief of staff in 1964. He later served as Israel's ambassador to the United States. Appointed to succeed Golda Meir as prime minister, in 1976 he approved the Entebbe rescue operation. He was forced to resign the prime ministership due to his wife's financial impropriety, but he remained active in Labor Party politics and was elected prime minister in 1992. A recipient of the Nobel Peace Prize, along with Shimon Peres and Yasser Arafat, for negotiating the Oslo Accords in 1993, the following year he signed a peace treaty with Jordan. He was assassinated on the evening of November 4, 1995, following his participation in a peace rally held in Tel Aviv.

Yossi Ben-Aharon   I remember making speeches in Washington mentioning Rabin—that finally the banner of the governorship of the state was being delivered from the hands of the Zionist settlers of the Diaspora into the Sabras, and here was the first general who was so typical of the new generation of Sabras, who took the mantle of leadership.

Eitan Haber   I was eighteen years old when I went to the army. I came out of three years of experience with the Herut paper, and then I asked to join the *Army Weekly* of the IDF. There was a big problem: I was from Herut, and in 1958 it was not so popular to be part of it, especially in the *Army Weekly*. My father had a friend who was the head of Shin Bet, and my father told him, "Don't stop Eitan. He is qualified more than others, and you can't blame him because he was educated in my spirit." They decided to give me the job. They sent me to the north because every two days there were incidents with the Syrians on the border. I went there with a photographer, and somebody ordered me to meet the head of the Northern Command, Yitzhak Rabin. I found him in a forest. There was an army exercise there, and the correspondent whom I replaced because he was leaving the army said, "General Rabin, please meet my successor, Eitan Haber."

There were dozens of Syrian attacks then, and I stayed there. We called it then the Syrian Hill, not the Golan Heights. Rabin was my commander; I was in his office, and I stayed with him, and I went with him in his car. For weeks we were together day and night. Because of the Syrian attacks, my articles were the headlines. So, unfortunately, I made my career on the blood of the northern settlers and because of the Syrians, not because of my qualifications. Rabin was very satisfied so we became friendlier and friendlier.

Dan Pattir   In 1966 [former vice president Richard M.] Nixon came to Israel with his wife [Pat] and two daughters [Tricia and Julie] on a visit. Many Israelis and many Americans forgot that he was once the vice president, and nobody paid attention to him. The American DCM [deputy chief of mission]—the ambassador wasn't here—threw a dinner party for Nixon. He invited all the number-one VIPs of Israel, and they didn't show up, only *Rabin*, the chief of staff, did. Nixon, I was told, didn't know what small talk was, and Rabin didn't know what it was. But they started to talk strategy—remember, in '66, half of Jerusalem is in Jordanian hands; the Syrians overlook the Golan Heights, and Rabin tells him what the situation is. And Rabin told me that he told Nixon, "Tomorrow, you will see it." Nixon stays silent, and then Rabin suspects something is wrong. He asks, "Mr. Vice President, are you scheduled to tour the country?" and Nixon says he doesn't know. On the spot, Rabin arranged for Nixon to tour the country in a military helicopter, with an escort, a crash course about Israel. Nixon was a forgotten man, and suddenly he was paid attention.

He was *nobody*. Two days after he was elected president, in November '68, I'm sitting with Rabin in his office at the embassy [in Washington, D.C.] and a call comes in. Nixon's on the line: "I hear that you are the ambassador here." Rabin doesn't recognize his voice, and Nixon says, "This is President-elect Nixon calling you. Are you free for coffee?" So Rabin says, "Yes," and Nixon says, "Come over to the Mayflower Hotel."

Yossi Ben-Aharon   I happened to be seconded to the Prime Minister's Bureau from the Foreign Ministry during the Yom Kippur War because [Mordechai] Gazit, the guy who was the director general of the Prime Minister's Bureau, knew me and valued my reports from Washington. He wanted someone like me to help him to deal with the diplomatic issues resulting from the Yom Kippur War, so he asked the Foreign Ministry to loan me to the Prime Minister's Bureau. I stayed there until Golda resigned along with Moshe Dayan.

In April 1974, Rabin was appointed prime minister. I had worked with him five years earlier so he kept me on. But I immediately saw that Rabin was a novice; you could see that he wasn't sure of himself because he was very hesitant. He tried to make as if he knew what he was doing, that he was sure of himself, but that wasn't the case. And his choice of people to help him in his office was very poor. That was his failing, his weakness. He just couldn't judge character and choose the right person for the job. Subsequently, he paid a price for that.

Gazit decided he could no longer work with Rabin. They were very different characters: Gazit was an intellectual, a diplomat's diplomat, but also a weakling in terms of appreciating the power of an independent, sovereign state and what it can and cannot do, and Rabin had kind of recoiled from the mentality of the Foreign Ministry types personified by Mordechai Gazit. Soon enough, I saw that Gazit was tearing himself inside and thinking that he couldn't make it anymore, and he decided to leave. He was sent to be the ambassador in Paris. I stayed on, and when I heard that Rabin was again choosing another person who was completely not made for this job, I decided that was it. He wasn't capable, so I asked immediately to be returned to the Foreign Ministry.

Dan Pattir Maybe he came too early to power because as prime minister in the aftermath of the '73 war, he didn't have experience as a politician. He had for three months been the minister of labor and he immediately jumped into the leadership of the country. He was unprepared and should have gone into the job of defense minister. He wasn't built for the infighting of a politician, so he suffered badly and didn't perform so well, although he did do one thing: he made the Interim Agreement with Egypt, which, in retrospect, was regarded to be the introduction into the peace with Egypt. Even Begin considered that. So his first term, in which I served, was quite miserable.

And then, with great dignity, he went down, was respected for his behavior, and regained power in 1992 as prime minister and did much better as a leader in his performance. You can agree or disagree with his policy—that's another story—but the performance was better, more confident. He was knocked out by an account that was unnecessary altogether. But he behaved in a moralistic way; he said, "I could have put that responsibility on my wife's shoulders," but he *didn't*.

The Reverend Jerry Falwell   I was impressed with him; he was a very bright gentleman.

Ronald Godwin   He was a very intelligent, articulate, well versed, kind of a Newt Gingrich Israeli, very well educated in Israeli-American and Israeli-European global relations. This was a sophisticated, intelligent, well-versed, highly competent gentleman.

Eitan Haber   Rabin reflected, first and foremost, authority; then unbelievable experience. And if I say that Begin was not an Israeli, Rabin was a number-one Israeli; everything in Israel was known to him. But the most important thing was that Rabin was such a serious man, not only in the Northern Command. For example, you couldn't tell him a joke; it was a waste of time. He reflected seriousness, and you couldn't speak with Rabin any gossip; gossip was not for him. "Don't waste my time. We have to take care of the State of Israel; let's speak about Israel. Don't give me any information about who slept with Moshe Dayan yesterday."

Dan Pattir   He was a man of tragedy, tragic because of his fate as a leader, because he was assassinated, but also because he was forced to resign [during his first term as prime minister] because of his wife's greediness. Holding a foreign currency account in a foreign bank was then contrary to the rule of Israel—two thousand dollars, four thousand dollars, it didn't matter. Three months later, after the elections of '77, one of the first things the incoming Begin government did was to reappraise the rule, and these accounts were allowed.

Menachem Begin (June 21, 1977–October 10, 1983)

Born in Brest Litovsk, Poland, in 1913, Mr. Begin headed Betar in Poland, was imprisoned by the Soviet Union in the Siberian gulag, and made aliyah in 1943. He served as commander of the Irgun Zvai Leumi. Elected to the Knesset in 1948, he served as leader of the opposition until his election as prime minister. In that office he signed the Camp David Accords; ordered the bombing of Iraq's nuclear reactor; launched Project Renewal, a program improving the conditions of Israel's underprivileged citizens; and was responsible for initiating the redemption of Ethiopian Jewry. Following both the First Lebanon War and the death of his beloved wife, Aliza, he retired and went into seclusion at his home in Jerusalem. He died on

In 1965, Prime Minister Levi Eshkol (left) and future prime minister Menachem Begin (right) drink a *l'chaim* in celebration of fifteen years of Jewish settlement. Matityahu "Mati" Drobles stands next to Mr. Begin.

"Begin was a real democrat, a real liberal. When it comes to human rights, these people will not compromise. That is what I will always remember about Begin."—Akiva Eldar

March 9, 1992, and is buried on the Mount of Olives, next to Mrs. Begin and two heroes of the pre-state underground.

Eitan Haber   I saw him first, along with twenty thousand people, when he first came from the underground—I was seven or eight years old—and he appeared for the first time in public in Tel Aviv, in an open cinema, with no roof, on Ben Yehuda [Street], opposite Betar. There were so many people there, and my father took me on his shoulders to see the hero. I remember only that he shouted from the stage and that he was very skinny, like somebody who came from a refugee camp, with a big mustache. I don't remember what he said, but I remember that the crowd around me was in such an excited mood that he had come from the underground.

My second meeting was two or three years later—I was ten years old— when he came to the Jabotinsky Institute, where I worked. He looked at everything, and he met every employee there, and he shook my hand. For me, it was like something from heaven. Later on, I met him so many times, and I wrote his biography in five or six weeks. I was asked by Dell Delacorte when he came to power, "Can you write a quick biography?" I said, "I know everything about Begin; ask me about Menachem Begin. Even the size of his shoes I can tell you!"

Yossi Ben-Aharon Sometimes I was astonished at his kind of flowery speech making—it was a little bit too much for my ears—but I was sympathetic to his views and, like many youngsters at that time, I thought Begin was the great orator. It was always an experience to come and listen to him. He used to address people in the middle of the city in Tel Aviv or sometimes in a hall, which they would rent when it was election time. I enjoyed listening to him because he gave a proud, particular Jewish education about the great learning of the Jewish people. There was a time when he succeeded in telling the public, he was implying that you had to fight force to take over the government control because the government was so wanting, so inadequate. And I remember very clearly, "Only through the ballot box; only by an election. You want a change? Vote for Herut!"

Eitan Haber Menachem Begin was the most *Jewish* prime minister of Israel, no doubt about it, but the number-one *non-Israeli* prime minister. Menachem Begin lived in the State of Israel, but he never, *ever* was a part of the State of Israel. For example, I prayed every Rosh Hashanah, Yom Kippur, Sukkot with Menachem Begin in the same synagogue. He lived six hundred meters from Metzudat Zev, in Rosenbaum 1. After the end of Kol Nidre on Yom Kippur, I accompanied him home. It's only six hundred meters—you have to cross two roads—and I can assure you that without companionship, he didn't know how to go home!

Maybe I exaggerate, but he never, never was a part of Israeli life. He never carried money, not even *one pound* in his life. When he had to pay, somebody found money. He never bought a gift. He never sat in a coffee shop. He liked movies very much, especially Westerns, and twice a week he went to the cinema, but his driver came and took him to and from the cinema.

Look, Rabin and even Shamir were part of Israel. Ask Menachem Begin, "Where is the Mediterranean?" Menachem Begin lived twenty-five centimeters above the floor—a little bit higher than the usual people. Maybe it's the same with Ben-Gurion. Rabin, you can ask him—there is a wadi; in a minute he will tell you the name of the wadi, the name of the mountain. He was *there*. Shamir, the same; Shamir was part of the life. Why did Israelis like Shamir? Because he was among us. Begin was always a picture on the wall. Begin was the number-one honest man. But you know what? Menachem Begin lived in Diaspora in Eretz Israel.

I could speak before Menachem Begin in Hebrew in such words that he would never, never understand because he understood the language of Eliezer Ben-Yehuda [the founder of the modern Hebrew language] but not the daily language. Rabin was the opposite, but not only Rabin, the same with Ehud Barak and Peres and Bibi.

Zalman Shoval   Begin to me was a stranger. He was a real Israeli, of course, but he was *different*—his mentality was *different*. He was also very legalistic, which most of us were not. I had some discussions with him, and he was very, very intent that every agreement with the Palestinians or Arabs had to be codified with article one, article two, and he was right, certainly, on the Egyptian thing—contrary to Rabin, who said, "Oh, another agreement, another agreement . . ."

But on the other hand, where I was coming from, it was more of creating all sorts of de facto situations. Once when I had a debate with him, he said, "The only way to end war is to have a written peace agreement." I said, "Look, in Europe there was no final peace agreement; that was signed much later. But you had the de facto situation of peace—you had the Marshall Plan; you had economic cooperation; you had the beginning of the Common Market." But on the whole, we had good cooperation because Begin was very proud of the fact that people who came from the other camp had joined, and he used to say, "My proudest moment is that the followers of Ben-Gurion and the followers of Jabotinsky are in the same party."

He was also a much better politician than Dayan. He didn't have the same aptitudes that Dayan had in other things; I think Dayan was a greater statesman than Begin, but Begin understood how to utilize him when he needed to. But as a politician, Begin was better—to arouse the masses, there was no one like him. He was also a very honest man, straightforward, which you didn't always see on the other side. So I had a good working relationship with him.

Maybe, also, Begin, like many other political leaders—like Ben-Gurion and perhaps Sharon—hated his own entourage. He was fed up with them; he didn't trust them; he thought that some of them were too much interested in their own political careers. He felt better sometimes with people who came from a different background than with people who had been with him all those years. I'm not talking about the people who were very close to him, but on the whole, if he could have been rid of the party organization, the functionaries—the same thing with Ben-Gurion and with Sharon and with Bibi—the better it was. And from that point of view, it was easier for Begin to put me in charge of writing the platform than some of his own court.

Dan Pattir   I knew of him when I was a political correspondent in a rival paper, the Labor paper. He was fair; I didn't believe he was a "clown," as some people said on the street. I thought that he was "Mr. Clean" in his own way.

I didn't know him face-to-face until he asked me to join him in 1977. It was a surprise. I mean, I was *shocked* when he said, "In the meantime, stay." I said, "I'll stay until you have a successor and ask me to leave." I went to Mr. Rabin, for whom I had worked for three years before that, and I said, "He asked me to stay." And he said, "Stay until you are not wanted there; I don't believe in leaving behind burning logs." Later I learned that he lived in almost austerity, *self-inflicted* austerity, in modesty. He was a politician like others, more skilled, maybe, but with tricks, too. He didn't like opposition from within; he dismissed, fired, some good rivals, too, because he had to survive.

But in terms of an exemplary way of life, it's almost unparalleled in what I read about people. Also, I must say for me, it was a great surprise that he asked me to stay because he knew where I came from, on loan from a Labor paper, and the man told me in certain words—he gave me three reasons why I should stay, and he was honest up to the iota for four years. I can't tell you how much I admired his way of behavior.

Akiva Eldar   A few months after I started working for *Ha'aretz*, in 1979 or 1980, I had a visitor in my Jerusalem office, a Palestinian journalist who had just been released from administrative detention. He had been arrested for being a member of the PLO. He showed me some bruises and told me that he had been tortured. I told him, "I can write the story, but I must call the Shin Bet and get their response. They will deny it, and it will be your word against theirs. But I have an idea: I will take you for a lie detector test." The test showed that he was, 100 percent, telling the truth. After some initial hesitation, the newspaper ran the story. It came up in the Knesset, and Begin, who was the prime minister, appointed Aharon Barak to conduct an investigation. That led to the firing of the Shin Bet people who had tortured the journalist. That was Begin. I don't see anybody else like him—not [Yitzhak] Shamir, not [Shimon] Peres, not [Yitzhak] Rabin.

The Reverend Jerry Falwell   My real hero of all the prime ministers I knew was Menachem Begin. I felt closer to him than I did to anybody else over there, and we exchanged private telephone numbers—I had his number in the apartment where he lived, and he had all of mine.

I remember spending some time with him in his office. He had a map on the wall, and just the two of us were standing there, talking. I said, "Mr. Prime Minister, I believe the Abrahamic Covenant," and I took my finger and put a line way beyond the boundaries of Israel on the map, and I said, "I believe you're going to get all of this. Do *you* believe that?" And he said, "Of course. We're both men of the Book." And when we got outside, an NBC [television] reporter began questioning both of us, and the question was posed to the prime minister, "What possible affinity do you have with American evangelicals, and especially *this* man?" And he said, "We're both men of the Book." I have never forgotten that.

Ronald Godwin   He was a charismatic figure to me. I was able to be in his presence three or four times, and, of course, I was completely aware of how close he and Dr. Falwell had become. And I was struck by his humility. All those Israeli leaders wore those open-neck shirts and were so unpretentious and so absolutely down to earth and practical, and I just had a huge admiration for that lack of pomp and circumstance. Of course, I read several books about Mr. Begin in his early life and the various roles he played as he was coming up. This was a historically huge figure. He was a man of immense determination, and it always struck me as logical that he and Dr. Falwell, two warriors in their own right, two men of huge willpower and intellect and both having a great sense of history, would have an affinity for each other. That was a genuine friendship, as much so as a prime minister of Israel could afford, and then perhaps a little extra.

The Reverend Jerry Falwell   On his last trip to America [in November 1982] he was supposed to speak here to the student body at Liberty, and we had purchased enough Star of David flags and American flags to put them all the way down the long drive from the highway to the auditorium. We had taught our band and choral group to sing the national anthem of Israel, and they were going to line up all along the road, and inside, and play and sing both national anthems, and have him speak to the students. But when he arrived on the West Coast, he got the news that his wife had died, and he returned home. And he never came back [to the United States].

Shlomo Ariav   Begin got the support of the poor people. It's not known today, but after 1977, he started to help the poor people to build. He was the first person to come up with this program, Project Renewal.

Yehuda Avner   Why did he leave office when he did? It was too much; he had had a stroke, a broken hip; Aliza; casualties; maybe Sharon. It all became too much. You could see that the man had lost weight, the gleam had gone out of his eye, that he was *tired*.

Yitzhak Shamir (October 10, 1983–September 14, 1984; October 20, 1986–July 13, 1992)

Born in the Russian empire in 1915, Mr. Shamir made aliyah in 1935. During the pre-state era, he served as one of the three leaders of Lehi. He later served with the Mossad, as speaker of the Knesset, and as foreign minister. As prime minister, he participated in the 1991 Madrid Peace Conference. He left office in 1992, following the election of Yitzhak Rabin. He now lives in retirement.

Moshe Sharon   Shamir was a simple man; when he didn't want to do something, he stood firmly, with both feet on the ground, and said, "I don't want to; I'm not going to do it." The language is understood.

"Shamir was part of Israel; he went by bus; he bought in the grocery shop; he went to the cinema, to theaters; he swam in the Mediterranean."—Eitan Haber

Prime Minister Yitzhak Shamir (left) with former refusenik Anna Paukov at the Prime Minister's Bureau in Jerusalem during the summer of 1990. (Left to right) Gerald Strober, Harry S. Taubenfeld, a former chairman of Herut U.S.A., and Deborah Hart Strober are also in attendance.

Shimon Peres (September 14, 1984–October 20, 1986; November 4, 1985–June 18, 1996)

Born in Poland in 1915, Mr. Peres made aliyah in 1934. After serving in youth movements, he held major posts in Israel's Ministry of Defense. First elected to the Knesset in 1959, he served as minister of defense during the Entebbe rescue mission. Following his first term as prime minister, he remained in the Knesset and was a major figure in the Oslo Process. He succeeded the assassinated prime minister Yitzhak Rabin but was defeated in 1996 by Benjamin Netanyahu. He joined in coalition with the Kadima Party in 2005 and was named vice premier in 2006.

Tzipora Ariav   I served together in the army with Peres's [future] wife, Sonya. We were both drivers, and we shared our lives for four years. I used to always get news about Shimon, and we even started to knit a sweater for him together—I half and she half. I know that he loved her very much. Then after four and a half years we separated. I met her once in Tel Aviv—she was the mother of three—and we talked, and that was it: she lived in Tel Aviv and I lived in Binyamina. But Peres gave a speech here in Binyamina once, and the head of the city council knew that I knew them so he asked me to come and see him and to send regards to his wife.

Uri Avneri   Peres was a nincompoop and a totally worthless man, without principles, without conviction, without anything at all, the very opposite of Rabin, really, a mere politician in the bad sense of the word.

Benjamin Netanyahu (June 18, 1996–July 6, 1999)

Born in Tel Aviv in 1949, Mr. Netanyahu spent much of his adolescence in the United States. Returning to Israel in 1967, he served in elite units of the IDF; in Israel's embassy in Washington, D.C.; and as Israel's ambassador to the United Nations. In 1993, he became chairman of the Likud Party and was elected as prime minister three years later. He later served as foreign minister and finance minister under Prime Minister Ariel Sharon. Today he is the leader of the Likud Party.

Uri Avneri   Bibi is nothing! He's a Jewish vacuum cleaner salesman in the United States, a man who had a certain knack of working on television—that was his only talent. I don't think he has many principles. Neither

"The good side of Bibi was his economic policy. The bad side of Bibi is that he didn't have a feeling for the poor people. He moved too quickly and he lost the support of the poor people."—Shlomo Ariav

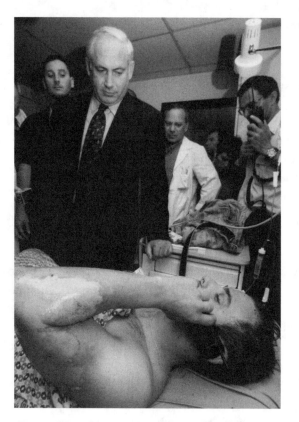

During Prime Minister Benjamin Netanyahu's visit to Sha'arei Tzedek Hospital on September 4, 1997, to comfort victims of the suicide bombing on Ben-Yehuda Street in Tel Aviv, he gave his own cell phone to one of the injured men.

he nor Olmert nor Peres are in any way people who have an interesting personality or have anything much to say. They are people who want to be in power, that's all.

The Reverend Jerry Falwell, after a meeting with Mr. Netanyahu in Washington, D.C., during the Clinton presidency, praised the Israeli prime minister, saying that he was "the Ronald Reagan of Israel."

Ronald Godwin   I don't know that I would be quite *that* effusive. I just didn't feel that he had the depth and the fierce commitment that Mr. Begin and Mr. Reagan had. Underneath all the geniality of Ronald Reagan was unbelievable courage and willpower, and I don't know that I saw quite that level of commitment in Mr. Netanyahu.

Moshe Sharon   The press doesn't like Netanyahu; they *hate* him. Second, he has got a very bad record: he could never stand his ground *properly*; he never spoke the language of the Middle East. Sometimes he *did*, but when he went to America, he never spoke this language. There is a point; you have to come sometimes as a leader and say, "I don't want to; this is against our policy, this is against our interest. Thank you very much; we are not going to do it!"

Ehud Barak (July 6, 1999–March 7, 2001)

Born at Kibbutz Mishmar HaSharon in 1942, Mr. Barak served with great distinction in elite units of the IDF, becoming chief of staff in 1991. In 1999, he formed a political party, One Israel, and was elected prime minister. After losing a special election in 2001, he remains active in the Labor Party and in 2007 was elected as its leader.

Uri Avneri   Barak was a disaster for Israel. In the army he was considered brilliant, one of the very, very few Israeli army officers who read books. I enjoyed having discussions with him about European military history, which happens to be a hobby of mine, too.

Very early on, he became a complete megalomaniac, convinced that he is a genius, convinced that he knows everything. He does not listen to anybody *at all*. When he left the army, he became a politician and, very shortly afterward, prime minister, without any real prior political experience. *He* knew what to do—he just *knew*—and his idea was: if Arafat has got a Palestinian state, they will be so grateful and jump into the air and accept everything else that I say we must have.

He had not the slightest idea! He had never in his life spoken with an Arab! So he promised in his election—we all voted for him; we were all very enthusiastic, the chief of staff of the army; he wants to have peace with the Palestinians within nine months. So what did he do? He pressured President Clinton, who is a nice guy but not serious, into convening this Camp David conference, which we all knew, from the beginning, was a completely idiotic idea because there was absolutely no calculation.

Ariel Sharon (March 7, 2001–January 4, 2006)

Born in Kfar Malel in 1928, Mr. Sharon served as a career soldier with the IDF, retiring with the rank of major general. He served in the government of Menachem Begin as minister of agriculture and played a major role in the development of settlements in Judea, Samaria, and the Gaza District. He served as minister of defense during the First Lebanon War and was forced to relinquish that post after a government commission found him to have been indirectly responsible for a massacre of Palestinians that took place in 1982 in Beirut, Lebanon. As prime minister, he directed the removal of Jewish settlers from Gaza. In November 2005, he left Likud and established the Kadima Party. In mid-December 2005, he suffered a minor stroke, followed several weeks later by a severe one, after which he lapsed into a coma.

Zalman Shoval   About Sharon, we don't have to talk. These people were like the Wild West in America: we are doing the right thing; we are doing it ourselves; and all these nonsense rules don't apply to us.

Uri Avneri   He was a clever person; he was very sociable—he could be very captivating. He made friends when he needed them and forgot about them when he didn't. He was a real fanatic, basically, but a real open-minded tactician in day-to-day politics—he could tell you exactly what you wanted to hear. For him, there was absolutely no difference between truth and lies—he used words in order to achieve the tactical objective of the moment, and I could not believe a single word that he ever said. He was very much above the level of an ordinary politician. He was an egomaniac in a different sense. He was not an egomaniac in day-to-day behavior, like Barak; he, from the beginning, was completely convinced that he was the only person who could save the State of Israel and who had in his hands the fate of the State of Israel for generations to come.

Akiva Eldar   Look at his ranch. Where did he make the money to buy this huge ranch, which is worth millions of dollars? And look at the fact that he wanted to bury his wife there. There is a law in Israel that you can't bury anyone in your backyard. What are you, a *king*? He allowed himself the chutzpah to do anything he wanted; there were no limits.

Uri Avneri   I knew him very well. Sharon was the prototypical Zionist in the negative sense of the word, the product of a very strong mother, in a moshav, a mother who not only hated Arabs—that would be an understatement—but was mortally afraid of Arabs. Just to give you an idea, when he moved into his farm, his *palace*, his wife [the late Lily Sharon], whom I very much liked, once told me the story about when his mother came to visit them at the farm. They had a flower bed in the front of the house, and in the flower bed there were little holes for irrigation. The mother said, "Ah, that's very good for shooting when the Arabs come!"

Raanan Gissin I knew him as a soldier when he was still the most well-thought-of commander and one who received adulation even when he was a young officer. And I followed his military thinking. Later on, I became a student in the United States, and I wrote my dissertation; I did something on the style of his command and on the measures that he used and his tactics and strategies as a commander—"Command and Control on the Future Battlefield"—which, by the way, later carried on in public life, where he moved to be a public figure and a leader. In 1996, I first joined his office when he became minister of national infrastructure in the Netanyahu government. And then I followed him throughout the years. And the more I knew him, I developed not so much of a personal liking, but an intellectual affinity.

Amira Dotan He really loved this dual identification of a very strong Israeli, in heritage all the Bible stories and all the feeling that this is where we should be—this is our *home*, and we have to make sure that this home will be the best in the world. And he was—is—a very warm person. He loved life. I talk about his eagerness; he had this powerful eagerness, and it had to do with everything, with people who were around him, with his family, with his officers. For me, he's really like a leader, and I never had these very intimate, private conversations because I couldn't reach this kind of conversation with him—he was very high above me. But I have to tell you, in 1971, when he was chief of the Southern Command, he lived in Beer-sheba. He understood that in order to command, you have to be there; you cannot command something and live in Tel Aviv. When I think of him, his mouth and his heart were on the same level. Because of that, politically speaking, we had a lot of fights. But as a person, as a leader, as somebody who really loved this state and the people, his strength was unquestionable.

Ehud Olmert (January 4, 2006, to the Present)

Born in Binyamina in 1945, Mr. Olmert, an attorney and a career politician, served as mayor of Jerusalem for ten years. He helped to establish the

Kadima Party and served as minister of trade and industry and as deputy prime minister in the Sharon administration. When the prime minister was incapacitated in January 2006, Mr. Olmert succeeded to the prime ministership and was elected prime minister in his own right later that year.

Shlomo Ariav We speak to him at least once a week. He was the youngest man in the Knesset. Once in a meeting he attacked Begin—Ehud was maybe twenty-three years old—and they told him, "Step down. You are not to bring this forward." But Begin, who was sitting in front of him, said, "Don't touch him; he has the full right to attack me." He [Mr. Olmert] was eventually very close to Begin and to Shamir.

Uri Avneri I've known Olmert since I was eighteen years old. In Hebrew we have an expression for a political aide—"weapon-bearer"—and Olmert was all his life the weapon-bearer for different political personalities; he has been riding the coattails, jumping from one coattail to another in order to advance. He is a pure politician, with no principles at all.

So how did he get into power? People forget. He was not very popular

"Growing up, Ehud was a very lovely boy, a nice young man, playing soccer."—Shlomo Ariav

Prime Minister Ehud Olmert (second from left), taking a respite from his increasing difficulties, and Mrs. Olmert visit with Tzipora and Shlomo Ariav, Olmert's childhood neighbors in Binyamina, during the fall of 2006.

in the Likud Party—they considered him an opportunist, too—and the Likud people are believers; they have an ideology. So because he could not advance in the party, he became a candidate to become mayor of Jerusalem—that seat opened at the time. There had been a very popular mayor, Teddy Kollek [1912–2007], and by a fluke Olmert was elected. And he was conspicuous, but not a very good mayor.

When he became famous enough, he went back to the party, and they put him way, way back, and he realized that he would not become prime minister by remaining in that party. So when Ariel Sharon had his idea of creating a party of his own, he jumped to this party. He was one of the first to jump, and being one of the first, he thought he would become minister of finance, which is one of *the* most important ministries in Israel, competing in importance with the Ministry of Defense—the treasury gives the money to the Ministry of Defense.

But Bibi had to be brought into the government, and Bibi said, "I am the leader of the party; the most important portfolio belongs to *me*." So Sharon could not give this ministry to Olmert, and he gave him a second-class ministry, Trade and Industry. As a consolation prize, Sharon gave him the completely empty title of deputy prime minister; his sole function was to preside over cabinet meetings when the prime minister was abroad. And Sharon was *never* abroad. If he was abroad, he was away for two days—he was not a traveling person.

And then Olmert had the incredible luck because Sharon had his stroke, and Olmert slipped into his job before anybody could think twice, quite naturally, being the deputy, and he became the prime minister. He then started and conducted a disastrous war. And, adding to his corruption affairs, he has incredible chutzpah to appoint as minister of justice the chief of police, all of this done quite openly. I hope they will get rid of him after this board of inquiry into the war. However, people who detest him want him to remain prime minister because what is the alternative? The only viable candidate is Bibi. And who wants to have *Bibi*? Therefore, he is there. And people don't want new elections because in new elections, the right wing could come out stronger, and they don't want a new coalition in this parliament, so he's there by default.

Chapter 10

WARS OF DEFENSE, ATTRITION, AND PREEMPTION

Following their victory in 1949 over five hostile Arab armies in the War of Independence, the Israel Defense Forces have been forced by circumstances to fight five additional major wars—Suez, in 1956; the Six-Day War, in 1967; the Yom Kippur War, in 1973; the Lebanon War, in 1982; and in the summer of 2006, a devastating, thirty-four-day confrontation in Lebanon. In addition, the nation was traumatized by the physically and emotionally harrowing War of Attrition following the Six-Day War, and by the Scud missile attacks by Iraq during the First Gulf War in 1991.

*The Israel Defense Forces: The Men and
the Women of the Citizen Army*

Joseph Hochstein   In earlier times, when people were asked which institutions they respected, the army came out either on top or near the top. So many people serve in the army that there is a personal element. The army gets a high degree of respect, but there are changes. The First Lebanon War and its aftermath had an effect on the army because for the first time you had a lieutenant colonel who refused to take his troops into Beirut.

It used to be that the army was led by people from the kibbutzim who went into the paratroopers, so you had an army that was led by people from the ideological left. It's still that army, but the young officers are coming increasingly from the modern religious groups and from the settlements.

What has developed over a period of time is that the army's mission has changed. It used to be there to fight for the survival of Israel. At some point this was no longer particularly the mission of the army or of the soldiers who were going into combat units.

I know people in their forties who were in the army in Gaza as soldiers living where later settlers came to live. When they were there as soldiers, they were doing their duty and defending the country. When they had to go back as reservists and defend the settlers, it was a different mission. What started to change the mission was the complication of the intifada, the first one of which broke out in late 1987. Rabin, the defense minister, gave the order to break bones. The IDF troops regarded themselves as soldiers; now they were in a police role. It's not a job they were trained to do. It changed from an army that was protecting us to an army that was doing distasteful things.

Amira Dotan   First, we have compulsory service so when you command other people, those people are there because somebody has ordered them to be there. Second, those youngsters are part of your family—the kibbutz, the moshav, the city—they went to school with your sons and daughters; they were part of the youth movement with your uncles. They *belong*. There's a kind of continuity. Third is the morale; it has to do with trust, with the understanding that it's not me who lives, but it's me and *you*; without you, *I* won't be able to live, and without *me*, you won't be able to make a difference. So there's a kind of togetherness; the basis of that is really trust.

The other element is that we continue to see our officers as [going] first [into battle]; it's not that they send somebody to check what's going on and *then* he goes, but he or she is the model. According to this model, we brought up all kinds of elements and morale. And the most important thing is that we fight for *our home*. We have never fought for somebody else's; we are not sending our children to the west, to the east, and not to the south. I'm talking about work—we are guarding *our* home; we are *Defense Forces* and the Israeli military is not a military, it's the Israeli Defense Forces and still is. Unfortunately, the fact is that we face not a war with our neighbors but with terror; it's a war with intifada. So the war presents itself to Israelis in this model, but we are guarding ourselves; we are not asking anybody to do it for us. And because of that, it's really a kind of family.

Even now, in 2007, when those young people are drafted into the Defense Forces, on the one hand there is worry—we know it's not going to be easy. But on the other hand, it's a kind of pride; you see your child in uniform; you see your child part of this organism, which is so important—it's really the backbone of who we are. Those things are quite unique to Israel. Because of them, we will continue to be so proud about the IDF.

When Ben-Gurion said that compulsory service will be for women and for men, that was a very good idea. And for the first years it was okay. The fact that no women—or not *enough* women—are the decision makers of the IDF harmed the IDF and harmed the society. It's not enough for women to really serve in other jobs when they leave the Defense Forces. My criticism of the IDF is that we can do it *better*. And we *should*; it's not just that we will, but we really *should*, as a society, push for more women, not just in the compulsory service, but as professionals, in all junctures of command and decision making, because people know now that the way women think is different, and it's very important to understand the other voice, as well as the voice that is heard ultimately, because men control the Defense Forces.

Service in the IDF as a Rite of Passage

Amira Dotan   I hope you lose something if you don't serve, although there are some groups in Israel who do not serve—Arabs do not serve; the ultra-religious do not serve. There is a kind of feeling, because we became very selfish and we want to be as other nations, so there is a kind of feeling that there are some people who present themselves as incapable in order not to serve. The way to handle that is to make sure that every citizen of Israel at the age of eighteen to twenty or twenty-one will serve the country, partly with the Defense Forces, partly with other vocations. I see my job in the Knesset as making sure that the feeling of contributing to Israel, to your community, will happen. The government just passed a law last Sunday [February 18, 2007] to make sure that a vehicle for national service will be in place. We are now building the unit that will be in charge of that. I hope the Arabs, as well as the Haredim [ultra-Orthodox Jews], will understand that it's not just for the niceties of the world, but that it's part of making sure that all the young people will understand that life is a lot more than just being an egoist.

The IDF as a Societal Leveler

Amira Dotan   It's such a part of who we are that I didn't even mention it. It's something in the stage of when you want to market something, people speak about it, but this is part of the basis of the whole idea: it's really all Israelis, except the Arabs and the Haredim, and when we have Ethiopians or when we used to have North Africans or Iraqis or Polish or you name it, people are coming and becoming citizens. By making sure that they contribute as part of the IDF, we will help them understand what citizenship is all about. Not to mention a lot of young American and European Jews who look forward to coming to Israel—we will make them feel as if they are part of the IDF. There are all kinds of wonderful programs for three months, six months, that will let them contribute and feel that they are part of the Defense Forces. Still, I think that the IDF is something to be very proud of, and the Ethiopians and the Russians are also part of it. Judging now to see them in one tent, I hear different music, different tones of voice, different observances of Shabbat—everything. When you live together, side by side, in those units, you see home only once in two or three weeks. But home comes to you for Shabbat with the very wonderful food that the mothers cook: in one hand, you have gefilte fish, and in the other hand, you have kibbeh. This is the mélange; this is really *who* we are and *what* we are, and it's so much a part of it that for me it's a given.

The First Woman Appointed a General Officer

Amira Dotan   I was very happy; it was wonderful. It was really fulfilling everything that one wished for. On the other hand, I really worked hard; it wasn't that I sat in the coffee shops and waited for somebody to do something for me. You really worked very, *very* hard. There was no stone that I knew of that I didn't turn—some I changed; some I left as they were—but it was really a kind of evolution. I owe it to thousands of people, to people who were in the Knesset, to Sarah Doron, who was a minister then and thought that it was about time for women to have that; of course, Rabin; Sharon, who was then the chief of the Ministry of Defense; and thousands of other people who really made it happen. Unfortunately, it was twenty years ago, and in twenty years, no other women were promoted to major general, and it's about time to make it happen.

In the police, we have done it. Part of a job that I've taken as a volunteer was to make sure that women will contribute not just in the Defense Forces, but in the police and in other places. Shahal, who then was the minister of police, was able to promote a woman to be a major general in the police. So if the police can, of course, the Defense Forces—it's about time to do that. It hasn't happened; there are all kinds of answers. But the thing in the Defense Forces, when you need to explain, it's not good, okay? So when we started to explain, things are not correct. So I hope that the new chief of staff will understand the method and that things will be changed.

Women today are going to the senior staff colleges, but, again, the numbers are very few, and when they then finish, I don't see them enough in the juncture where decisions are made. And this is very important because when a young Israeli woman is enlisted in the Defense Forces and she sees that there's no way for her to become more than a major or a lieutenant colonel or a colonel, it's not enough. The abilities of those women are tremendous, so I think that it's time.

Why Was the Decision Made to Restrict Female Soldiers from Combat?

Amira Dotan   These are some of the things that I really started to deal with when I became an officer and then, of course, when I was the chief of the Women's Corps. What I learned from the first women who were the commanders of Chen [Women's Corps] was that the model was the British army, and the British army was *auxiliary*. *Auxiliary* was a great part of Jewish understanding that women are *women* and that they are very well equipped and they are very intelligent, but, first of all, they are *women*, so we have to protect them. If they want to be part of the Defense Forces, they can be *auxiliary*—nurses and working in communications and as secretaries. Of course, we, Chen, fought to change it, and we are *still* fighting to change it, because combat is one phase. In the Defense Forces only a very small percentage of women have real combat duties. The units consist of other duties that are not combat, like communications and intelligence and all kinds of things that women, according to my view, should be and are doing now because of the changes that we have made. The idea was that we need to read the map of the needs of the Defense Forces as they are and be able to really put women soldiers in those professions, not just combat, that the Defense Forces need, which means thousands of other vocations, such as computers and electronics and intelligence and educators and instructors.

The first time that we put instructors in the armor, the idea was: they can't do that. My male friends said, "No, no, no! She cannot stand there, petite and nice, and instruct the men how to do that." You know the phrase of that song [from Irving Berlin's *Annie Get Your Gun!*]: "Anything you can do, I can do better"? That came to my mind and I said, "Do you know this?

If they will see her doing that, they will show her that they can do it *better!*" So that was the beginning—this was part of the strategy: you know what you want, and you need to translate it to other people's understanding, not because they are bad or because they think that it cannot be done. It's just a way of thinking, and this makes me modify my ideas all the time.

Attributes of People in the Special Units

Muki Betser   The special units are made up of the very best people in our country. But even among this group, in the year and a half of training, 40 to 50 percent drop out. The qualities that I look for are, first of all, honesty, dependability, good physical condition, intelligence, high technical ability, and people who integrate well into a group because, after all, in the final analysis, they are a group, a team, a body—a combination of all of these things. And, also, a sense of humor is desirable. That gives the best result for a fighter.

Suez: A Rare Instance of French, British, and Israeli Cooperation

In the fall of 1956, a most unusual instance of military cooperation occurred between Israel and two European powers, Britain and France. The three nations acted with the avowed intention of reoccupying the Suez Canal Zone in order to restore free navigation of the ninety-two-mile-long canal, the link between Africa and Asia. Their action caused pandemonium in Washington and ended in the withdrawal of the invading forces.

The military venture began on October 29 with Israel's invasion of Egypt. Then, less than two days later, on the afternoon of October 31, the air forces of Britain and France launched a bombing offensive against military airfields in Cairo, Alexandria, Port Said, Ismailia, and Suez. The joint air-land operation took place following the expiration of an Anglo-French ultimatum that had been issued twelve hours earlier to Egypt's president, Gamal Abdel Nasser (1918–1970). He had come to power earlier that year and would rule until his death.

Yossi Ben-Aharon   I was in charge of a small special communications unit attached to the Ninth Brigade, under General Avraham Yoffe. The brigade was sent for the first time from Eilat down the coast of Sinai, right

"This war was finished before it started."
—Simcha Waisman

On November 1, 1956, three weeks into the Suez campaign, an Egyptian soldier surrenders to an IDF patrol.

down to Sharm el-Sheikh. In preparation for this campaign, one officer and two or three people were secretly sent to see the possible course because we were in regular trucks—we had just two tanks that were sent later. The problem was: could we pass through the desert area, beginning in the north, outside of Eilat, and cross the border? So my unit was providing the only means of communication between this brigade and the Central Command. Why? because we had no communications that could cover the distance of two hundred miles from Eilat to Sharm el-Sheikh.

Dan Pattir   I was exempt because of a disability, but I was involved in 1956. I was a military correspondent at that time for a newspaper, and on the eve of the war, I was sent to London to work with the Hebrew section of the BBC. We felt far away, and we wanted to be alert to every word of what was going on in the Straits of Tiran. But we were very close to the [Israeli] embassy, and we were informed directly from the embassy what was going on.

Raanan Gissin   We saw it from afar, and it was clear: something is happening in Israel. I was old enough to understand that this was a war, and I could feel the concern of my parents. Remember, this wasn't the age of television; you had, maybe, a couple of pictures coming over, in delay, from the area, showing that the Israeli forces are charging. Although we were in the Diaspora, for us, as Israelis, it's second nature. You have to get up in the morning and defend yourself, and you're raised in a country where being able to defend yourself and stand up for yourself is part of the essence of being a Jew and being a Zionist. And, in a sense, when you're out there, it reinforces your identification with the land, with the people, with what is happening there.

Not only did the unusual joint military operation amaze Middle East watchers, it caused consternation in Washington, when the visibly furious U.S. president Dwight Eisenhower demanded that the invaders cease and desist. It seems that the American president had not been informed in advance of the original ultimatum to the Egyptian president, a supposition confirmed at the time by the British prime minister, Sir [Robert] Anthony Eden, Earl of Avon [1897–1977; prime minister, 1955–1957], who on November 2 told the House of Commons when asked to confirm or deny reports that the United States had been blindsided, "From the beginning, I have declared that the French government and ourselves have taken action on our own responsibility."

By November 2, following additional Anglo-French air and naval attacks in the Suez Canal Area, the way was cleared for a full Anglo-French land invasion. The allies intended to occupy the Canal Zone temporarily, only until free navigation was achieved. After the invasion, they planned to cease operations and await action by the United Nations, presumably the insinuation of a police force, to ensure free navigation through the canal.

Simcha Waisman   It actually was something that built up, that started with the British, the Americans, and the French. In Israel it was kind of low-key for a while until they really put the ships to the test, and that's when this whole thing took motion, the wheels started moving. In those days, we had the best leaders in the military, who really thought it out very carefully and really went to war prepared and knowing that they had an 80 percent chance of losing it. But since everybody else got involved, they felt much more comfortable. It wasn't much felt in the big cities because everything was [taking place] *away* from the big cities. But everybody was in the military, and a lot of things were closed.

Dan Pattir   Eisenhower was a great disappointment for many Israelis because he was portrayed here by Ben-Gurion as the commander in chief who liberated the camps, so he was a hero for many Jews. Were we surprised by his action on Suez? Maybe we were carried away by our dream, the First Kingdom of Israel. At the time, it was a big disappointment because the collusion between the British and the French and us was regarded as a French-Israeli operation; the British were regarded as secondary. They didn't want to be involved, but they wanted to protect their own interests in the Suez Canal. The French were regarded here as the great partners because the French socialist government of [Prime Minister] Guy Mollet and the others were very friendly, politically. True, they were also interested because of [their presense in] Algeria. But the way they sent planes to help us—we saw the French Mystères here flying over—it was felt that we were in good company with the French at *that* time, that it was the great Americans we regarded as the "bad guys." Thus, the *French* were the "good guys. "

Yossi Ben-Aharon   We were very upset. We admired Ben-Gurion in his capacity to stand up to whomever. But there was something very wrong in what Ben-Gurion did—that he agreed to double back and return for the deployment of the U.N. forces and the total withdrawal from Gaza. Even at the beginning of 1957, when I wasn't there—I was studying at the Hebrew University—I knew enough about the Arab world, having lived in Egypt, to know that this was a terrible mistake. There was a kind of pressure, an outright threat by Dulles and Eisenhower, that if we didn't move back, they would send in the marines. I have thought many times since then that Ben-Gurion should have told Eisenhower, "Look, all we want is peace, and these people want to do us in. We will not withdraw until, and unless, the Egyptians are willing to negotiate peace with us. If you think we should withdraw before, *send* the marines! We will fight *anyone* who pushes us back because we are fighting for our existence!" That would have shaken them up. Eisenhower, much, much later, before he died, said that he and John Foster Dulles may have made a mistake.

June 1967, The Six-Day War: Acquisition and Its Bloody Aftermath

In May 1967, Egyptian president Gamal Abdel Nasser ordered his army into forward positions in the Sinai Peninsula, while at the same time, Syrian troops moved along the Golan Heights. On May 22, Nasser closed the Straits of Tiran, a strategic waterway that afforded Israeli ships access to the Port of Eilat. He repeatedly declared that "Our basic objective will be the destruction of Israel." Then, on May 30, the Egyptian dictator signed a defense treaty with King Hussein of Jordan.

On June 5, Israel, faced with the imminent threat of destruction, launched a preemptive strike. By day's end, nearly the entire Egyptian air force and half of Syria's had been destroyed. During the following days, the Israeli army advanced far into the Sinai and drove the Syrians from the Golan Heights. Upon Jordan's entry into the conflict, Israeli troops conquered the West Bank of the Jordan River and, on June 7, liberated the Old City of Jerusalem, which contains Judaism's most sacred site, the Western Wall of Solomon's Temple. At war's end, the United Nations Security Council passed Resolution 242, an ambiguously worded statement that is still in play, calling for Israel to return land in exchange for peace.

Malcolm Hoenlein   I went [in 1966], as a guest of some of the Arab countries, to Lebanon and Syria and Jordan. I had two passports so I could travel on one or the other [Arab countries would not admit travelers with passports bearing Israeli stamps]. The Algerian government, I think, had extended the official invitation, and I got arrested in Jordan for being a "Zionist spy and a CIA agent." I stayed at the American Colony Hotel [the legendary Swiss-owned establishment located in East Jerusalem that was, and remains, *the* favored gathering place of journalists, intelligence gatherers, and intriguers] and collected a great deal of information. I just happened to be in the wrong place at the wrong time. When the Israeli troops were coming in, to go to [Mt.] Scopus—they used to come twice a month or twice a week—I just happened to be there and saw things I shouldn't have seen and got pictures of it, so they came out of the woodwork and arrested me. They put me under house arrest at the American Colony, but I snuck out the back [by walking through the hotel's rear door and making his way to the Mandelbaum Gate, the official crossing point between Jordanian-held East Jerusalem and Israeli-controlled West Jerusalem prior to the unification of the city]. It was very exciting.

When I walked through the Mandelbaum Gate—you come around the bend—the Israeli soldier looked at me and said, "I think I can say, 'Welcome home,'" and I literally got down and kissed the ground. For me, it was a very, very exciting trip and the love affair has only intensified.

The next year, I was a Middle East specialist at the Foreign Policy Institute [a New York–based think tank], and I had taken off from college to work on an aid package for Israel in the weeks *before* the Six-Day War. Then, on the last day of the war, I went to Israel, and Shlomo Argov [the

Israeli Foreign Ministry official whose shooting by PLO terrorists in London in the spring of 1982, when he was ambassador to the Court of St. James's, sparked Israel's decision to carry out its Peace for the Galilee campaign] was actually supposed to process me. I came there, and they started laughing and saying, "How could you pull this off? You think we're going to be *fooled*? You're twenty-one years old and you come here and . . . ?" And he refused me the first time, so I had to go and get all sorts of documentation to prove I *was* who I *was*. And it led to a really close relationship until Argov was shot.

Simcha Waisman   The Arab nations—the Arab League in those days, Syria, Lebanon, Jordan, Egypt; the ones really close to our borders—had a big meeting and made a united front. One of the worst things that came out of it was that Gamal Abdel Nasser vowed [in a speech at] Sharm el-Sheikh that he was going to rape women and children and throw the men into the sea.

For each soldier—it didn't matter which branch you were in—it was *your* family, *your* country. If you ask Israelis, that's one of the main things that registered in their minds. Soldier or *not* a soldier, a red light started flashing: we have to do something about it! Each person became a mere machine. You just kept going and you said, "If those people are going to do it to us, we'll make sure that we protect our women and children, and we will protect *our country*, and we're going to win. They're going to do this to my *wife* or my *sister*? Are you *kidding*?"

And that's what happened. It was the biggest loss to the Arab world, and I believe that antagonizing the people was one of the biggest mistakes that they made because all of a sudden the people became like a machine.

Yehuda Avner   I was terrified! My wife had already lost her sister, and I was thinking in terms of her parents in London, and her father is cabling me: "I've already given one daughter to Israel! Don't put my other daughter and my grandchildren in danger!" Now, my wife's brother was living in Haifa, and we had arranged that the family would be together there.

Dan Pattir   I was in Canada at that time because President [Zalman] Shazar, of Israel, paid an official visit to Canada. Canada was celebrating its centenary, and that night, the mayor of Montreal was having an official dinner with *tails*. We felt that something was going on. In the middle of the speech by President Shazar, a correspondent of the Montreal English-language paper showed me the Reuters ticker: "Nasser Cuts Off the

Straits." I went to the military secretary of the president, and we decided that we weren't going to tell the president about it because if he heard that, he would want to go right back to Israel. So we kept the message from him until the dinner was over. We went to the hotel.

At five o'clock in the morning, I get a call from the security man: "The president wants to see you." I see the president of Israel in his tails, unshaven, red eyes, and he says to me, "I called the prime minister and nobody answered; I called everybody and nobody else answered." They didn't want him to go back because we hadn't yet decided what to do. He said, "The only thing I can do is to write a poem to mobilize the Jewish nation all over the world to the help of Israel." He showed me the poem. It was written in Yiddish. I said, "Mr. President, why is it in *Yiddish*?" He said, "Because I want as many Jews as possible to understand what I want to say." I said, "But Mr. President, most of the Jews in the world *don't know* Yiddish; you have to turn this into English." So his other secretary, she was American-born, translated it. And at six o'clock in the morning, we sent it by our network to our embassies all over the world.

I went back to Washington, and the rest was a celebration because the war was won quickly. I can't forget the scene: there stood at the [old Israeli] embassy [located at 22nd and R Streets] all the great stars of the American media—Martin Agronsky and the Kalb brothers [Bernard and Marvin] and [Walter] Cronkite—everybody was sitting on the stairs with microphones and waiting for some news from Israel. We fought in the war on the streets of Washington.

Amira Dotan   I wanted to be a doctor, and the military was not part of my thoughts at all. I finished my compulsory service at the beginning of the Six-Day War, and nobody left then. It was the tension before the war, and then the war broke out, and I was an officer, of course, and I stayed. Then after the war, the triumph and the winning and the feeling that you are part of a very strong and a very promising kind of Defense Forces and the glory of being a part of Israel—it was really a very wonderful time. And it was very successful, so there was no question that I was not leaving.

Then I was in the Southern Command, and the lady who was in charge of the Women's Corps was wounded very badly in Gaza. I came to [General Ariel] Sharon, who was then the chief of the Southern Command, and I asked whether I could replace her, although she was a major and I was only a lieutenant. And then it all started because he said, "You have very good grades, and everybody says you are a good officer, but there are two things that are minuses in your career: one, you started to learn in the university"

(I had started psychology and behavioral sciences at Ben-Gurion University) "and you have a daughter"—I was the mother of a very young girl, my first daughter. I don't think it was chutzpah, but with frankness I said, "General, with all due respect, those are the two big advantages that I have." And the "love story" started then with Sharon. I learned most of what I know about strategy and the way to read a map, not just a geographical map but a map of what's going on, and see the macro, not just the micro. To be able to plan ahead with all kinds of variations—if it goes this way, it's okay; if it goes the *other* way, it's okay—I learned from him, and I owe him a lot because of that.

Yehuda Avner   A week before the war I am in Tel Aviv, and the war correspondents are coming in droves. The government press office asked me to help out, when I can, with briefings and translation of communiqués. I meet with a clutch of journalists at the Hilton. On the way there, I pass a small beachfront park, and a hearse drives up. Out come a half-dozen *chevra kaddishem*, undertakers, with all the garb—beards, pipelike hats. I recognize the driver from funerals in Jerusalem, so I ask him what's going on because two of these undertakers are calling out measurements to a third fellow, who is writing them down, and two are walking around and around, wailing at the top of their voices. He says, "We have been asked to help out the Tel Aviv *chevra kaddisha* [burial society] to consecrate parts of cemeteries." I had seen a warehouse full of plastic rolls [of plastic sheeting] for burying bodies—and he says, "The word is that there are going to be anywhere between ten thousand and forty thousand dead!" I get very angry and say, "You shouldn't spread such pernicious rumors!" But it hits me. By the time I get to the Hilton, the journalists have smelled a rat and I have a hard time. Then I get back to Jerusalem, and the secretary tells me that Levi Eshkol wants me. I go to the outer office, and his secretary is sitting there, and there are two big cartons next to her desk. She says, "He wants to talk to you about these; we're getting letters of support in *sack loads*, and he wants to know what to do with them." So I go in to him—I've never seen him look so grand—and he says, "We're getting lots of these letters; I want you to go through them carefully—they must be coming from very important people—and those that are important, then I want you to tailor the responses."

I am about to leave when Ya'akov Herzog comes barging into the room and says to Eshkol, "I just received a message from our embassy in Washington that Johnson is saying he needs more time to put together an international coalition and that if we fire the first shot, then we'll be alone." And he then adds, in a totally different tone of voice, "and our intelligence is spotting gas equipment in the Sinai. This is war! Nasser will use it as he used it in Yemen." And Eshkol says, "If he does it, blood will flow like water!"

And then, on Herzog's heels, in comes Yisrael Lior, his military secretary, a colonel, and he says, "We have no stockpile of gas masks." Eshkol looks at Herzog and says, "We have nothing at all." And then he says, "I have to talk with the foreign minister [Abba Eban]." Now, there was a dissonance between him and Eban, a South African, Cambridge educated. These others were down-to-earth Zionists, and they considered Eban something of an incongruous outsider and a windbag. Eshkol thought of him that way, Golda thought of him that way, Rabin thought of him that way, and in his heart of hearts, if Begin had been asked, I think he would also have thought of him that way. But I adored Eban; I learned so much from him. And Eban was beloved by Jewish communities the world over for his oratory at the United Nations, his brilliant speeches; and by high society, for his scholarship.

Eban was about to meet with Johnson at the White House. Now, you are not invited to stay in the room when all this is going on, so I leave. So I pick up the first carton—it is quite heavy—and Herzog sticks his head out and says to the secretary, "Find Eban immediately in Washington; the prime minister needs to speak to him." So I shlep this box to my room, and one door has been left open so that I can hear Eshkol screaming into the phone to Abba Eban, "It's no longer blocking the Straits of Tiran [near Eilat]," telling him about the gas, reminding him of the commitments Johnson had made him "during my visit in 1964 to the White House that the United States will always back Israel, if attacked." He says, "Write it *down*! Write it *down*!" Then he bursts out, in Yiddish, "Tell the goy that we're dealing with Arabs! Do you hear? *Arabs!*"

Israel's Surprisingly Swift Victory

Simcha Waisman   You're halfway into the Golan Heights, three-quarters into the desert, and three-quarters into Jerusalem, and you listen to the *Arabic* radio, and they say they are marching into Tel Aviv and Haifa. The way they did this thing backfired—that's *their* language. I was surprised, but, at the same time, I believed in our commander in chief, and I knew that they [the Israel Defense Forces] are one of the best [armies] in the world. You have to know them to appreciate them. They have led us through a lot of hard times and to victories that we sometimes didn't expect to happen so rapidly. Yes, we had casualties, but it could have been worse.

Akiva Eldar   I was in the reserves. We were very anxious, very concerned, *petrified*; we were fighting for our lives. I remember Levi Eshkol's famous speech, where he mumbled and stuttered. I lived in Jerusalem, which was attacked. No one thought it would take only six days—that it would end so quickly and in such a heroic way.

Liberation Day in Jerusalem

Joshua Matza   On that day I was serving in the army, and there came to me a cable from the army: "Jerusalem was liberated." So, of course, there was great joy, and we all celebrated. I was a member of the Jerusalem Municipality in those days, a councillor, and on the same day I sent to [the mayor of Jerusalem, the late Teddy] Kollek a telegram—I couldn't find him by phone—"Please call for a meeting of the entire Council of Jerusalem to celebrate."

Visiting the Kotel, the Western Wall

The Western Wall supporting the ancient Temple Mount, which dates from the destruction of the Second Temple in the year 70 of the Common Era, is also called the "Wailing Wall" because it was a focus of Jewish grief and lamentation over the centuries. Yet it is also revered as a place for prayer. Access by Jews to the Western Wall had been interrupted in 1947, following attacks on Jews by Arabs. After May 1948, following the new Jewish state's loss of the Old City's Jewish Quarter to Jordanian forces, the holy site lay in Jordanian hands for nineteen years. It was liberated on June 7, 1967, the third day of the Six-Day War, by Israeli paratroopers who broke through the Zion Gate.

The liberating troops discovered just how severely their holy site had been desecrated by its occupiers: the access way whereby Jews had once thronged to the Wall now lay fouled by garbage.

Dan Pattir   We were privileged to be youngsters who had visited the Wall before 1948, so we saw that it was narrow and poor. There was a wall between the women and the men. And it was filthy, shabby, and dilapidated; no one took care of it. But we had an urge to be there.

"For me, the liberation, the reunification, of Jerusalem was the liberation of Jewish history, the Jewish soul—coming to the Kotel, being free to go to the Kotel."
—Malcolm Hoenlein

On June 7, 1967, two days into what would go down in history as the Six-Day War, the jubilant Israeli defense minister Moshe Dayan and Commander Uzi Narkiss pose in the newly liberated East Jerusalem under a street sign, in Arabic, pointing to the Jews' holiest site, the Western Wall.

For us, 1967 was a great event because suddenly a dream became reality. Those who had never been there maybe didn't feel that strong emotion as we did.

Joshua Matza   I went to the Kotel. I wasn't alone—all the councillors of the municipality went with Teddy Kollek to inaugurate the new road that they opened. It was a day or two days before Shavuot [a Jewish summertime festival that historically marked the end of the barley and the beginning of the wheat harvest]. They prepared this road, and we came especially to inaugurate it and to cut the band [ribbon] there.

Malcolm Hoenlein   I had visited the Kotel in '66, and I started to clean it up because the conditions there were really awful. And then a policeman came so I had to put the stuff in my pockets. Then it was very narrow, and when I came back the next year, they had just plowed one part of the plaza area.

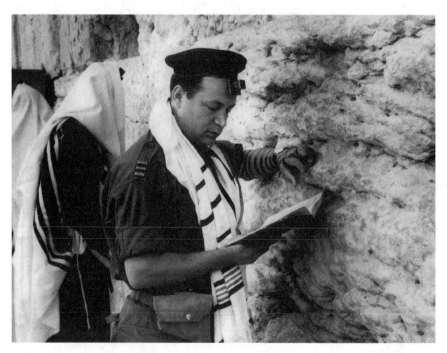

"It was a great celebration, of course."
—Joshua Matza

Joshua Matza prays at the Western Wall in June 1967, immediately after the liberation of Jerusalem.

"We thought the resistance would be much stronger."—Simcha Waisman

On June 14, 1967, three days after Israel's stunning victory, Prime Minister Levi Eshkol—future prime minister Menachem Begin stands behind him (right)—visits with a reserve unit at Jebel Livni, in the Sinai.

A roadside in mid-June 1967 as it appeared to journalist Philip Hochstein and his wife, Leah Hochstein.

"You can see shot-up military vehicles everywhere."—The late Leah Hochstein, in correspondence with her daughter Deborah Hart Strober

Simcha Waisman   The only time that I had seen the Kotel before was through binoculars, through pictures, and through other means. You thought you were never going to get there. A lot of us said, "Maybe, finally, we're going to have peace." It didn't happen—we had another war afterward—but everybody's heart was full. Even today, I go there, and I still feel the same thing.

Malcolm Hoenlein   Jerusalem is a very special place, and too often we take it for granted, including now. This is the fortieth anniversary year [of the liberation], and it's hard to get people to really do what they should do to celebrate it. If we don't proclaim to the world our connection to Jerusalem, we're going to lose it because *they* [the Arabs] proclaim it all the time—whenever you see a picture of an Arab leader in Jerusalem, it's always a picture of Al Aksa Mosque behind him; when you see an *Israeli* leader, there's always a picture of Al Aksa Mosque behind *him*! So I told them, "What the *hell* are you doing? You know, more Americans identify Jerusalem with Islam because in every picture they see, there's a picture of a mosque." We have not asserted *our* connection and *our* ties.

When they opened the tunnels, Arafat said that the problem of the tunnels was the Judaizing of Jerusalem. And he was right! There's no one who goes through those tunnels—and I've been with a hundred congressmen and senators and Margaret Thatcher and Giuliani and D'Amato, everybody—there isn't *one* who doesn't come out and say, "I get it!" Because there is three thousand years of Jewish history—you see where Abraham brought Isaac to the sacrifice; where the Maccabees marched—all of Jewish history is *right there*, along the two temples.

The Postwar Economic, Political, and Demographic Upheaval

Simcha Waisman   It was a gradual thing. You didn't feel the changes right away. In Israel, you're so occupied with your job or whatever you do that it's very hard to feel a lot of the time. And a lot of us in Israel live on one assumption: you live for today because you don't know what tomorrow will bring. Today it is quiet; tomorrow you can be blown out of the sky.

Shlomo Ariav   We grew up with the idea of *Shtei Gadot* [a Jewish state on both sides of the Jordan River] so in the moments after '67 it was like the Messiah was coming; we were free to do anything. Then people started to push for settlements, and Arik Sharon—he was the mastermind of all these things—immediately established a special committee to start buying Arab land.

The Role of Keren Kayemeth
(the Jewish National Fund)

Shlomo Ariav   A woman from the Department of Justice had to check everything, and many times she didn't let us [Keren Kayemeth Le Israel] buy it. She had an excuse; she was afraid there were going to be problems. But at the time we started to work to buy land. Eighty-five percent of the land for settlements in Judea and Samaria was not bought directly by Keren Kayemeth. I was only the middleman; anything that we bought, we bought for the government because the government couldn't do so itself. We went all over Israel at that time to find land.

We really put in so much money, so much effort, at that time. And the same money and effort could have been used for something very different, the Negev and, especially, to keep a section of the Galilee. You come there today, and everything is Arab—you come to some villages, and you wouldn't believe it. And they keep coming and coming: somebody marries someone from Jenin or Ramallah, and they are coming in. Many ideas that we had before we are unable to do now because it's not the right time.

Yossi Ben-Aharon   There was no plan for taking over Judea, Samaria, and Gaza and incorporating them. It may have been in the thoughts of people who belonged to the Herut Party under Menachem Begin in the early sixties. But the Mapai, the establishment, had plans that were military in nature, in case of an attack, but nothing, to the best of my knowledge, in terms of incorporating Judea, Samaria, and Gaza. If we do have to take over parts, how do we manage them? The only experience we had then was with the military governorship of the Arab part of what we call "the Triangle," the Arab villages in the north.

Yehuda Avner   When Eshkol was taken to the Wall, he was alleged to have said to somebody: "What do we *do* with this?"

Dan Pattir   Dayan at that time was saying, "We are waiting for the phone [to ring] with the Arabs. Until then, we are the masters of the area." And nobody actually came out and said we must return, because there was no need for that; people felt very comfortable with the situation.

Yael Pattir   Israelis, all of a sudden, enjoyed the space. With the settlements, we became a big country. And you could go up to Egypt with no problem whatsoever.

Dan Pattir   You should have seen the weekend souks [the Arab market] of Nablus and Ramallah and Hebron, people from Israel proper, not so much from the settlements, driving back and forth. So there was some kind of belief that this was a new era with new realities. Nobody envisioned the intifada at that time.

Akiva Eldar   They didn't have a *clue*. First of all, the cabinet made a decision on June 19, 1967, that Israel would withdraw to the international borders with Syria and Egypt for peace. A few weeks later, this decision was reversed. In the West Bank there was no international border, so this was left open. I recall sitting in the university dorms with fellow students when we discovered that for very little money we could get nice apartments in Ramat Eshkol, which was in no-man's-land. Even poor students could get what was called a standing loan, which after five years turned into a grant. We laughed at people who bought those apartments because we thought that Israel would give those areas back in a few weeks or months. We thought that it was not possible that the international community and the Americans would let us keep those territories, including East Jerusalem. The common wisdom was that we would have to give the territories back in return for peace. In 1956, Israel had been pushed by the United States to withdraw. I recall that in the 1970s, when I was a young reporter visiting Alon Moreh, we didn't believe this was serious. But if you go back to the documents, the government didn't have a strategy.

Look what happened in Hebron at Pesach. The settlers were smart enough to realize, How can you stop a Jew from going to Hebron for Pesach, or to Gush Etzion; where the survivors wanted to go back, and they did this on Rosh Hashanah? Eshkol couldn't deal with their tears. The government leaders did not see how things were going to deteriorate or, in a way, escalate the way they did.

At the same time, there weren't checks and balances. Peace Now started only in 1978; the Americans did not use their diplomatic influence to stop the settlements until 1992, through the loan-guarantee issue. After a while, the Israeli government realized they could get away with it—that the sky was not going to fall. The price of fighting the settlers and the settlements seemed higher than the conflict with the United

States and with the international community. They concluded that it would cost more to stop the settlements than to allow them, so they allowed them.

Let's imagine that there are no settlements and that we will not build new neighborhoods in Jerusalem. There would be tremendous pressure on Israel from inside and from outside to go back to the 1967 lines because then it would not require moving people out of their houses. Let's go back to the '67 lines: it's no big deal; we will get peace. This was the dream, that one day the Arabs would come to terms with our existence and with our right to exist—with reality—and we would all go back to the 1967 borders.

Joshua Matza   This policy of creating settlements was accurate and right, and they should have done it even more intensively, hoping that one day we would even be able to annex them. Because of the criticism of the world, we didn't annex them, but we started to build these settlements. This was the right way, being Eretz Israel, to have back our lands, while, of course, taking care of the Palestinians living there and not abusing them. We couldn't send them away; they learned from '48 not to leave their places, so they stayed there, and it was our duty to take care of them. We could, and we did it in Gaza, and we did it in Judea and Samaria, in a lot of settlements. I know that today we don't have any other choice but to find a compromise, only because of one issue: authority.

The War of Attrition

In the years following the Six-Day War, Israel tightened its hold on the West Bank—the biblical regions of Judea and Samaria—and established settlements outside Arab population centers, where eventually more than two hundred thousand Jews would live. The Arab states continued to refuse recognition to Israel and would not negotiate a peace agreement. Hostilities resumed in 1970 as Israel and Egypt traded artillery fire along the Suez Canal, that conflict coming to be known as the War of Attrition.

Dan Pattir   I could have envisioned it because Egypt couldn't absorb this kind of a shock. The humiliation was absolutely devastating—the pictures of their airfields being completely cut off and demolished. And Nasser was at that time carrying the flag of mutiny in Egypt—the kingdom was definitely not the choice of the Egyptians and never the choice of Egyptians.

The War of Atonement

Full-scale warfare erupted on October 6, 1973, Yom Kippur, with Egypt and Syria's launching of surprise attacks in the Sinai and on the Golan Heights, respectively. While the Egyptians and the Syrians initially had the upper hand, the tide soon turned as Israeli ground and air forces, despite very heavy casualties, defeated the two Arab armies.

In the war's most dramatic battle, an Israeli division commanded by Major General Ariel Sharon crossed the Suez Canal after an all-night fight. At war's end, Prime Minister Golda Meir was sharply criticized for not having made a preemptive strike in the hours just prior to the Egyptian and Syrian attacks.

The Pre–Yom Kippur War Political Scene

Arie Lova Eliav   After the great victory of '67, I thought that the leaders of our government took a dose of political LSD or political heroin—they were drugged with victory. I said, "You're drugged, and you will take a big dose of LSD, and that's where you'll end." They thought that now that we had won the '67 war, we were the strongest and mightiest; we had an empire. And, eventually, this kind of concept brought on us the Yom Kippur War.

I left the Labor Party because of that—because of the clash with Golda Meir and her friends. I was convinced that they were dead wrong, and I created a small party called "Sheli" [Israel Peace Party]. We had two members in the Knesset.

Yehiel Kadishai   After the Six-Day War, for two and a half years or more, we had only two ministers, Sapir and Begin, in the government of [Levi] Eshkol. But then Eshkol passed away and Golda Meir took over. She established a new government with six ministers of the Likud [formed by Herut and the Liberals]—Haim Landau, Ezer Weizman, and Begin of Herut; and [Simcha] Ehrlich and [Aryeh Leon] Dulzin of the Liberals—and in 1970, we had six ministers for nine months.

Then, when the Rogers initiative came, in August 1970, there was a cease-fire on the [Suez] Canal, with Egypt, [arranged] by [Dr. Gunnar] Jarring [Sweden's ambassador to the Soviet Union, who was appointed by the United Nations secretary general U Thant as his envoy to the Middle East under the mandate of Security Council Resolution 242]. The government of Golda accepted the cease-fire—that it would be okay with Egypt, and we would move from the canal, and we would have to fulfill Resolution 242 of the United Nations. The Liberals wanted to accept it and to remain in the government, in spite of the fact that Pinhas Sapir and Golda asked Begin to "Stay in the government; vote in the Knesset against it."

He said, "No, if we stay in the government, we are responsible for the results and"—he said it openly, in the Knesset—"you say that the decision to accept this cease-fire will bring peace, and I say that there will be war. I don't know when, but this will cause a war." Almost two years after this came the Yom Kippur War.

Amira Dotan   I was with Sharon in the Southern Command through 1972, and then I was with the one who replaced Sharon. Then the war broke out, and I was very eager to take every woman soldier and officer out of Sinai. I persuaded everybody, and there was an order that came from the chief of staff. Part of what I had done was to go from unit to unit and make sure that no women would be there.

It was quite a war, I can tell you. No one can explain, first of all, the surprise, and then the actual war, which was really very, very bad. And we tend to forget, because of what Sharon did afterward, that there was a lot

On October 13, 1973, Israel Defense Forces soldiers moving along the Kuneitra-Damascus Road flash V for victory signs.

of tension between Sharon and the other generals over what was right and what was wrong.

Why Didn't Israel Launch a Preemptive Strike?

Dan Pattir   We considered a preemptive strike very seriously, but Golda was waiting—as she said, "We didn't have to produce an excuse to the Americans to start the war." We came very close, with Syria, mainly, because the intelligence was indicating that something was coming up. Sinai was far away, and it wasn't a physical threat.

Yossi Ben-Aharon   A commission of inquiry was appointed subsequent to the war and determined [in the Agranot report, issued by the Agranot Commission, which was chaired by the American-born Dr. Shimon Agranot, the president of Israel's Supreme Court; it submitted its finding to the government on April 2, 1974] that the blunder was committed by our military intelligence. There was no pluralism in our intelligence at that time, and the people in charge of our military intelligence thought you had to decide whether the Egyptian-Syrian concentration of forces on the border was an exercise or a preparation for an assault. And the guy in charge, [Major] General [Eliahu] Zeira, whom I knew—he was in Washington before that—decided that on the basis of all the accumulated information, it was an exercise. Although there was a challenge to this on the part of the Mossad, it wasn't strong enough in the eyes of the political leadership, Golda and Moshe Dayan, and they opted for what the military was saying. We were caught unprepared, and we paid the price.

Simcha Waisman   It's very easy to judge afterward, and I was surprised that a lot of the judgments came out. I think that the country learned from the past that the mistake everybody makes—and who knows whether it was a mistake or *not* a mistake—could be that somebody fell asleep at the switch. In the end, they did what they were supposed to do. It was a bad call. I'm not going to judge. Golda Meir was *Golda*. This is my perspective, but if you go back—people forget about a lot of the history—it's very easy to point fingers. Somebody fell asleep at the switch; that's the only thing that happened. And it taught everybody that your best intelligence is the intelligence on the ground. And a lot of the intelligence got destroyed because people said, "Oh! New technology! We don't need them [the intelligence assets on the ground]!" There's nothing better for intelligence on the ground than what you *see*; it's not what you hear.

Would a Preemptive Strike Have Deterred Egypt?

Dan Pattir   I don't know. I can tell you one thing. I was one of the first Israelis who officially went to Egypt after Sadat had been here. We discussed the pullout from the Sinai Peninsula, and I had a talk with General

On August 10, 1982, more than two months into what, two and a half decades later, would come to be known as the First Lebanon War, IDF troops engage in mopping up operations in southern Beirut under the gaze of a Fatah terrorist whose image is depicted on the poster at left.

"Nothing affected morale."—Amira Dotan

[Abd al-Chany al-] Gamazy, who was then the defense minister of Egypt. I asked him, "How did you do it to us?" I said it against the background of everything in 1977: Egypt was falling apart; machines were shabby, telephone lines were not working, everything was contrary to what we expected of the Egypt that could have launched the '73 war. And I can't forget what he said in metaphor:

> You know, the alarm clock: you load the spring—you load it, you load it, you load it—and then when you lift it, a certain kind of energy is released until the spring is not loaded anymore. So this is what I did. For three years I selected from our military might, manpower, the best, to train and to train and to train. And I thought that if we loaded a spring to the maximum, we can release the energy after crossing the Suez Canal, and beyond that.

This was the action, the maximum that the Egyptian military could have done. And then I realized that the major part of the war was *our* fault.

Dayan was in a very defensive mood. He said, "The destruction of the Third Temple." He was made out to be the great hero, but the great heroes were the lower echelon of the military. This was definitely a time of big trials for Israel, the first time after 1948 that we had a real physical threat to our existence.

The First Lebanon War: Peace for the Galilee

In the 1970s, the Palestine Liberation Organization (PLO), a terrorist organization founded in 1964 and devoted to the destruction of Israel, held sway over Lebanon, persecuting the Christian community and using that nation's southern region as a base from which to launch attacks against Israeli civilians living in the Galilee.

Then, in early June 1982, terrorists from a PLO-affiliated organization shot and severely wounded Israel's ambassador to the United Kingdom, Shlomo Argov. On June 6, Israel responded by launching Operation Peace for the Galilee, with the intent of driving the PLO back to the Beirut area.

Although Israel dislodged the PLO, which, with its leader, Yasser Arafat, was exiled to Tunis, fighting continued until 1985. Then, in 2000, Israel withdrew completely from southern Lebanon.

During the summer of 1982, the authors brought a group of Christian clergy to Lebanon to show them the truth about Lebanon. Arriving later in

Israel, the authors attended a reception for the Christian group at the Prime Minister's Bureau in Jerusalem. When Prime Minister Begin came into the room, although suffering the aftereffects of a broken hip and walking with great difficulty, he made his way through the assemblage and paused to greet each member of the delegation. Then, moving to the front of the room, Mr. Begin addressed the group. He spoke eloquently of his aspiration for a new Middle East—namely, that the coastal highway connecting Egypt, Israel, and Lebanon would become an open road toward a relationship of friendship. He was so visionary, and then, of course, it all fell apart.

The Decision to Allow Female Soldiers into Lebanon

Amira Dotan   It was a process. First of all, I became very feminist, and I had a lot of very good teachers, my good friends in the United States, who, when I became the chief of staff of the Women's Corps, really gave me the ideas and backed me up because I sometimes really asked myself, Am I meshuga or am I a normal person? They really were the backup of lot of new ideas and achievements within the Defense Forces.

When I became the chief of staff of the Women's Corps, the Lebanon War was happening. The reserve military men had already been away from home for ten months, and the economics of Israel were, of course, in trouble because of that. On the other hand, I saw those young Israeli soldiers, who are very capable, and I said, "Okay, let's trade them off; the men will go back to their vocations, families, et cetera, and the women—at least in some of their vocations—will replace them."

I was very lucky because the chief of staff then was Moshe Vachetsi [literally, "one and a half;" Levy was so nicknamed because he was extremely tall], Moshe Levy, who was very open and very courageous, very low key, but very, very courageous. And it was the two of us who really changed everything.

But in 1981, it was the first time that women soldiers were crossing the border and doing those jobs. We mapped what vocations would be there. And after we mapped the vocations, we did another thing: I interviewed every soldier who went in because I wanted to make sure that the women who went in would be very strong, psychologically and mentally, on the one hand, and that we would really be able to hold together, with all the pressure of the unit, of the war, of the surroundings, and everything else.

Fortunately, no woman was wounded; no woman was killed. And the fourth thing that we did was that we rotated them with other women after six months. It was a real achievement because then nobody could say: it cannot be done. And it opened a lot of other ways for to us really integrate women into the Defense Forces.

IDF Morale

Amira Dotan   Part of my job now in the Knesset is in foreign affairs and security, so we interviewed some of these soldiers and the officers. I can say that their morale is one of the beauties of those wonderful people. I think nothing will break it, and this is, I think, part of being Israeli, of being able to live here and to really take upon our shoulders the fact that Israel will continue to be a Jewish democratic state.

The First Gulf War: Scuds Fall on Israel

Yossi Ben-Aharon   Bush had a point there; he didn't want Saddam Hussein to adopt the guise of the "Great Savior" of the Arab world against Israel—the "Great Fighter" against the Jewish state. Therefore, he wanted no involvement of Israel in this attempt by the Americans to do him in and throw him out of Kuwait. Therefore, Bush kept sending delegations and letters to Shamir: "Please do not involve yourself even if you are attacked. We will take care." Of course, we, with our experience, knew that the American air force, with little experience, didn't have the expertise, the know-how, the experience with the Arabs, to do what was necessary. To an extent, I can fill in these letters because they knew from the beginning that we cannot be attacked and do nothing, so they estimated initially that in a certain situation, they would give us the wherewithal in order for us also to participate and at least hit the ground-to-air missile batteries. But they *didn't*. When the Scuds came on a Friday night in February 1991, when a whole salvo of missiles hit the north of Tel Aviv and Ramat Gan, we had a big meeting, and Misha Arens and the military commander had prepared a plan: we would send the army into Iraq and try to pinpoint where these locations were where they had the missile launchers. But after Arens listened to everything that they said, and what the cost would be, and how wide the conflagration would be, he decided to wait. And he was right because, eventually, clearly this was the last burst of the Iraqis. Of course, Bush was very effusive in his appreciation.

July 2006–August 2006, Hezbollah's War against the Jewish State: The Second Lebanon War

Sharon's removal from the political landscape in January 2006 had enormous repercussions when, during the summer of 2006, the Iranian-backed, Lebanon-based Hezbollah "militia," which had taken over southern Lebanon following Israel's withdrawal in 2000, killed a number of Israeli soldiers and kidnapped two others. Olmert, who had never served in a combat unit, and his defense minister, Amir Peretz, a former leader of the Labor Confederation, badly blundered in their response to Hezbollah's provocation.

The resulting Second Lebanon War revealed weaknesses in the IDF's planning and preparedness and caused serious disruptions in Israel's northern region, where many Israelis were killed and hundreds injured as more than four thousand rockets rained down on their towns and cities, some reaching the center of the country.

Joseph Hochstein There is a consensus that the soldiers fought like heroes but that the supplies weren't where they should be, that the planning wasn't what it should have been. The soldiers as soldiers were fine, but the army as an army was rotten; there was this inner rot.

A building in Haifa's Bat Galim neighborhood, located near Rambam Hospital, where many of the conflict's wounded were taken, as it looked after a Katyusha barrage on July 17, 2006, only days into the Second Lebanon War.

"The Israeli air force destroyed the heavy rockets that they had on the first day and that was intelligence, so it's not right to say that our intelligence failed."—Rafi Eitan

Raanan Gissin   The government did not function as expected and did not prepare the people. But the *people were* prepared, and when there was no government, they knew what to do. This capacity for collective action, for total mobilization in times of emergency, is something that is part of our upbringing and culture and heritage. I wouldn't want to test it too many times, but I think that when you look at the balance, the ability of the Jewish State to survive, despite all the challenges and all those tsunami waves we have to ride, is today much greater than ever in the past of the Jewish people.

———

On January 17, 2007, more than five months after Israeli air and ground forces had fired off their last salvos in a war that had lasted thirty-four days, the chief of staff, Lieutenant General Dan Halutz, stated in a letter to Prime Minister Ehud Olmert, that "For me, responsibility is everything." He thus resigned, leaving in his wake charges that he had badly mismanaged the battle by not having sent in sufficient ground troops and having relied too heavily on air power.

The conflict began on July 12, 2006, when Hezbollah terrorists stole across Israel's border with Lebanon, killing three Israeli soldiers and abducting two others. Responding immediately, the Israeli air force conducted massive operations and, despite heavy bombardment, was unable to destroy the enemy's rocket-launching apparatus. Hezbollah was able to fire at will, sending off more than a hundred Katyushas a day across the border and devastating northern Israeli cities and towns.

Complicating matters, on June 25, less than three weeks before hostilities would begin in the north, Palestinian terrorists on Israel's border with Gaza had abducted a shy, French-born, nineteen-year-old IDF corporal, Gilad Shalit, to Gaza.

After the firing of more than four thousand Katyushas into Israel, with 159 deaths in Israel and, according to Israel, 500 Hezbollah terrorists dead, hostilities ended on August 14, 2006. The cease-fire followed the United Nations Security Council's passage of a resolution calling for an international peace-keeping force to be deployed in southern Lebanon, as well as oversight of the Lebanese seacoast and border with Syria, with the aim of stemming the rearming of Hezbollah.

Dan Pattir   It [the failure to destroy Hezbollah] definitely didn't contribute to the empowerment of the country. I don't believe this was the critical point of weakness. Maybe we lost some face in not demolishing

Hezbollah altogether, as we should have. But, on the other hand, I am one of those people who say, "I am happy that it happened; it happened at the right time, before we would have faced a new situation—of the Iranians and the Hezbollah more entrenched in south Lebanon with much more weaponry."

Did Israeli Intelligence Fail?

Rafi Eitan   We were not prepared enough for the war in Lebanon. To say that intelligence failed is not true because the intelligence was very accurate for giving the air force the targets to diminish all the heavy rockets that they had. But to say that we were prepared all the way is also bad. We were not prepared *enough* for what happened in south Lebanon.

Chapter 11

REDEEMING ENDANGERED EXILES

From the very beginning of the state, Israel had been determined to ingather as many Jews as possible from throughout the world, an aim directed particularly at the Jewish communities of Arab nations, as well as toward countries espousing virulent anti-Semitism.

Operation Magic Carpet

In May 1949, Israel initiated Operation Magic Carpet, a series of flights that eventually brought forty-five thousand Yemenite Jews to the Jewish homeland. Then, in the 1950s and 1960s, hundreds of thousands of Jews from other Arab lands were brought to Israel and absorbed into its society.

Ernest Stock I accompanied one of the [Magic Carpet] flights. The people brought on board their treasured possessions—their Torah scrolls. We hired one of the Yemenites, a young woman, as a maid. Later, she left us to take a position with a bank, and we lost touch with her. We believe that that happened because she was ashamed that she had once worked as a maid.

Yemenite Jews rescued from their precarious existence in 1950 during Operation Magic Carpet look dazedly into the camera en route to Israel on board a DC 4 flight organized by the American Jewish Joint Distribution Committee.

"They were very poor and carried little in the way of material possessions."
—Ernest Stock

A five-year-old Yemenite boy (left), the brother of Bracha and Ernest Stock's housekeeper, poses with his good friend, the Stocks' son Adlai (right), also five, at the Stocks' apartment in Jerusalem.

"They were good friends despite the differences in their social and economic backgrounds, and the Yemenites were very proud. Adlai's friend was dressed for that visit in his best clothes and shoes."
—Bracha Stock

Soviet Jewry

By the early 1970s, the Jewish community of the Soviet Union, numbering more than one million, was in a desperate predicament. Although it had been roused by Israel's stunning victory in the Six-Day War, its leaders were either exiled or imprisoned in the notorious gulag, while ordinary citizens were forbidden to exercise their basic human rights of freedom of emigration and the observance of their Jewish faith.

Springing into action, Israel and the Jewish communities of the West launched an intense public campaign to win freedom for Soviet Jewry. The movement reached its climax when on December 6, 1987, more than two hundred fifty thousand Americans gathered on the Mall in Washington, D.C., to participate in Freedom Sunday for Soviet Jewry, a demonstration of support and advocacy.

One of the speakers was Natan Sharansky, who had been imprisoned in the gulag for nine years as a prisoner of conscience and who had emerged as the movement's symbolic leader. By the late 1980s, the gates of the Soviet Union began to open, and with the implosion of the Soviet empire, more than one million Jews were allowed to emigrate, most of them choosing to live in Israel.

Arie Lova Eliav   I was the first secretary in Moscow [in the late 1950s]. The operation [to smuggle handwritten copies of Leon Uris's book *Exodus* into the Soviet Union] was a Mossad operation, and I was the head of this Mossad unit, which was part of the embassy. We did very important work, not only *Exodus*, but by talking with tens of thousands of Jews, under very difficult conditions—for them and for us—and bringing in *Exodus*, as well as hundreds of thousands of prayer books, and going all over the Soviet Union, from coast to coast, and meeting Jews and going to their synagogues or wherever we could. We were sent to be the torchbearers of Neo-Zionism and Judaism, under very difficult conditions, behind the Iron Curtain. It was a very important service in my life.

Bobby Brown   One of the most glorious modern struggles we've had is of the Soviet Jews coming back to being Jewish. It's incredible when you think about it! And they were certainly one of the major factors in creating awareness, which helped to bring down the Soviet state. Even kids of Russian families don't know about that struggle! It reminds me of the Irgun at one time; now nobody knows about it.

Of the heroes of that period, Sharansky may be known because, although I don't think people know what he did, they know him because he was in politics. But [Vladimir] Slepak and Ida Nudel and [Yosif] Mendelevich, people who were unbelievably brave in the face of a totalitarian system that could crush them at any moment, where is their story? Where is that part of the Jewish consciousness? Soviet Jewry who came here changed Israel—and changed the world, for sure. If you want their kids to have a sense of pride in their own origin, you have to tell that story. It's not told.

Raanan Gissin In the nineteenth century it was the pioneers who came for ideological reasons; they left behind everything they had in Russia, and came and wanted to build socialism. Later on, other immigration waves came—from Poland and from Germany—the Third and Fourth Aliyahs; and the Fifth one [of Soviet Jewry] really established the industrial infrastructure of Israel.

Malcolm Hoenlein I was involved with Soviet Jewry from the early sixties, so there's a whole history. I went to Russia in '71 and got arrested there

Natan Sharansky (center) listens, as Shoshana Cardin, then chair of the National Conference on Soviet Jewry, the American Jewish community's umbrella organization for advocacy on behalf of the Soviet Jewish community, makes a point during a break in meetings of the Jewish Agency for Israel, held in Jerusalem in the 1990s.

"I organized the first demonstrations outside New York, in Philadelphia, where I grew up, and was involved in the founding meeting of the American Conference on Soviet Jewry [the predecessor organization of the National Conference on Soviet Jewry], in Philadelphia, at Constitution Hall."
—Malcolm Hoenlein

for being a "Zionist provocateur." They threw me out, actually, but we did a good job in talking our way out of it. We were in Kishinev, and there was a trial, and they had to postpone the trial because somebody ratted on us. It was a little bit strange; I mean they just said, "You're a Zionist provocateur." And I said, "Bring me *proof*; show me *proof*." And he waved some letters. And I said, "Let me read them." And he said, "No, I can't, I can't." And I said, *"That's* what's wrong with the Soviet Union! I'm leaving this country *right away!"* And he said, "No, no. Wait a minute!" And he had already thrown us out! It took us fifty-five hours to get home.

I told this to [former KGB official, now Russian president Vladimir] Putin in 1998. We were having a meeting and there was a guy giving a forum, but they didn't introduce him. I said something about Islamic fundamentalism and the impact on Russia, and this guy went off like a rocket: Israel! It's the biggest danger! So I said, "Excuse me, are you going to introduce us?" He said, "My name is Vladimir Putin; I'm head of the KGB." And I went, Whoa! And afterward, they brought out vodka, and he came and poured me a glass. I said, "You know, this is really strange for me because last time I met you guys, you arrested me!" He said, "Where?" And I said, "Moldova." He said, "That's why we got rid of it [in the dissolution of the Soviet Union]!"

Abraham Foxman During the cold and hot war periods, it was the issue of freedom for Soviet Jewry that determined our relationship. The American Jewish community stood up for Soviet Jewry. We gave Secretary [of State George P.] Shultz an Elijah Cup. We gave it to him so that he would always remember the seder that he had in the American embassy [in Moscow] for refuseniks. And he said to us, "I'm only allowed to take five or six things home, personally, after I finish [being in the Bush administration]. This is one thing that I will take home."

Arie Lova Eliav In 1965, I wrote in my book *Between Hammer and Sickle*: "One day, when the system will implode, one million Jews will come to Israel." And people said, "You are out of your mind! What are you talking about? And what would we do with tens of thousands of doctors and engineers and mixed marriages?"

There are many problems. If you bring a million people from *anywhere*, there are problems—you'll find whores and pimps; you'll find smugglers—but all in all, you cannot envisage Israel today, 2007, without the million Jews who came from the Soviet Union—they are in every layer of life. It is one of the greatest treasures that we have gotten.

Natan Sharansky There is always a difference between people who are guided by ideological drive and their desire to fight for something, and that's what defines their decisions, and people who didn't share this ideology but whose main drive is coming from daily needs. Sooner or later, for every group of immigrants, although the majority came to Israel because of the circumstances, in every movement, in every group, you'll find people, and usually those who were the first, who came because of ideological reasons. So there is a difference in absorption. Of course it is easier for people who are coming because of ideological reasons to take the hardships.

On the other hand, they can be more difficult for society because they are very demanding in their desire to fight for their principles, and when they find out that society is not exactly working out this way, they become dissidents *here*. And it is more difficult for the people who are coming because they have to, or they felt pushed because of material or other needs, to accept hardships because they came here in order *not* to have

Prime Minister Shimon Peres poses with a young Israeli "Ghostbuster" redeemed from Ethiopia during Operation Moses.

"I haven't seen any other country but Israel that has taken black Africans with no skills, often with health problems, into their bosom."
—Bobby Brown

hardships. On the other hand, they can be much more accepting of society as it is. It is true about the Russians. But it's also true about any other group of Israelis.

Operations Moses and Solomon

Operation Moses, the first of two airlifts to redeem Ethiopian Jews, occurred between November 1, 1984, and January 5, 1985, bringing 8,000 exiles to Israel via the Sudan. During the second airlift, Operation Solomon, a thirty-six-hour mission that took place in late May 1991, an additional 14,325 Ethiopian Jews were flown to the Jewish state.

Bobby Brown   When the Ethiopians came, people were going to absorption centers, to deliver up-to-the-sky piles of clothes that people had brought in. And that was the beautiful Israel, the great Israel. There are a lot of good people here.

But the problem was not only how do you integrate them into society, but how do you integrate them into the *middle* of the society? If they all get entry-level jobs, then you create a black-white problem, and, automatically, in the more expensive areas, you can't settle them because the costs are too high.

And then there is the standard of living: they turned off all the hot water in the absorption centers because they didn't know what hot water was and they were burning themselves. And they took out all the gas stoves because they were scared of them.

We failed to do what we had to do—maybe it was impossible to do—you can't blame the country so much on the first generation. There are signs that the second generation is beginning—there are now Ethiopian Jews who are lawyers and doctors and diplomats. Is it representative? No. Is it enough? No. But I do believe there is a beginning, and I don't feel that the race problem is at the same level that it is in the United States. Don't forget, a generation ago, the gulf between the Ashkenazim and the Sephardim was so great that people thought there was going to be a civil war. Their problem is now solved.

Arie Lova Eliav   We have Ethiopians in Nitzana. It's a problem, but when I was minister of absorption, you had problems. One way or another, with any community, you are uprooting and want to replant people with a different language and culture. Every Jewish community that was absorbed had its problems, some more and some less. Ethiopians have their own difficulties. But if you ask me, "Will they be good citizens?" Yes. They will have a fringe of people who will not be absorbed and will have real problems, but it's a process. It's not only because of their color, but it's a process of absorbing newcomers with old-timers; old-timers hate newcomers—you have it everywhere.

PART THREE

Seismic Changes

Chapter 12

MAY 1977: A POLITICAL AND DEMOGRAPHIC EARTHQUAKE

The election of Menachem Begin in May 1977 as the first Likud prime minister of the State of Israel, following nineteen years of rule by the Labor Party, was perceived by many, both at home and abroad, as a political earthquake. Within Begin's own movement, however, many of those closest to him were not shocked. Rather, they viewed that seismic event as the inevitable outcome of their years of struggle for recognition.

Yehiel Kadishai   I didn't believe that we were going to win the election. Begin *did*, but he didn't say it. I was present when Hart Hasten [an American Zionist activist and a longtime Begin supporter from Indiana] told Begin, "You are going to be the next prime minister." And Begin didn't deny it. I *did*. I said, "I don't believe it." I never believed that Herut, or the Revisionists, would take over.

I've never said it's better to be in opposition, but I didn't care much. I have always thought that the opposition plays an important role in the life of the country, that there must be an opposition *always*. Of course, any opposition should strive to become the leadership, the government, because then it can prove that its policy is right; that's the object of any party, any movement.

Joshua Matza   Even when we had failures, we believed. Herut was eight members and discriminated [against]. You couldn't even say that you belonged to the Herut Party. We didn't know when it would happen, but we were with him. We had seen his path, how he was bringing us to power—

"I didn't believe we'd manage to win, but Begin believed in it."
—Yehiel Kadishai

Prime Minister–Elect Menachem Begin speaks to supporters at the Likud Party headquarters after his election on May 17, 1977.

after Herut, he went with the Liberals; after the Liberals, he allied with other parties, so that we were legitimate. Being legitimate, we succeeded being in the government—and he was a genius.

But it wasn't the victory of the Right Party; it was the failure of the Labor because of the new party, with [Professor Yigael] Yadin [a former military chief of staff and commander of Israeli forces in the War of Independence, later an eminent archaeologist, who in 1976 accepted the leadership of the DMC, the Democratic Movement for Change, a political party that had emerged in the aftermath of the Yom Kippur War of 1973], and they took a lot of votes from the Labor Party. Dash [DMC]—Shinui ["change," a faction now allied with the DMC]—took a lot of seats, and with these seats Begin could create a government. If it hadn't been for the split of Mapai and the Labor Party, and the creation of this new party, history could have been different.

Matityahu "Mati" Drobles   The election of Menachem Begin in 1977 as prime minister was the realization of a dream. It was something that we thought maybe would happen or *not*, but for me it was the realization of the dream.

Joshua Matza   We looked at him as a god; we didn't even come close to him. When you came close to him, you felt you had achieved some of your real highs. He was entirely a believer in Eretz Israel, really a *believer*. I had the opportunity to accompany him to many, many events, presenting him as a speaker. In Jerusalem there wasn't even one speech that I wasn't close to him from the moment that he was on the stage 'til the moment that he finished and 'til the moment that the people in the crowd took him on their shoulders. Always the people took him on their shoulders: Begin, to power! Once, when I didn't appear at one of his events in Jerusalem, he called home to ask my wife what had happened to me.

Yehiel Kadishai   It was a very good feeling. And when we came the first time into the office and Begin sat in Rabin's seat, he said, "Yehiel, *avodah* [work]."

Eitan Haber   I was watching television with my father, and the minute it was said, "Begin will be the prime minister," my father cried like a newborn baby. Many years after, when I wrote an article about him, I said that he cried not only because they did it after so many years of suffering, but because for many years he had dreamed of being ambassador of the State of Israel somewhere under a Begin regime. And I think that on May 17, 1977—and I wrote it—my father cried bitterly because he understood then that the dream about being an ambassador was over because he was too old. It was the same with Menachem Begin. He came to power more than ten years too late.

Forming the Cabinet

Mr. Begin surprised many people, among them Shmuel Katz, by bringing in General Moshe Dayan as minister of foreign affairs. By rights, Mr. Katz should have succeeded to that position.

Yehiel Kadishai   He [Begin] was still living at number 1 Rosenbaum Street, near Habima. It was not a cellar but was one step down from the level of the street. He was in his apartment, and outside there was a demonstration of bereaved families going on—their sons had been killed in the Yom Kippur War four years earlier. Dayan was blamed for the Yom Kippur War, and about twenty-five people or so were demonstrating against Begin's choosing Dayan as the minister of foreign affairs. They were throwing stones at the windows, and some windows were shattered.

I said, "I know two of the families outside." I brought them in, and another family came in and sat down. There were two sofas—one was the [Begins'] bed—this was the studio, the salon, and the bedroom. They were sitting there—there were chairs from the kitchen, and he was sitting in his armchair. He said,

The government that I'm building, the State of Israel, should have a minister of foreign affairs that when he comes to a prime minister or a president—or a president comes to his office—before he enters [pointing to the seam of his own pant leg] should check this part of his trousers if it is neat, if it is straight, if all the buttons are done up, because that means that he has got [self] respect. He will continue with this bandage on his eye [Dayan lost his left eye in combat while fighting alongside the British army in Lebanon during World War II].

Here, with us, he lost his halo from the Yom Kippur War, it's true. But abroad, he's considered the hero of Israel and the ministry of foreign affairs is for abroad. It's true that with *us* he's lost his halo, but abroad he is considered a hero of Israel, and we need such a minister of foreign affairs in this government, so that [when] the goyim [non-Jews] check their crease, they are properly dressed and properly shaven, and their buttons are done up. That's what we need.

That's all true. But there was another reason. Our party, Likud, plus Herut, was a conglomerate of three parties, and the main counterpart of the Herut within this body was the Liberals. The Liberals are a coalition; everyone wants a piece of the cake. We, Herut, had got the prime minister and the defense minister—Ezer Weizman [a nephew of Chaim Weizmann]—and they had finance, [Simcha] Ehrlich, and in accordance with the distribution of power, they should have the Ministry of Foreign Affairs.

Then there were others. The ex-Mapainiks with Yigal Allon—these were the splinter groups, but the two main parties were Herut and the Liberals. So we have a prime minister and a minister of defense, and they should have the two other pieces of cake—defense and finance. So finance goes to Ehrlich. The man who wants—and is entitled to be—is [the late] Mr. Aryeh [Leon] Dulzin. He is a very nice man; he's properly dressed, always with a tie, speaks nicely, looks nice, is very nice to people, and he wants people to be nice to him. It's very important to him; he's full of himself, very important. He could represent Switzerland, Finland, Holland, but Israel, with its complex problems with the world, he can't represent. He would represent us, but as a good Mapainik; he will use the language of the Liberals.

Besides, this same Dulzin had said openly—it was in the papers—in a meeting in the Holy Land Hotel in Jerusalem, six months earlier, before we won the election, "We, the Liberals, must get rid of Begin; he is destroying our party [Likud]. We will never be in power because he left the government in 1970."

Staffing the Administration

Yehuda Avner   Begin asked me to work for him—I had worked for Rabin and before that Eshkol—on the basis that he wanted to establish once and for all the integrity of a permanent civil service on the British model. My first communication with him was sitting opposite him at his desk. He's showing me a letter of invitation to visit Washington that he's just received from President Jimmy Carter. A sentence reads, "I therefore invite you to visit the United States during the week of June the Nineteenth with a view to our establishing a partnership of peace that will between us lead to a just and lasting peace."

Begin told me that Rabin had recommended to him that he show me this letter because part of my job was to draft responses to letters. Begin told me that he didn't need anybody, that he wrote his own letters and his own speeches. So he said, in English, "I want you to polish my Polish English, to Shakespeare-ize it." And from that day forward, he called me "my Shakespeare." He says, "I'll prepare my own draft, and let's meet at four o'clock this afternoon, and we'll go over it together." Nonetheless, I was used to preparing a draft, so I went back to my room and I prepared a draft. [Eli] Ben-Elissar was the director general [of the Prime Minister's Bureau] so I thought: this is an opportunity for me to get to know him better. I said that I'd drafted a reply to Jimmy Carter's letter and said, "You can't show that to Mr. Begin; Menachem Begin has never put his signature to anything he has not written himself."

We came to him at four o'clock—and this was classic Begin; any paper that came to hand, any pen that came to hand, he reviewed. This was cheap, lined paper, and he had this very cramped style of handwriting, crab-like, and I was trying to decipher it. There were words written in red ink, and I had a normal pen. His English was excellent, but Begin didn't know syntax so I was stylizing. Within two minutes he looked over the desk and saw a lot of my black ink, and then he said, with a twinkle in the eye, "I hear from Dr. Ben-Elissar that you've written a draft of your own." So I said, "I happen to have it on me." I pointed out this sentence, and I said, "It's not part of the standard lexicon of dialogue between ourselves and the United States and, therefore, maybe we should say "*To* establish a partnership of principle," meaning that now we *don't* have a partnership. There was something else. Begin had begun the letter with "Your Excellency," and I told him you don't address President Carter that way. "*Ma, HaGadol*"? ["What, the Big Man"?] He didn't believe me; he himself referred it to the Protocol Department of the Foreign Office. That was on day one.

Sending a Message Regarding Future Settlement

In May 1977, on the day following his election, Menachem Begin traveled to the Territories, where he visited Kadum. The new prime minister's gesture was a signal that he intended to expand existing settlements and establish new ones. Matityahu Drobles would become the major government official in effecting that demographic upheaval.

Matityahu "Mati" Drobles   Menachem Begin's ideology was there. When he was elected prime minister, he said, "We have to do something; my ideology will now become reality. I am going to settle Judea and Samaria." When we judge history, the world will know that there were various political constellations—that Begin sometimes regressed from his ideology—but it was his ideology right after he was elected to settle all of Judea and Samaria.

Yehiel Kadishai   I don't know whether he saw it as exactly systematic. I remember traveling with him on the helicopter over the whole area on a few occasions, and we saw land that was empty, and he said, "Here is an Arab village; there is an Arab village, but there's plenty of land to settle, to build new settlements." On many occasions—at least four or five times—I was sitting next to him on the helicopter, looking down on the empty land, and he sounded meshuga in 1977; it was ten years after the Six-Day War.

There was a judicial debate about a certain *yishuv* [settlement] that was called Alon Moreh. It was an Arab village called Adjoor, on a hill, and the Beit Mishpat [high court] in Jerusalem said that we should not settle there because it was the private property of an Arab. Ninety percent of the land belonged to the government of Jordan; it was state land—public property. When they heard the verdict of the high court, they had already built some shacks there and said that the settlers should be transferred to another place. They called this place Alon Moreh. Then Begin said, "There are judges in Jerusalem; we have to recognize the ruling of the high court, and they [the settlements] will be taken up and put back, and there will be more and more in the neighborhood." This was his declaration. And there was dancing there.

Tekoah: An Example of Settlement Pluralism

Bobby Brown   I grew up with a certain ideology—that the Land of Israel belongs to us. I made aliyah eleven years after the Six-Day War, and we basically felt that we wanted to do the maximum we could; we don't want just to live here, we want to *contribute*. Since Judea and Samaria were areas that were in danger of being taken away, and we felt that there was no way of defending them, they would not stay part of Israel unless Jews lived there. So we thought that by living there, we were making a statement with our lives.

We wanted to live close to Jerusalem because, like every good Jew, we fell in love with Jerusalem, and because employment was probably going to be better for both of us [Linda Brown, Bobby's wife, is a physical therapist] in that area. We went to a lot of places to look, and we found this magical place called Tekoah—it's exactly where the Judean Mountains and the Judean Desert separate.

There were four families and they told us about this idea they had, where religious and secular Jews would live together. And we always felt that there are not five Jewish people—there's not a "religious Jewish people" and not a "nonreligious Jewish people" and not an "Ethiopian Jewish people" and not a "European Jewish people." We felt that we were *one* Jewish people, and this idea of living together in Israel sounded very normal, coming from New York.

It's a magical place. It's right next to King Herod's palace, Herodion, and every morning when I wake up, I have Masada [the mountain where, dur-

"In Israel it was a revolutionary thing that all different kinds of Jews would live together. But we loved the idea, and we became the seventh family to live in Tekoah."—Bobby Brown, former mayor of Tekoah

A view of Tekoah.

ing the Roman occupation, Jewish residents committed mass suicide rather than being forced to live in captivity] outside my window, and Jewish history just comes. In New York, somebody explained what a garden was [Mr. Brown was raised in an apartment building in Washington Heights, in upper Manhattan], and they gave me a tree and said, "You have to dig a hole and put it in and cover it with soil and then put water on it," so I went outside, and my little daughter went with me. We started digging a hole, and all of a sudden, she said, "Daddy, Daddy! I found some money!" So I figured one of the guys building our house had dropped a coin. I looked at it, and it was a coin from the Herodian period. From that, we had a wonderful discussion about who dropped this coin—what happened to that person, why no one lived there, and why we came back. Just from the earth we had a whole history lesson. It was very natural; you get your Judaism here from the air, from the language, from the holidays.

I always loved America and always felt that America was very good to me, but it wasn't really the country whose tradition was my tradition—you know, you kind of squint a little in the Christmas period, and you see all the trees and the Santa Clauses. You don't resent it, but it's not *yours*. And here, the Jewish holidays are just in society, and that's a lovely thing.

Today, the population is about four hundred families, and it's still mixed, religious and secular. It is probably, in a country that has too much government involvement in people's lives, a place where people can follow their dreams. And it works. It's got the framework similar to what a kibbutz or a moshav had at one time. If someone needs help, if someone has a tragedy, if someone is left alone because her husband is in the army, the community closes in and helps. And yet, from an economic point of view, everyone is independent and nobody relies on anyone else.

Akiva Eldar   In 1992, Arik Sharon took me and a few other journalists to see the West Bank settlements. He was so proud. There was no organic logic in what he did. He threw up settlements and roads everywhere to cut the territory so that no future government would be able to give back the land.

Prime Minister Begin's Very Controversial Relationship
with the American Evangelical Community

Abraham Foxman   I remember the conversation with Begin when he went to the church in Dallas and he was asked about it [the belief of many in the Jewish community that evangelical support for Israel stemmed from their desire to convert Jews]. He said, "Okay, I understand that. But I'm not going to worry about it now."

Yehiel Kadishai   He said openly, "We have to become friends to everyone who is helping us. They help us with our rights to Eretz Israel." And when he was told that they wanted us to become Christians in order that the Messiah would come, he said,

> It's stupid; they help us now. They come to Israel, they support our needs to be recognized as those who own the country and they say it, and they are forty million and more in the United States, and they support us, so we should be friends with them. They are friendly to us and we'll be friendly to them. That's all.

He was attacked in the press in 1978 and '79. And he met Jerry Falwell in Washington [in two sessions, one of which, at Blair House, the authors attended]. There is in Jerusalem a Christian from Holland—he's lived here for the last forty years—of the International Christian Embassy. He speaks Hebrew, and his wife is a Muslim. He is a great friend, and he does very nice things in Jerusalem. And the officialdom there doesn't like him. I know him, and he's a very nice man; he was very friendly with me. He was coming to the office [the Prime Minister's Bureau, in Jerusalem], and I was having coffee with him. He helped us. They [Begin's critics] were looking for those who hate us, to make them love us. But if someone loves you, why shouldn't you love *him*?

Abraham Foxman   The hesitancy is historical: Christians have not been our friend; they've been our enemy. Christians killed Jews *before* Arabs killed Jews. So you come with the baggage of history, and whether these were Christian states and Christian rulers or secular rulers with Christian populations, the history of the relationship between those who stood up as Christians and as Jews gives Jews good reason to be anxious and nervous when Christians all of a sudden embrace us. Why was there antagonism throughout the years— because we rejected Jesus, we killed Jesus? It was because we didn't want to be Christian. Why was there an Inquisition? If you accepted Jesus, you weren't burned at the stake, and then there was friendship and embrace.

And in all honesty, they do have another agenda. I have relationships with them and we talk, and they don't hide the fact that it is a principle of faith for them to convince you of *their* truth. A significant number believe that they possess *the* truth, not *a* truth, so there's enough reason to be wary; there is reason to be concerned. Christians come to the Holy Land as *Christians*. We would be disrespectful of their faith if we just ignored it.

Now, once you recognize it, you look at a certain reality. I have, and the ADL [Anti-Defamation League] has and has taken a position that is basically, "Respect them and suspect them." Just as we don't say to them, "If you want to love Israel, you have to give up your hope of proselytizing us and converting us," we've said to them, "We will accept your embrace and your support of Israel, but don't you tell us what our social agenda should be." They're learning, but too frequently they have chastised us. But there is also no reason *not* to accept their support. Certainly, we need it.

The Reverend Jerry Falwell   I came to faith in Christ in January 1952, when I was an eighteen-year-old college sophomore. I did not own a Bible, but my pastor suggested that I purchase a King James version, the *Scofield Reference Edition Study Bible*. Dr. Scofield, who was a Zionist and died at about the turn of the twentieth century, wrote extensive notes in about every chapter, sometimes in every verse. I began reading the notes, and it was in doing that that I became very aware of the key role Israel played in world affairs and in biblical prophecy. Until that time, having no knowledge of the Bible, my only impression of Israel was that they had recently become a free nation and were surrounded by a lot of enemies. I didn't know anything else about the significance of Israel. Dr. Scofield points out the importance of the Abrahamic Covenant and the promises to Abraham, and to David, the Davidic Covenant. It became very clear to me, as a young Christian, that Israel was the most important piece of real estate on the planet.

And when I arrived at Baptist Bible College in the fall of 1952—I had just turned nineteen in August—fortunately for me, every one of the Bible professors was a very strong believer in the significance of Israel in God's economy. There was not a person there whom I would not consider a biblical Zionist. So I got literally immersed in the importance of Israel throughout history, that everything had begun in the region, and as an evangelical Christian, everything would conclude there. And I also came to understand, in a more emphatic way, that God deals with people and nations in relation to how those people and nations deal with Israel.

The Moral Majority: How Did Israel's Security Become One of the Major Planks in Its Doctrine?

Ronald Godwin   It can be traced back to Dr. Jerry Falwell, our founder, and his vision and his convictions and his principles. Dr. Falwell took advice and counsel from other Conservatives in Washington and came up

"I really believe that every time we've been involved in any kind of pressure play on Israel to trade land for peace, that America has been judged for it."—The Reverend Jerry Falwell

An enthusiastic Reverend Jerry Falwell, flanked by (left to right) *Israel at Sixty* coauthor Gerald S. Strober and Defense Minister Moshe Arens, is applauded by delegates to the 1983 Moral Majority convention held that November in Jerusalem, in solidarity with the people and the State of Israel.

with being pro-life, pro-family, pro–strong national defense, and pro-Israel and in favor of its right to exist and prosper, and that fourth plank of the Moral Majority doctrinal statement was non-negotiable. Basically, we didn't care whether you were a Mormon or a Catholic or a Jew or what flavor you might be; if you could support those four planks, we welcomed you into the Moral Majority. And for that reason, I found myself often speaking in synagogues and in Catholic churches, and we had a lot of strong friends from the Mormon Church. They were what many, many people in those days considered amazingly strange bedfellows, kind of agreeing to disagree on other issues and to mute those disagreements in favor of agreeing on those four issues.

Why Do Evangelicals Support Israel?

Ronald Godwin   We have to remind ourselves that the Conservative movement as a whole is made up of at least three branches and that has to do with the fiscal Conservatives, the political Conservatives, and then what some call the "social" or "value" Conservatives, and evangelicals would fall into that branch. And though evangelicals tend to feel that supporting Israel is part of their theology—that brings up another issue—there's a growing schism, often not talked about, between fiscal and political Conservatives, and value Conservatives, in that the entire country is becoming more secular, and the Conservative movement, along with the country, is becoming more secular, and those two branches of the Conservative movement are far less tolerant today of those issues that are most important to social Conservatives—they just eat the fish and spit out the bones, but there's no longer an enthusiastic amen to what we often consider to be of jugular importance, as there was a few years ago.

The Reverend Jerry Falwell   There is a small minority of evangelicals who, for whatever reason, are not Christian Zionists, at least to the degree that most of us are. But most take the Abrahamic Covenant literally; some of us are evangelical and believe in the premillennial, pretribulational Coming of Christ for his church, and many do not. But the real issue is not that the Lord is coming and that Israel is going to play a key role in the last days. It is rather that God promised the land to Israel and to Abraham and his genealogy, and that God will bless those who bless Abraham and curse those who do not. There have been several thousands of years of history to prove that, from the pharaohs to Hitler or, more recently, the Soviet Union.

Ronald Godwin   Evangelical support for Israel is critically important, located as Israel is in a sea of increasingly hostile, increasingly violent Arab nations. Israel and the Israeli people are at grave risk, and it's only the will of American evangelicals that gives some promise of security in the future in regard to the American government's support. Once your enemy determines that they can carry out their agenda without catastrophic losses, you've increased the likelihood of extremely provocative behavior. Somehow, we've got to keep the social branch of Conservatism involved. I've been spending a lot of time talking to our Conservative friends in Washington and reminding them that if we let this schism among fiscal and political and social Conservatives grow unattended, the ripple effects of that will not only directly affect the future success of the Republican Party, but could also affect the future safety of the nation of Israel. The people I talk to all acknowledge that. But I don't see anybody coming up with a coherent strategy to combat it.

Chapter 13

SADAT IN JERUSALEM AND THE CAMP DAVID ACCORDS

In the fall of 1977, Egypt's president Anwar Sadat signaled his interest in meeting with the Israeli leadership. On learning of Sadat's wish, Prime Minister Menachem Begin, who had been elected less than six months earlier in a stunning political "earthquake," invited the Egyptian president to address the Knesset in Jerusalem.

The Reverend Jerry Falwell We flew into Cairo, and President Sadat was down at Aswan, in the south, on the Nile, in his palace, and we went down there to spend some time with him that day. Then he and I talked privately, and I told him we were going up to Jerusalem the next day and that I'd be meeting with the prime minister. He asked, "How are you going?" and I said, "Well, we're going to have to get a flight from Cairo to Amman and then get into an automobile to go across the Allenby Bridge." He said, "Oh, no! You don't need to do that," and he loaned us [the Egyptian equivalent of] Air Force One, and it flew us there [to Amman].

But talking to him—we had some private talk on spiritual matters—he gave me a note that he had written to Mr. Begin and asked me whether I would give it to the prime minister. I never mentioned that at all until both of them were dead. I took that note with me, and he flew us up there in Air Force One. When we landed, those people didn't have any *idea* who was on that airplane. At that time, Sadat was king of the hill everywhere, and as they lined up, they said, "It's got to be the vice president, or somebody," and they treated us like royalty. We never told them who we were, and we came down that red carpet, and the next day we were up in Jerusalem. And after the conversation, I just slipped Mr. Begin the note from Sadat. I have no idea what was in it. I've never discussed it, and I've never seen that in the press anywhere.

Preparations for a Historic Journey

Yehuda Avner   I was in London with Dan Pattir; we were the advance party to set up a meeting between Begin and Jim Callaghan, the [British] prime minister. Amazingly, Begin asked us to stay on, as we were the only ones who had experience in arranging the prime minister's overseas missions.

Then Yehiel Kadishai called us early Thursday afternoon, saying, "Come back. Sadat's coming on Saturday night!" We couldn't get a flight back on Thursday, but we did manage to get a flight first thing on Friday morning to Geneva and catch the El Al flight, which arrived minutes before Shabbat. Yehiel had arranged for a border police jeep to meet us at the foot of the plane and stamp our passports and then drive me immediately to Jerusalem.

By the time I got to Motza [on the outskirts of Jerusalem], I was beginning to feel a little uncomfortable because the sun had set, so I left my baggage in the jeep and said, "I'm going to walk." So I walked, faster and faster, up to Jerusalem, singing *zmirot* [songs of blessing] as I went, and I walked into the house just as they were *bentching* [praying].

There was a big envelope from Yehiel waiting for me there; in it were the various stickers for free passage, and there was a note from Begin, asking me to go to the address of the safe house of the Palmach to pick up a friend of Begin's who had flown in especially. So immediately when Shabbat was over—I had an old Peugeot, a 404—I went to this house, knocked on the door, and an elderly gentleman wearing a coat (I didn't even ask his name) got in the car, and we drove off toward Ben-Gurion Airport.

He told me as we drove that Israel was full of shale oil—that we were going to be oil independent. He was an American with very close ties to the Kremlin. It was Armand Hammer. I had no idea that he was that close to Begin and that Begin had invited him especially.

There we were, all assembled in the old terminal, upstairs. There was the chief of staff, Motta Gur; Begin's military secretary, Ephraim Porat, known as Froika; and your own humble servant, too. Now the new road had not been completed—the first part of it, from Ben-Gurion to Shar Haggai, was still being paved, and that's where Froika and Eli [Eliahu] Ben-Elissar, rest their souls—they were the ones who oversaw the whole operation—had arranged for the entourage to travel up to Jerusalem.

When Begin heard that, he got very angry and turned to Froika and said, "Under no circumstances! Only by the King's Highway!" In other words, "Take the old road, which is still the official road; the new one is not yet open." So at the last minute, Froika had to shift all the forces, all the security, all the police, all the army, to the old highway. And then Yehiel sent me ahead, in my old Peugeot, to the King David Hotel to make sure that everything there was in order.

Sadat's Arrival

In the early evening chill of Saturday, November 19, 1977, the Egyptian president arrived at Ben-Gurion Airport, then known as Lod, outside Tel Aviv, where Israel's political and military leadership, who for more than a generation had regarded Egypt as their nation's chief adversary, had gathered to receive Sadat.

On November 19, 1977, moments after Anwar Sadat's historic landing at Ben-Gurion Airport, the Egyptian president (center), Israeli president Efraim Katzir (right), and Prime Minister Menachem Begin (left) stand at attention as the two nations' national anthems are played.

"What was going through my mind? I looked at the man who had tried every means to destroy us—by blockade, by boycott, by war—and there he is."—Yehuda Avner

Yehuda Avner   Out of the blackness of the sky emerges this aircraft, taxis to the floodlit area there on the tarmac, and there is the guard of honor and the trumpets. The door opens, and there he stands! And to the sound of trumpets, with enormous dignity, he descends the steps. There are two rows in the receiving line; one row is the cabinet, and the other the Supreme Court judges and the chief of staff, and, for some reason, yours truly, under the heading of "prime ministerial adviser."

Begin is introducing each one. He introduces Golda to Sadat, and Golda takes him by both hands, and he takes Golda by both hands, and he says to Golda, "I've been wanting to meet you for a long time." And Golda says to him, "And we've been *waiting* for you for a long time."

A Last-Minute Glitch: The Suggestion
of a Trojan Horse

Dan Pattir   Ah! That was the great excitement. We had an arrangement with the Egyptians that they would fly out of Suez City, northwest, Ismailia [on the Suez Canal], a military base. Why? His [Sadat's] people were afraid to take off from Cairo because of security, domestically. He arranged therefore to fly about eight to ten minutes in a direct line from Ismailia to Ben-Gurion Airport.

Suddenly, we saw, contrary to previous agreements, that the plane was flying a detour over the Mediterranean, which prolonged his flight and delayed his landing. Some top security people of ours, most experienced security people, said, "Maybe the whole thing is a trap: out of the plane will come a suicide group and kill all our leadership," because for thirty or forty years we were learning how to deal with our enemy. Suddenly, it's too much of a quick change; overnight, almost.

General [Mordechai "Motta"] Gur, the chief of staff, had, three days before Sadat's arrival, published an interview in the paper here that the whole thing was a trap and flew to Iran for a secret visit. He didn't tell anybody about the prospective publication of the interview except his secretary and she kept silent, so it was a big shock here, three days before Sadat was coming.

The day before Sadat arrived, General Gur came back, and Begin wanted to fire him. There was a meeting called in Begin's office, and he called in the top-ranked people. But Ezer Weizman, the defense minister, while going to Jerusalem, had been involved in a car accident, was badly wounded, and went to Tel Hashomer Hospital. Motta Gur was saved because without the defense minister you don't fire the chief of staff.

Then—this is not known—thirty-six hours before Sadat's arrival (Sadat arrived on Saturday night, the nineteenth of November), there was military intelligence that the Egyptians were moving massive forces from western Egypt into the Suez Canal, toward the fire line. Begin summoned the chief of the Mossad, the chief of our internal security, and Ezer Weizman was missing, but General [Yigael] Yadin, and the former chief of staff and deputy prime minister were there, and it was very dramatic. The people asked for partial mobilization of Israeli forces. Imagine that thirty-six hours before Sadat came there would be general mobilization! It wasn't only that the Sadat visit was going down the drain; there would likely be a military clash! Begin made a bold decision. He said, "No mobilization, no partial," and we continued with the plan to receive Sadat. This was the prelude to Sadat's visit!

Yehuda Avner   And then came Motta Gur, and Sadat said, "It is not a trick, General! It is not a trick!"

Dan Pattir   I went behind the receiving line, to face in, listening to what Sadat was saying. First was Motta Gur. He was standing behind Yitzhak Rabin, and Rabin said, "Mr. President, this is General Gur," and he said, smiling, "General Gur, is this still a *deception* game?"

Greeting General Sharon

Dan Pattir   He [Sadat] told Arik Sharon, "Next time, I won't let you come to the west side [of the Suez Canal, in reference to General Sharon's heroic crossing of the canal during the Yom Kippur War]; I'll catch you *earlier*."

Greeting Golda

Dan Pattir   The most thrilling greeting was with Golda, kissing each other. It lasted a few few seconds, but I wondered, Who is going to move first? Then she said to him, "Mr. President, I was waiting many years for this moment." And he said to her, "Me, *too*, ma'am."

Sadat's Wardrobe Faux Pas

As Anwar Sadat deplaned in Israel, an enterprising photographer with a close-up view of the Egyptian leader had noticed, and taken a picture of, his necktie, which was emblazoned with swastikas. Needless to say, many Jews in Israel and the Diaspora were amazed at his choice of neckwear.

Dan Pattir   Nobody paid attention to it; only at the dinner at the King David, where there was a close-up picture. It was the Indian swastika. People didn't know how to treat him: Is he *real*? Is he being truthful? Is he playing a game?

Yehiel Kadishai   It was a foolish thing. I was watching Begin; he saw this. Sadat took it off and didn't wear it anymore. From a certain angle, it looks like one swastika and another one. When you see a picture of him, you can also recognize them.

Yehuda Avner   When Begin, a long time later, visited Cairo, the traditional Egyptian guard of honor were wearing semi-Wehrmacht uniforms and high boots, and they were goose-stepping! I attach more significance to it.

Dan Pattir   I asked Sadat, two years later, sitting in his home in Alexandria, "How come, Mr. President, you overlapped with Golda for five years and you went through a bloody war; you overlapped with Rabin as prime minister for three years and hardly made an interim agreement in 1975; you come to *Begin*!" He said to me, "You know, I'm not a historian, but I'll ask you a question: who made the détente with the Soviets, the agreement with the Chinese? Nixon, didn't he? Who made the withdrawal of the French from Algeria? De Gaulle, didn't he?" I said, "Mr. President, what do you mean by that?" He said, "Look, I learned that it's better to do business with the right-of-center people rather than the left-of-center people because they have more power and more authority to make concessions."

He was right, in the historical sense. Mubarak told me later that when Begin won the elections in May 1977—Mubarak was the vice president then—and he got a message that Israeli television reported, "Begin won," he didn't know what to say. "Sadat was asleep," he said. "Should I wake him up? Maybe he'll be cross with me. If I let him sleep until the morning and don't give him the information, maybe he'll be cross with me," he said. "I waited for twenty minutes and then I started to wake him up. I said, 'Mr. President, bad news. Begin won the elections.' And what did he tell me? He said, 'Good news.' Why? 'We can do business with him.'"

Sadat Sends a Message to the Arab Street

Dan Pattir   Sadat asked us to enable him to pray in Al Aksa Mosque on the morning of the twentieth of November, '77, which happened to be in the Muslim calendar the Feast of the Sacrifice, one of their most cherished religious events. [Hosni] Mubarak told me later that he had advised Sadat, "Go and pray at Al Aksa Mosque after you arrive in Israel and show to the Arab world that you really have the first gain as a civilian leader of the Arabs from your move toward peace with Israel."

Sadat was supposed to go to pray about six or six thirty in the morning. I got a call about four thirty from our security people, and they told me there was a big problem: the authorities of the mosque, the Palestinian authorities, demanded that Israel remove its television car and cameras from the mosque because it was a desecration of Islam, although we had done it many times before.

The whole visit of Sadat was handled by Israeli television; the feed was given to all the networks in the world, so there was one set of cameras. I was shocked by that, and I realized that there was some power game in it. I didn't wake up Begin for that—I had the authority to decide on this kind of thing—and I told security: "Don't you *dare* move the cameras out. Don't go into conflict; try to remove the mobile car outside, four hundred yards away, with longer cords to be used." And the pressure was very heavy; it was the brink of crisis. Begin was aware only after the prayer was over, and so was Sadat. So you can imagine if we had yielded to the Arab effort. It could have been a disaster if we had yielded to this pressure, and the programs would have been cut off from the entire world.

A Lighter Moment

Yehiel Kadishai   On the second evening of the Egyptian delegation in Jerusalem, all of a sudden they made a decision to go back to Egypt. At the same hour that they were packing their suitcases to leave, I was asked by Menachem Begin to go to the Hilton Hotel—the old Hilton [now a Holiday Inn] at the entrance to Jerusalem—to bring a document to a person who was there. I took the document there, and as I was leaving the elevator, more than a hundred journalists—they knew that the Egyptians were packing—were there and cameras. "Yehiel, Yehiel, *what's happening?*" So I told them, "I said, '*Am Yisrael chai!*' [Long live Israel!] and they left the place!" And the next day, it was on the radio—they repeated it, "Yehiel: *Am Yisrael chai!*"

The Camp David Accords

Within two years of Anwar Sadat's historic visit to Jerusalem, on March 26, 1979, as the result of negotiations held at Camp David in Maryland, Sadat and Begin signed a formal peace treaty, the first such agreement that Israel had achieved with an Arab nation. Then, in 1994, Israel entered into a peace agreement with Jordan.

Dan Pattir   The Americans came with the suggestion; nobody knew exactly how long it should take place, how long it would last. Nobody had an agenda; nobody had any idea of what the outcome should be. Everybody minimized the expectations. Begin said, "We will come out with some kind of a general statement, and then we'll have to invent the best way to go about the negotiations."

Yossi Ben-Aharon   I was in touch, by phone, during the course of Camp David with Eli Rubinstein and also with Kadishai. On the evening that the agreement was reached, I was making a speech at one of the big hotels in New York, and in the middle of the affair, I got a phone call, and they said that they had signed an agreement.

It was only subsequently that I began to learn the details and got some of the documents, and it was clear to me that although Begin was a very strong nationalist, the pressure on him was threefold. You had Carter, who was two-faced and applied immense, brutal pressure. Then, unfortunately, Begin had picked the wrong people to join him: Aharon Barak, Weizman, and Dayan, who were defeatists. And this was the beginning of people's saying, "There must be a way; and we need America, and if we come away from this investment that America has made for peace without a break-through, it will be a disaster; and Sadat towers over the other Arab leaders, and we have to really go with him and not wait."

I was very upset, even in New York. General Abrasha Tamir, a worka-holic, prepared various options for an agreement. And when I saw this doc-ument and the kinds of options he was preparing, I saw that he was a weakling, taken in and enslaved by this concept that had obtained since 1947, that there has to be cease-fire, an armistice, a demilitarized zone.

I saw that he was an "expert" in maps—I don't want to say "idiot"—and he preferred the map with disarmament lines on this side of the border and the other side of the border, as if we were playing a game—a repeat per-formance of what we had done in 1949 with our neighbors. And I said, "If this is going to be the peace, why bring a third party into this?" His planning was for some kind of international force and observers and troops, and I said, "It's crazy! Why go back to the previous border? This will serve as a terrible precedent to the others. They will say, 'You gave the Egyptians everything; you have to give us also'—Jordan and Syria and so forth." It was a disaster! This is a country that attacked Israel in '47–'48, again in '56, and again in '67, under Nasser, three times! And then you give them exactly everything they ask for?

In any case, Sadat made bombastic speeches. He said, "This is territory that belonged to the Egyptians for seven thousand years!" Sheer baloney! I had traveled through Sinai by train in 1946, and once you crossed the Suez Canal, it wasn't under Egyptian control. The British were controlling it; *they* were in charge of Sinai; the Egyptians had nothing to do with Sinai. They never *did*; Sinai for many generations belonged to the empire that ruled Palestine. Why do you have to take this *baloney*?

Dan Pattir   I'm very critical of Carter because I think he didn't understand the whole process, *whatsoever*. He believed, in his messianic way, that if the person says something, it must happen. Basically, what happened in that respect was that Camp David was the meeting point of two leaders out of three—Sadat and Begin—whose interests came into convergence, although the interests were different, on three levels. One is the full political-military. Second, this agreement served political domestic needs— Begin comes home with a paper, the first ever, with the Egyptians, the Arabs' number-one country, and Sadat could wave the paper and say, "I get Sinai back." And the third one—not to be belittled—is that each man wants to go down in history as a peacemaker in his own right. They achieved these three levels of convergence of interests.

The Americans' input was important because it happened on American auspices, on American territory, through presidential hospitality, but *not* with American input, although some people want to portray it that without *Carter*, nothing would have happened. That is absolutely wrong.

Yossi Ben-Aharon   The coup de grâce was many years later—in 1994— when a man called Kenneth Stein, who had been very close to Jimmy Carter in the White House [in 2007, Mr. Stein resigned from the board of the Carter Center in protest of comments made by Mr. Carter in a book], right here, in this chair [Ben-Aharon was referring to the chair in a hotel lounge in Jerusalem in which he was sitting for his interview with the authors], interviewed me, and he said, "You know, Carter told me long after Camp David that Sadat had come to him before and said that for him the election of Begin as a revolutionary change in 1977 was a "terrible development," as Sadat had been preparing for some kind of approach to the Rabin government because he was desperately in need of doing something for the economy, to reopen the Suez Canal, to open Egypt to international tourism, because his situation was desperate. He told Carter, "I need this desperately, even if I have to give up part of Sinai." Carter heard this and never said a word to anybody that Sadat was willing to give up part of Sinai!

For me, this wasn't news; I was convinced that if Begin had had the kind of support, not from Dayan, Weizman, and Barak, but from Yehiel Kadishai and Meuki Katz and Ben-Elissar, had he taken *them* rather than those other three, the situation could have been handled had he stood firm to Carter and said, "We will not go back to the status quo ante, because that would be suicide; it would deliver a message to all the Arab world that if you hit us, *you'll* get compensated, not us."

I learned this subsequently, over Taba, in April 1982, because exactly the same situation repeated itself. And I told Shamir—I was then already very close to the leadership; we were in Cairo and I whispered in his ear, "The Egyptians are making a big to-do about Taba." It's small, a hundred square miles, with a hotel, and they said, "No, this belongs to us since time immemorial." And I told Shamir, "Tell Begin to tell [Sadat's successor, Hosni] Mubarak, 'I don't want this to cause friction between us and you after we've got the peace treaty. Therefore, we will not retreat from the last portion of Sinai until the question of Taba is finally resolved.'"

And I told Shamir, "I have no doubt, whatsoever, that if Mubarak is faced with one of two alternatives, that we do not carry out our obligations, we will withdraw by May of '82 until the Taba issue is resolved, he will say, "No, no, take Taba, just let us make something, and I'll tell my people that this was the right thing," over and above the fact that we had every reason to believe that Taba, according to the British determination of the border in 1906, was exactly on the border—in other words, it should have been given to Palestine.

Begin wouldn't hear of this: "We have committed ourselves to withdraw, and we *will* withdraw. Taba will be resolved subsequently through negotiations." We lost Taba, and I subsequently asked an ex-Egyptian Jew who became our ambassador, Ephraim Newman, "Had we followed the advice I gave Shamir, what do you think would have been the Egyptian reaction?" He said, "You're exactly right. Mubarak, given this choice, would have opted for giving up Taba."

"Carter knew Begin and Begin knew Carter. But he was the president of the United States and he tried to do harm. He caused harm, but not too much; it could have been worse."—Yehiel Kadishai

Egyptian president Anwar Sadat, U.S. president Jimmy Carter, and Israeli prime minister Menachem Begin take a break from tense negotiations on September 6, 1978, during their meeting at Camp David, and relax on the porch of Aspen lodge.

The Atmosphere at the "Concentration Camp Deluxe"

Matityahu "Mati" Drobles There were two smart people meeting: on the one hand, Begin, and on the other hand, Sadat. Until the 1977 elections, all the Mapainiks—Ben-Gurion, Levi Eshkol, Golda Meir—were very, very average, and they agreed to do everything they were asked for: slowly, we will see what will happen. Everybody knew what they were asking; everybody was asking us to give in to the Arabs; they were moving over the years to hear: "Okay, you want to get rid of this."

They knew the minute Begin was elected that the situation would be completely changed. Begin was very smart and strong; he stood on ideas and ideology, with ideas that were absolutely the opposite of Eshkol's and Golda Meir's. Sadat knew, If I have the chance to meet Begin, and we speak about Sinai or about peace, this is a chance—we will miss the chance.

The only problem was with the settlement of Yamit [located in the Rafa salient, on the northeastern tip of the Sinai Peninsula, and developed by its Jewish settlers into a verdant enclave, Yamit would be forcibly evacuated following the closing of all northern Sinai roads on February 26, 1982, on the orders of Defense Minister Ariel Sharon. While most of the residents eventually agreed to evacuation in exchange for compensation and left on April 1, diehards remained unwilling to budge for several weeks, and it wasn't until April 25 that reversion to Egypt would take place] and the area surrounding Yamit. Begin was ready to sacrifice Yamit to get this peace—a moment between Israel and Egypt that would be a model for the Arabs. And he was ready in a peace commitment to give back the Sinai. But Begin would never, never consent to [cede] Judea and Samaria.

Yehiel Kadishai   Camp David was in the woods, in the mountains. Begin called it "a concentration camp *deluxe*." Jimmy Carter is anti-Jewish, anti-Israeli. He was from the beginning, yet they played diplomatic games there.

Dan Pattir   The excerpts that I read from his last book were not surprising. Carter warned us at Camp David, "If something fails here, I won't blame the Egyptians; I'll blame *you*. I'll go to the Congress and the public and put the blame on *you*." It was as simple as that. And he didn't like Begin because Begin was different—the difference in personality between Begin and Sadat was less than [between] Begin and Carter.

"Sadat was very much interested in affecting the other Arab countries. He was opposed by all of them."—Dan Pattir

On October 10, 1981, the procession of Israeli mourners, Prime Minister Menachem Begin (second from left), government ministers (left to right) Yosef Burg, Ariel Sharon, and Yitzhak Shamir, and Yehiel Kadishai (far right), as they walk, because it is the Jewish Sabbath, from their lodgings to the funeral of the assassinated visionary Anwar Sadat.

The Reverend Jerry Falwell Jimmy Carter came the closest [of any U.S. president] to selling out Israel. In my opinion, Carter is an anti-Semite.

Abraham Foxman I believe that it's part of his religious worldview. You have the evangelicals and you have the Southern Baptists, and the evangelicals in their religious worldview about Jews and Israel see us as important—if not essential—to bring about the Second Coming. And, therefore, they want to see us strong and independent, and they have forgiven us for rejecting the First Coming.

The Southern Baptists, where Jimmy comes from, have *not* forgiven the Jews for rejecting the First Coming. And if you read the book [Mr. Carter's recent and controversial book], it's very revealing of who he is. Whether you start with the conversation that he had with Golda Meir, where he said, very clearly, "I've always been taught, and I taught the Bible, that God punishes those who reject Him." Well, he wasn't talking about Jehovah; he was talking about Jesus. That's where it comes from, and it's that Christian preoccupation with suffering. Proselytizing may be part of it. I'm not shocked—he was never a clear friend—and he was tough in his relationship with Begin. But what I find so sad is that the Jewish people and Israel provided Jimmy Carter with his only success on the world stage, and that is the Camp David Accords and the Nobel Prize, and yet he is still so angry at Jews and at Israel.

Yehiel Kadishai But the relationship between Sadat and Begin was very good. And Jihan Sadat even flew to Los Angeles for a dinner for the Assaf Harofeh Aliza Begin Hospital, and there were many other non-Jews there, as well.

Dan Pattir It was very interesting. Begin gave me a present before he departed, the whole collection of his exchanges, in writing, with Sadat, and they came out as close friends in the sense that they used to talk on their hotline [telephone] connection, about their families and what's going on.

But was also it destiny because Sadat was assassinated not too long after what happened with this terrible, bizarre thing of six American helicopters landing in the Persian Desert to try and save the hostages, and it was a disaster, a calamity. Sadat was so furious. There was a meeting between Begin and Sadat, and Sadat said to Begin, talking about 1981, "I'm so sorry that I tried to help Jimmy [Carter] to be reelected." And Begin asked him why, and he said, "Because look what happened here: if fifty hostages to be salvaged out of Tehran was in the national interest of the United States, a superpower sends the Sixth and Seventh fleets, together, to Persia, not *six helicopters*."

The calamity meant that as the result, America became, so to say, a paper tiger in the eyes of the Arabs, and "We," Sadat said, "Arab moderates, are being looked upon in the same way because we are friends of the Americans." A few weeks later, he was assassinated by the fundamentalists.

Yehiel Kadishai [former U.S. Department of State official] William Quandt in his book—it's a very good book of about five hundred pages—writes the most unbiased and correct assumption; he said in the chapter about the achievements of Begin that he was the most able negotiator, and he knew exactly what he wanted and was playing his cards close to his chest and was showing them only at the last moment, when he knew what the position was with the Egyptians and the Americans.

Begin did sacrifice the Sinai Peninsula, which was not part of Eretz Israel, for the sake of keeping Judea and Samaria in his hands. He passed away without seeing [the result of] his ceding—what will happen in the future. Meantime, we are still there.

But he never agreed to cede the Gaza Strip because it's *ours*. He said that it's very important, not only because it's part of Eretz Israel, in accordance with the Mandatory border, but it's very important for our security that we have a border all around, with Egypt, from the sea to the east, to the Jordan.

Dan Pattir Two days before the end of Camp David, Begin sent for me and said, "Let's have a walk." I said, "Mr. Begin, why do you want to?" He said, "Because my house is bugged." He said, "Don't worry; *everything* is bugged in Camp David; even the *trees* are bugged."

Then he said to me, "You don't understand me; you come from the other side"—he meant not from the Likudniks—"We already have a great achievement: we've got a peace treaty here." I asked, "Why do you say that?" He said, "Because I made the greatest concession here." I asked, "*Concession*? What do you mean by *concession*?" He said, "You don't understand me. I was raised, and taught hard, by my informers that, nationally, Israel has the right over the Arabs over the land of Israel. And here, I said, I'm going to say that I deferred the right for the dream of the ideology."

Then he said, "I still do believe in the ideology, but in practice, I defer it or postpone it, in the meantime, to have some kind of a practical agreement." I understood that it was a great, great, great concession, his concession, with *himself*. And that is what made the agreement viable.

Chapter 14

FIGHTING TERRORISM: TAKING CONTROVERSIAL ACTIONS TO ENSURE THE JEWISH STATE'S SURVIVAL

Israel's battle to protect its citizens from increasingly brutal acts of terrorism by young male and female suicide bombers has been spearheaded since the state's inception by operatives of the vaunted security services, the Shin Bet and the Mossad.

Shabtai Shavit   As soon as I started to learn Arabic—I was five years old—it had a tremendous effect on my life. Then in high school—we didn't have one in Nesher, so I studied in Haifa—they had a special study group of Arabic history and literature, so I specialized in those studies. And during my compulsory military service after high school, for a year I was wandering around among the Bedouins in the southern part of Israel. Then I joined an elite unit in the IDF, where Arabic was a prerequisite, so all my history was rooted in the main topic of our existence in this part of the world. Then, after serving in the IDF, I went to the Hebrew University and graduated with a degree in Arabic and military history. And after graduation, I joined the Mossad.

What Does the Mossad Look for in an Operative?

Shabtai Shavit   The first quality is integrity, being a real Zionist Israeli, truthful. Now in an organization like the Mossad, if somebody wants to cheat or not exactly report the truth, you can check the reports that people are giving, so it is essentially important to rely on people's reports on their activities in the organization. So truthfulness and comradeship are important, that he's working in tandem with other people in the organization. Being able to work in a group is a very important element. On the one hand, you expect people to have blind obedience, but on the other hand, you expect people to ask the right questions in order to get the right answers about why you have given this or that instruction, or order. One word that summarizes it all is a Yiddish word: mensch [an honorable, decent person].

Separating Professionalism from Emotionalism

Shabtai Shavit   On the one hand, it is very hard to separate emotions and professionalism. But the task of serving in the Mossad is to be able to separate these two traits in order to achieve your goal. And that is to say that to be successful in executing a mission, you have to be a professional, and for the period when you are performing your task, you have to be totally professional, totally rational, not emotionally involved. In order to do it, everybody who comes into the organization undergoes a very long period of training and orientation and practice, and you develop it. If somebody cannot make this separation, he doesn't stay in the organization.

The length of the training period depends on the task that you plan to perform. There are tasks in the organization where the training is rather brief. And it also changes from time to time. I'm talking about the early sixties—that's not history; it's *archaeology*—and I'm sure that today it differs a lot because the foundation never stops developing according to the needs and tasks. You are talking about a period of time of preparing a person, between something like three months and beyond. The longest period of training and preparation and exercising to prepare someone for the more difficult, more dangerous tasks varies. To give you an example, some of those who were to be trained to live undercover in enemy countries had such a task; it means a longer period of training and a longer period of preparations, whereas somebody who was supposed to work as a researcher in one of the departments of the organization here in Israel, his time of preparation would be shorter.

Among the Visible Terrorists was Yasser Arafat, the Chairman of the PLO

Shabtai Shavit   When Arafat didn't want the fire to go up, it didn't go up. And there are other instances where he wanted the fire to be there. He generated it himself; I can hardly think of any terrorist activity without Arafat instructing them to do it or knowing about it or approving it, not necessarily that he knew of each and every terrorist act that was perpetrated, but the people under him always knew how to read him correctly, whether he wanted or *didn't* want it. I don't believe that he can claim any kind of deniability when it comes to terrorist activities.

A Daring Mission in Retaliation for the Munich Massacre of Israeli Olympic Athletes

On the evening of April 9, 1973, a tall man and a woman made their way to a house in Beirut. In the moments that followed, this "romantic duo" morphed into a two-man hit team consisting of a future prime minister, Ehud Barak, and one of the heroes of Entebbe, Muki Betser. In an operation that stretched into the early hours of the following morning, the two men and their team took out a terrorist cell affiliated with the PLO leader Yasser Arafat. The team consisted of soldiers from the Spring of Youth Operation who were fulfilling one of four operations of Operation Grapes of Wrath, which were executed almost simultaneously in Lebanon in retaliation for the massacre of eleven Israeli athletes during the 1972 Munich Olympics.

Shabtai Shavit   The decision, made by Golda Meir, who was then the foreign minister, was the result of very deep emotional feelings—the reaction to this horrendous massacre of the Israeli athletes in Munich was that the state and the people of Israel should prove to themselves, to the rest of the Jewish people in the world, and to the goyim that Jewish blood cannot be shed without paying for it. And there was the idea that even though Israel is a very small country, one of its responsibilities as the Jewish state is to do whatever is possible and necessary in order to prove that it stands by its philosophy of the existence of the Jewish people as a people.

There has, of course, been a long discussion interpreting the results of it. I don't think that it was a decision based on the aim of vengeance. There was much more an element of building deterrence. Putting the sentiments and emotions aside, the professional thinking was that we needed to bring some kind of deterrence in order to prevent similar things from being repeated in the future.

Muki Betser   Four operations in one night—two in Beirut, one in Tyre, and one in Sidon—is something they wouldn't approve today. Moshe

"The thought was that if we chase the perpetrators of this massacre and we either bring them to trial or do away with them, such an act will build immediate deterrence."—Shabtai Shavit, speaking of Israel's action in April 1973 against the perpetrators of the Munich Olympics massacre

On September 9, 1972, grieving relatives of the Israeli athletes held captive by Islamic terrorists at the Olympic Village in Munich and then massacred at the airport there gather at Ben-Gurion Airport, then known as Lod, for a memorial service before individual funeral services at local cemeteries.

Dayan, who was the defense minister, said that if we carried out our mission in Beirut, we wouldn't be able to go back to Beirut again, so we'll do two operations in the same night. That was Dayan's judgment.

Planning the Barak-Betser Operation

Muki Betser   The planning for an operation is ours, and we have to recommend it to higher authorities. If it's good planning, they approve it. Many times, the planning was good, but they didn't approve it for various reasons. In the case of Aviv Neurim, the Beirut operation, it began with a group of people brainstorming, throwing out ideas, and then it crystallized into a particular plan.

Look, the operation was very daring. We had to come in by the sea, dress up as tourists, and identify a certain apartment. And you think of all the possibilities of what might happen, and you have to remember that the most expectable element is the *un*expected. This was the only operation

I took part in where there was no extraction force. Ordinarily, there are soldiers who come in and take you out if something goes wrong. I don't know whether anything like that has happened since, where the prime minister, the defense minister, and the chief of staff have approved a mission without an extraction force.

The question is whether the government would approve such a thing today, when the concern for security and the self-confidence of the government aren't what they were. We conduct our missions according to where they take place, and today that arena is principally in the Territories—Judea and Samaria. In Lebanon, to our great regret, things didn't develop as they should have.

Who Came Up with the Idea of Dressing as a "Couple"?

Muki Betser   Barak says it was *my* idea. I'm not sure. Masquerading is part of the combat methods of our unit, Sayeret Matkal. But it has spread to other units, and you see it in the Territories today.

Getting Ashore and to the Target

Muki Betser   There were sixteen of us. The Mossad brought our vehicles to within twenty kilometers from there [our target], enabling us to move freely. And then, walking farther, we were able to blend in. My team's mission was to take out Arafat's deputy. He had a security guy downstairs, and the goal was to kill him quietly, with a pistol. He wasn't there—he was downstairs, in a car. When I was already upstairs with my team, on the sixth floor, he got out of the car, and Ehud Barak and Amiram Nadin shot and injured him.

Going back to what I said about the *un*expected, when Amiram shot the security guard, part of a bullet hit the vehicle and caused a short circuit in the horn, and it started blowing. It was midnight! People came out on their balconies to look around. They feared something suspicious was happening, so they called the gendarmerie, like our border police, and a battle began. We shot at their three jeeps, and to our good luck none of our people were hurt. One was hurt upstairs, but we were able to call to our vehicles that were only a hundred meters away, and they came and took us to the seaside.

Could Arafat Have Been Killed
in That Operation?

Muki Betser   I was badly wounded at Karami [in 1973] when we went to get Arafat. The story is that he got away on a motorcycle. Now, I *hoped*, I *prayed*, because we had intelligence that Arafat held meetings from midnight 'til two in the morning in that building, on the sixth floor, and I hoped that he would be there. I *would* have killed him. But, to my regret, he wasn't there.

Shabtai Shavit   In the second half of the sixties and the seventies Arafat was chased by us, similarly to other Palestinian terrorists. I don't recall that the Israeli security services made a decision to allocate an especially big effort toward him, specifically. He was just another terrorist whom we had to chase. But once he had become a recognized leader of the Palestinian movement, we stopped chasing him as just another terrorist and we tried to get him in Lebanon by bombing and destroying whole neighborhoods where he was hiding and moving from one place to another and never sleeping for two nights in the same bed.

There was a time during the First Lebanon War when Arafat had agreed to leave Lebanon with his immediate cronies. At that time we controlled the Port of Beirut, and we could have done anything we wished, but there was a silent understanding—I don't believe that there was any American pressure; it was an Israeli decision—that we would allow him to be evacuated from Lebanon and that he would sail with his people to Tunis.

When he walked to the boat, he was in the line of fire from Israeli machine guns and rifles, and had it been decided to eliminate him, it would have been possible. But the decision was: Let's allow him to leave Lebanon. Maybe the decision to let him go was based on the fact that for some time we had tried to eliminate him and we hadn't succeeded. Also, very many innocent people had suffered as the result of our having chased after him. No one at that time could have prophesied all the developments that would take place later on.

Was the Intelligence Community
Opposed to Arafat's Return?

Shabtai Shavit   Of course, there was opposition. The rightist political parties were very vehemently opposed to the proposition that Arafat would be allowed to come back. The more leftist and the center parties agreed to it. Since they were the overriding majority in Israeli political life he was allowed to come back, through the Oslo Agreements.

Within the security services, there were various attitudes and recommendations. I don't recall a unanimous recommendation as to whether to allow him or not to allow him to come back. But the decision to allow him to come to the Territories was a purely political decision, not a military or intelligence decision. That, of course, lent weight to all the pros and cons—the threats and dangers vis-à-vis the positive aspects of his return. And bear in mind that it was based on the Oslo Agreements that, at the time, the majority of people in Israel and the West were thrilled about: the agreements were considered to be the preamble to future peace.

Entebbe

Shortly after midnight, on July 4, 1976, Uganda time, the first of four Hercules C-130 transport planes touched down on a darkened runway of the airport in Entebbe, Uganda. Thus began the daring mission of thirty soldiers of the Israeli Defense Forces' General Reconnaissance Unit, the Sayeret Matkal, to rescue 105 Jewish hostages and the crew of an Air France Airbus. They had been hijacked by a band of Palestinian terrorists one week earlier, on Sunday, June 27, during a stopover at the airport in Athens, Greece, on a flight from Tel Aviv to Paris. The hostages were eventually flown to Entebbe, where the Ugandan dictator Idi Amin, once a friend of Israel, embraced, comforted, and abetted their captors.

Muki Betser The understanding that Idi Amin and the terrorists jointly initiated this operation developed during the week. At first, we didn't know that.

———————

By Wednesday, June 30, however, based on information supplied by non-Jewish hostages who had been released and debriefed, it was evident that Idi Amin had not only allowed the hijacked Airbus to land, but was also abetting them.

Learning of the Hijacking and Developing an Initial Strategy

Muki Betser In our unit, there were four commanders who were authorized to deal with hostage-taking situations, and on the twenty-

"At that time, it was very important that this action be carried out. You have to remember that in 1974 the world received Arafat at the United Nations. He appeared with a kaffieh and a pistol, and everyone stood up and applauded."—Muki Betser

The scene at Ben-Gurion Airport on July 4, 1976, as jubilant and relieved relatives of the passengers on an Air France Airbus hijacked by terrorists to Entebbe Airport a week earlier, joined by fellow Israelis, await the released hostages' return.

seventh of June, I was the duty officer. The first thing we do in such a situation is to go to our airport against the possibility that the hijacked plane will be flown here, as had happened before with a Sabena aircraft.

Taking Action

Early on, alternative plans were developed, all of them based on the assumption that Ugandan officials were not in league with the terrorists: sending a rescue force that would arrive by yacht on Lake Victoria, located a kilometer away from the airport; the painting of an Israeli aircraft to resemble an Air France jet—based on the terrorists' demands for Israel's release of Palestinian prisoners and their transfer to Entebbe on an Air France aircraft—and loading that aircraft with twenty Palestinian terrorists and twenty Israeli soldiers disguised as terrorists; a parachute drop by a combined force of naval commandos and Sayeret Matkal operatives on Lake Victoria that would travel by raft to the airport; and the so-called Army Plan, requiring a massive force that would overwhelm the terrorists and the Ugandan soldiers guarding the airfield.

Muki Betser   There were four plans, and one of them was to take an Israel air force plane and make it look like an Air France plane, and I didn't want to complicate everything with the French.

The hijacking was on Sunday, and the plane went to Benghazi [Libya], and it was only on Monday evening [June 28] that we understood that the plane had landed at Entebbe. Not everyone in the army knew then where Uganda was, or could say the word "Entebbe." But I had been there for four months as an adviser to Uganda's paratroopers. And officers could request equipment and it would come from Israel to Entebbe once a month on a Hercules aircraft, the C-130. So the idea was in my head that you could get there, that there were pilots who flew there.

On Monday night, Barak called me to a meeting of the general staff—I was brought in as a representative of Sayeret Matkal—and I understood that there was a plan and that it was top secret. No one other than Yoni [Jonathan Netanyahu, the commander of the operation], who was in the south, not even the men of Sayeret Matkal knew that this planning group was meeting.

Sending Barak to Nairobi to Negotiate the Postrescue Refueling: Was There a Power Struggle with Yoni?

Muki Betser   There was no argument. Ehud Barak was our ultimate commander and Yoni was his deputy, so it was logical that Ehud Barak would command this. Yoni didn't feel comfortable, as if people didn't trust him or wouldn't depend on him. He shared his feelings with me, and I told him to calm him, not to worry, that in the end, Ehud would go to another mission.

I didn't know that at the time, but that's what happened. Barak was a full colonel, and it was a very complex operation, full of all kinds of possibilities. In the refueling, there were only two possibilities: one way was to pump the fuel out of the underground tanks, and there was a team that knew how to do that, to essentially *take* the fuel; and the other way was to refuel at Nairobi. Barak, who was the one and only person who could arrange all this, went to speak to the Kenyans about other things and then about making this happen.

Finding a Mercedes, Dressing Up as Idi Amin, and Flying the Hostages Out

Muki Betser   The idea of using the limousine and dressing up as Ugandan soldiers was mine. In this operation, there were two points of primary importance: first, how to arrive and get past the Ugandan soldiers, surprise the terrorists, and overcome them before they could harm the hostages. Two years before that, I had commanded the operation at the school at Ma'alot. [In May 1974, three armed terrorists of the Popular Front for the Liberation of Palestine, having crossed into Israel from Lebanon, invaded a school in the northern Israeli town. They took 120 teenagers hostage, demanded the freeing by Israel of twenty-six terrorists, and threatened to dynamite the school if their demands were not satisfied. Israeli soldiers counterattacked, and when the shooting was over, twenty-two of the students (most of them girls), one Israeli soldier, and the terrorists lay dead.] There we did not surprise the terrorists, and there they killed twenty-two students and wounded sixty others until we eliminated them.

On the Ground

Muki Betser   This may sound immodest, but I was the only officer involved in the operation from the very beginning of the planning to the actual carrying out of the operation. Part of the plan was my idea, and from Monday through Thursday I was informed of the details of the plan—for *our* unit and the overall plan—and I was the commander of the force to break in, which was divided into five groups. While I was aware of the overall plan, I concentrated on *our* unit's mission, and I was prepared to take command when Yoni was killed in the first moments. I notified the units that I was taking command.

Why Was Yoni Killed?

Muki Betser We had great apprehension during our planning about the control tower. It was very tall, four stories high, and we knew that it commanded the field, that the Ugandans would see us from the moment we landed, during the ride to the terminal, and certainly as we were running to storm it. Everybody except my group was forbidden to open fire. The instant I opened fire, everyone was free to fire at whatever target they saw, so we set up a group that was to direct its weapons at the control tower but was not to open fire until my group had broken into the terminal.

Something went wrong. There was a mistake, and we lost the element of surprise. We ran toward the entrances but not according to plan. Yoni was with us, but before the team that was to cover the tower was in position, they opened fire on us from the tower and Yoni was hit. One bullet entered his right shoulder and exited from his back, at the left, and another hit his left elbow. In an hour or so he died. It was *fate* that he, of all people, would be killed and no one else.

I had hardly slept that week—I had gotten maybe one hour of sleep since Monday—and I was exhausted, but I had lost a good friend, Yoni, so what was in my mind was that if Yoni were alive, it would have been a perfect operation.

Osirak

On Saturday, June 7, 1981, Israeli air force jets flew over Iraq's nuclear plant at Osirak, destroying Saddam Hussein's capacity at the time to develop weapons of mass destruction. So targeted was the attack, that only one person on the ground was killed.

Rafi Eitan It was Begin's decision, and later everybody blamed him, [saying] that he did it before the election. The men pushing Begin to do the operation were Arik Sharon, who was at the time the minister of agriculture, and Ezer Weizman, the minister of defense.

The decision was made only when we had very good information that this would be the last time we could bomb the reactor before radioactive material was put into use. My main involvement was in bringing Begin this information. And we knew for sure that if the operation were to be postponed for a few weeks, the heavy water and the radioactive material would be put into the reactor. Then, if we bombed the radioactive reactor, we would endanger the whole area. Therefore, that was vital information—that we had a few weeks.

The Reverend Jerry Falwell In 1981, when Menachem Begin went down the smokestack of that nuclear reactor, he called me just hours after it happened and said, "I don't want you to feel that we are doing anything recklessly here, but this is the beginning of the creation of nuclear weapons in the hands of a madman." Of course, it was Saddam Hussein.

Simcha Waisman Why did it take them *so long*? If they hadn't done it then, I don't think Israel would be here today. When you give these kinds of weapons of mass destruction to unstable people, you open Pandora's box because you don't know where they're going. It was a matter of time; a lot of people's lives were at stake. And there was a lot of work; it was not just fly the planes in and bomb them. Somebody had to coordinate it on the ground, and that's a pretty heavy job.

It doesn't matter *what* Israel does; they're going to criticize Israel.

Iran's Nuclear Threat Today

Simcha Waisman The rest of the world will do what they have to do. And they're going to take care on their own to safeguard Israel. How is it going to end? I don't know. But I believe that it's going to end by doing something in Iran. I mean, this guy [Ahmadinejad] is really *nuts*! This guy is scary just for hosting the Holocaust conference [in the winter of 2006]. He was looking to stir the pot all over the world so they wouldn't focus on him. I don't think that the world is going to leave him alone. I think the world will come to understand very fast that this guy is more dangerous than he appears.

Why Doesn't Israel Act Now?

In January 2007, the *Sunday Times* of London ran a story in which it was maintained that Israel was preparing to attack Iran's nuclear facilities.

Simcha Waisman You have to do your homework; you don't want to do it too early and just destroy half of it. You want to destroy the whole thing so they cannot rebuild it there and they have to build it somewhere else. You know, there is a reason for everything, but I think the number-one reason is preparation. And I don't know how far they are in their level of preparedness. It's important; you want to make sure to take out *everything*. In Iraq, they didn't take out 100 percent, but they did enough damage that it took longer to put it back together.

Rafi Eitan   The Iraqis wanted to build a reactor, and the Iranians are doing it. But politically, there is no similarity. In '81, we had the political option to attack the reactor; today we don't have the political option. And I'm not going into the military option. The Iran of today is not the Iraq of '81, and the involvement of the big powers in Iran today—the United States, Russia, China, North Korea, and many others—is not the same as it was in '81. Then the Middle East was a remote area. Today it's not a remote area; it's heavily involved.

And, also, Iraq was a supplier of oil in '81, but it was *one* of the suppliers; the world as a whole could live without it. Today, if you stopped the flow of oil from the Persian Gulf, which might happen if you did anything against Iran—even if the Americans are doing it, they are risking the flow of oil from the Persian Gulf: Iraqi oil, Iranian oil, Kuwait oil, Qatar oil, and Saudi oil—and Israel is not in the political situation that it could allow itself to be responsible for that. Therefore, we don't have a political option.

Iran today is ruled by a dictator, as was the government of Iraq in '81, and there's no doubt that if Ahmadinejad had nuclear weapons today, he could give them to a terror organization.

Is Israel's Leadership Capable of Dealing with the Existential Threat of a Nuclear Iran?

Yossi Ben-Aharon   As has happened in the past, we are at our best, and our performance is brilliant, when our very existence is threatened. Then the "Jewish genius" is capable of devising a whole plethora of means of hitting back, and I am sure that we have the wherewithal for the performance necessary. And for those who will attempt to hit us, we'll give them a price that they've never paid since the beginning of the country. Of this, I have no doubt whatsoever.

Until then, we have a leadership crisis in this country, not just mediocre leaders. But we survive because the people have a better backbone than the leadership. It may sound simplistic, but they know that what we are up against is an attempt to do us in—all the rest is just sheer form.

The Reverend Jerry Falwell   The president of Iran is insane with hatred for Israel, and he's totally ignored everybody, including the U.N. It's going to come down that if America does not take care of the Iran problem, *Israel* will because there's no way that Israel, with its very existence at stake, can sit by any more than Menachem Begin did in '81 with Saddam Hussein.

The Abduction and Murder by Hamas
of a Young Israeli Soldier

A source who did not wish to be quoted for attribution told the authors of Prime Minister Rabin's passionate reaction to the kidnapping and murder of the young Israeli soldier Nachshon Wachsman by Hamas and of the resulting interchange between Rabin and Yasser Arafat.

> Rabin called Arafat—I was there—and he said, "It is your guys who kidnapped him. If you are not going to bring him back within twenty-four hours, I'll bomb Gaza; I'll kill *you!*" Rabin was so nervous and he shouted into the telephone. And Arafat said, "You know what"—Arafat never, never lied to Rabin—"He's not here; he's not with us. We didn't do it!" And Rabin shouted, "You are a liar! I'll show you! I'll kill thousands of you! I'll send tanks to Gaza!" And Arafat said, "I sent hundreds of soldiers to look and he's not *in* Gaza." And Rabin said, "He *is* in Gaza; we know that he is in Gaza and I'll do everything to destroy Gaza!" Two or three days after, the head of Shabak came and he said, "He is not far from Jerusalem; Arafat doesn't know anything about it." And then Rabin said, "So Arafat told us the truth!" And he called him and he said, "I'm sorry that I did that."

The authors' source also stated that Arafat personally identified the killers to the Israelis as Hamas operatives and told them, "The only thing I'm not going to do is to kill them; my people will direct you to the right apartment, but they will never kill their own people [meaning fellow Palestinians]. It's your job to kill them." And, the authors' source says, the Israelis eventually did kill many of them.

Shabtai Shavit   When it comes to Hamas, the separation between the military and the political is artificial because both elements are wrapped up

"What Fatah was not able to deliver diplomatically, Hamas was able to deliver militarily."
—Akiva Eldar

Eyewitnesses to Hamas's attack on a number 18 bus on March 3, 1996, as it crossed the intersection of Jaffa and Shlom Zion and Hamalka streets in Jerusalem, react as a rescue team removes the body of a victim.

in religious ideology, so everybody in Hamas understands what his job is: to eliminate the Jewish state.

When it comes to Fatah, it is harder to come to this conclusion because over the years one has been able to identify various factions within the entity that we call the Palestinian Authority. It is interesting to note that we're now talking about the Palestinian Authority and underneath this umbrella we have Fatah and the Al Aksa Brigades and different organizations. It proves that various factions within the Palestinian Authority represent a different thinking, a different philosophy, a different political objective. And I do think that this distinction does exist in the Palestinian Authority as compared with Hamas.

A Troubling Development: Doing Away with the Anonymity of Mossad Chiefs

Shabtai Shavit   I wish there had been thinking behind it. There was *not*. I'm sorry to say that the one who took off the lid was the then prime minister Shimon Peres. It was the wrong decision to divulge the identities of the heads of the services. In the case of the director of the CIA, the fact that it is a political decision automatically makes it a condition that his identity should be divulged.

The assignment of an Israeli to become director of the Mossad is a purely professional decision. I was assigned by Prime Minister Shamir, and after three and a half years with him I worked for three and a half years with Rabin, two people who represent entirely different political parties, with two entirely different political viewpoints. It has not disturbed them a bit, or me, to serve both of them, despite the fact that they represented entirely different parties, because I was a professional. That is one justification for keeping the identity of the Israeli heads of services secret.

Second, the length of the hierarchy in the Israeli system between the top of the organization and the combatants in the field is very short, whereas in the American or British or West European system, the distance is wide. And one of the secrets of the successes of the Israeli security services stems from our structure.

Now, to translate this structure to real life means that the number-one guy in the Israeli system does not sit in his office in Tel Aviv; most of his time is with his combatants, his troops, all around the world, where the dangerous activities are coming from. Now, how can the top guy wander around the world when his name and identity are known publicly? I used to wander all around the globe incognito, and it was very easy because nobody knew who I was. But today, I feel for the guy—wherever he goes, there's a tail of bodyguards. It was a big mistake. Israel is undergoing very many changes, and today, everything is transparent—whatever is being discussed in the cabinet is known.

Chapter 15

OSLO AND THE RESULTING "UNTHINKABLE" HANDSHAKE

On the sunny morning of September 13, 1993, during a ceremony conducted in the White House Rose Garden in the presence of Prime Minister Yitzhak Rabin and President Bill Clinton, Yasser Arafat and Israel's foreign minister Shimon Peres signed an agreement providing for Palestinian self-rule in parts of the West Bank and Gaza for a five-year interim period, during which time the parties would negotiate a permanent peace. While Arafat, Peres, and Rabin would receive the Nobel Peace Prize, the hopes raised by Oslo would be dashed due to the PLO's continued and intensified terror campaign, known as the First Intifada, launched in 1988.

Akiva Eldar You don't make peace because you are pushed, because you don't have other alternatives. Rabin realized that Israel was strong enough to make peace; he felt Israel could afford to make concessions. He wasn't strong enough to disturb the settlements—he was afraid of them—and I hold it against him that he didn't use the opportunity to evacuate Hebron after the February 1994 massacre. Instead, he kept a hundred thousand people under curfew to protect the settlers from revenge.

He believed in an incremental, step-by-step, confidence-building measure approach. He was very wrong because you cannot build trust under occupation. It is an oxymoron. He believed you have to feed the Israelis with a spoon, piece by piece. When you have elements on both sides who have a clear interest and have the power and ideology to undermine the process, to make sure that you won't reach the point where you make major concessions, then they will do this. Rabin was too careful; he didn't make the full transition from a military hero to a political leader. Part of him was still in uniform.

Yossi Ben-Aharon   As soon as Rabin was elected, he turned around and betrayed everything that he had said before, that "There's no such thing as leaving the Golan Heights. This will be a betrayal." Sure enough, he was willing give them the Golan Heights. And he said, "We will not negotiate with the PLO." That was the beginning of our disaster. What happened subsequently in May and June of '92 was a story of one disaster after another, in every respect, for the State of Israel. The leadership was useless; our policies were useless; the Arabs misread our capacity; they thought—with some justification—that we are a weakling that stage by stage would be eliminated.

And then we had American presidents who didn't understand the situation *at all*. It began with Carter and Bush the elder; then Clinton, another disaster; and finally, George W., who is better. But the situation has already gone so far that with all the problems that Bush faced after 9/11 and Iraq, he just kept the same boat going, without trying to do something more useful, more basic, to solve the problem.

A high-ranking American Jewish leader, who preferred not to speak on the record, told the authors that he was with Clinton when the president went out to the Rose Garden to make the announcement of the second Camp David talks, and that when Clinton returned to the Oval Office, he said, "I announced Camp David," to which the official responded, "Are you really *ready* for them?" The president said, "No, but [Prime Minister Ehud] Barak asked me to do it, and we're *doing* it."

Joshua Matza   I was chairing a committee of the International Parliamentarian Union, which gathered twice a year, going to places all over the world. The time came when we had to participate in Australia with Raanan Cohen from the Labor Party and two other members of the Parliament. I was at home, ready to leave—I was just going out the door with my luggage—when I heard the announcement about Oslo. I decided that I would not travel to Australia, and I called Raanan Cohen and told him so, and he started to shout. I said to him, "I cannot be there. They'll bring this agreement to the Knesset, and I have to be here." So he didn't have any other choice. The Oslo Agreement made me feel so bad.

Rav Shalom Gold   For the last thirteen years, since Oslo, there has been a great deal of pain in this country, and it has been getting worse and worse. The country is in a terrible state of affairs. We had always hoped that Israel would be a light unto the nations. We're not a light unto the nations—the corruption, the evil, the worst evil of all, the exile of ten thousand Jews from their homes. I don't understand it. After two thousand years of Jews being thrown out of their homes by Gentiles, how could a Jewish government have *done* that?

All of our attempts at peace have been wasted. Nobody wants peace with us. "Land for Peace" is an absolutely empty slogan; it never had any meaning. Another slogan, "Restraint Is Strength," is absolute nonsense. We have been living on slogans and haven't come face-to-face with the reality that they don't want peace with us.

That's why I say that at the top of the agenda should be a turning inward; we've got to talk to *each other* first, or we will never be able to talk to anybody outside of the Jewish people. We have to begin to heal and repent and rebuild and restructure and understand that our best friends are our fellow Jews and nobody else in the world. If we don't get to work on creating a truly decent society here, we will never have the strength that is going to be required of us in order to stand up against our enemies from without.

I don't think that another penny should be spent on that crazy wall that they are building until every Jew from Gush Katif has a home. It is a profound tragedy, and it's the worst sin of all—Jew against fellow Jew. There has to be an all-out war against traffic accidents and an all-out war waged against poverty. We have to do whatever we can for the underprivileged and the handicapped. I have a feeling that if we truly make ourselves a beautiful society, our neighbors living in Gaza and Ramallah and Hebron and Jenin may very well want to emulate what we have here and get rid of all the killer terrorists that we imported into Israel.

It is the most tragic error that we thought we were going to make peace with Arafat and bring in his forty thousand killers. I've never for a moment been able to understand how Jews could be so stupid.

Malcolm Hoenlein   Oslo was inherently flawed. For one thing, I don't know that people were ready for it. Two, you have to cross every "T" and dot every "I"; you can't leave all these things for later decisions when there are contentious issues, like incitement, that are simply ignored. They rushed into stuff for which there wasn't preparation because everybody was facing the time clock, and you saw how this frenzy developed, and you needed to get a deal before both of them were out of office. Some of the proposals were clearly not well thought out: there were things giving away significant

"There are facts that you have to accept. I was at the celebration of the settlement with King Hussein. We had to settle with him."
—Joshua Matza

On October 26, 1994, at a royal residence in Akaba following the signing of the milestone Israeli-Jordanian Peace Treaty at the Arava border crossing, a gracious King Hussein, cigarette in mouth, lights Prime Minister Yitzhak Rabin's smoke.

parts of Jerusalem, I mean, really endangering the future of Jerusalem that, thank God, were stopped at the last minute. Sometimes even good ideas, if they're not properly prepared, will fail.

There were other deals. For instance, what Peres tried to do with King Hussein was probably a better deal. I pushed for Peres to look at the Hussein deal more closely at the time. People rejected it right away, and he came to America, and he actually did a very poor job selling it. He said to me, "Just remember, every subsequent deal we make will be worse than the one before." And there he was right.

Uri Avneri   I was for Oslo; I had a part in convincing Arafat to accept Oslo. I still think it was a good thing, but it failed because on the Arab side and the Palestinian side there was a clear concept of what the solution is—it has not changed to this very day—and if today Condoleezza [Rice] talked with Mahmoud Abbas, it would be the same thing. Arafat told me more than thirty years ago, "The Palestinians have a clear-cut solution: they want a Palestinian state in all the occupied territories."

Rabin and his successors did everything they could to scuttle the Oslo Agreement. Every single part of the Oslo Agreement has been violated by

*"Rabin broke the
timetable, which was
inherent in the Oslo
Agreement. Oslo was
in the end a failure."*
—Uri Avneri

Future prime minister but then foreign minister Shimon Peres (right) with Prime Minister Yitzhak Rabin and PLO chairman Yasser Arafat on December 10, 1994, in Oslo, moments after each had received the Nobel Peace Prize for the Oslo Agreement.

the Israeli government. The Palestinians also violated it but far less, for the simple reason that they have no power and we have.

Joseph Hochstein   I'm not sure that the average person at any time thought peace was possible. It's more of a vanguard who think it can be done and are trying to make it happen who represent the peace movement. I don't think this movement is, or ever was, a majority. What did happen is that when the Oslo Agreements came down in 1993, everybody understood that the idea is, We will do this; the Palestinians will get a state and we will have to live side by side; we will be here, they will be there. As a result of the failure of the Oslo process—which came fairly quickly—almost nobody today will say the Oslo process can work. It is hard to find starry-eyed people now.

Preparations for the Rose Garden Ceremony

Eitan Haber   I took care of every second, and I dealt with the White House two or three days earlier. There were dozens of telephone calls, and

I told them who would be standing where and who would speak and what they intended to say. It was a huge, huge, huge story.

Staging the Handshake

Eitan Haber   I spoke with Martin [Indyk, the Australian-born U.S. ambassador to Israel], my liaison officer, about how long the handshake would take, and I warned him twenty times to tell Arafat, "Don't even dare to *think* about hugging Rabin." I told Rabin, "In case he decides to be close to you, shake his hand and push him back with your other hand." I gave the order about how Arafat should dress and what he would say. And the biggest problem was: what will happen after everybody leaves the Oval Office? Only Clinton and Arafat will stay in the office. What will they do? There will be two minutes that they will be alone. I told Martin, who then told President Clinton, "Don't even *think* of letting them speak in the room when they are waiting to go out [to the Rose Garden]."

Dan Pattir   Rabin told me later that he was in the Oval Office with Clinton and he said, "Mr. President, there should be no kisses," and Clinton's security people showed him how to shake hands with Arafat but to keep a distance from him, putting his elbow at a certain angle so that Arafat couldn't come near.

After the Handshake, Did Rabin Want
to Wash His Hand?

Eitan Haber   No, but he showed everyone that he was not happy. Two days earlier, I had suggested to him—it was not in the papers—that he should not go to Washington, and on Friday, I called the ambassador here and told him, "The prime minister has decided not to go." But on Saturday President Clinton called him and convinced him to come.

PART FOUR

New Realities

Chapter 16

THE BEGINNING OF PALESTINIAN
SELF-RULE

Uri Avneri   From the early fifties, I came out for the establishment of a Palestinian state next to Israel. At the time, the West Bank was under Jordanian rule and the Gaza Strip under Egyptian rule. In the Six-Day War, on the fifth day, after the army had conquered the West Bank and the Gaza Strip, I published an open letter, calling on the Israeli government to help the Palestinians to immediately set up the Palestinian state in these territories.

I also privately contacted the prime minister, Levi Eshkol, with whom I was friendly, and asked him to receive me so that I could explain this idea. He invited me immediately after the war, and I had a long, very unsuccessful conversation with him about this idea, which at the beginning was popular. But then Israel got used to the idea that we can keep it [the West Bank and the Gaza Strip] and settle it, and this idea (establishing a Palestinian state) became less popular.

Arie Lova Eliav   I wrote books and articles—that we have to meet the Palestinian people. They are our bitterest enemies, but you make peace with your enemies so, first of all, *meet* them, start talking with them. And that was not popular, and I and some of my friends, one of them Avneri— I came from the heart of Labor, right in the middle of the establishment, and he was a good man, but he was an outsider—made the first contact with Dr. Issam Sartawi [a senior member of the PLO, a moderate who in 1979 was the corecipient in Vienna, Austria, with Arie Eliav, of the Bruno

Kreisky Peace Prize], and we started meeting with PLO leaders in Paris and in other places [in 1976 and 1977]. It was heresy: "How come you are going to meet murderers, like Sartawi?" But I said, "Look, we have to start talking with them and see who they are." And, actually, Sartawi paid with his life for meeting with us because he was assassinated by extremist Palestinians later [in 1983, in Portugal].

Dr. Sartawi had a realistic idea about the concessions that the Palestinians would have to make for peace, and he paid with his life for understanding it. At that time—and some still harbor this idea—it was all or nothing. But at that time, men like Sartawi said, "Okay, you won the '48 war; you have a state of your own; now we will recognize you, but you have to recognize the Palestinians as a legitimate national movement. And, eventually, you'll have to recognize that our future state will be in the West Bank and Gaza. And then we will make peace." I believe that if the government had taken my road and that of people like me, we would have had peace by now. I paid with my career for my belief.

"Later, it was permitted, but it was a big thing at that period."—Arie Lova Eliav, speaking of his early overtures to the Palestinian leadership

Arie Lova Eliav, a pioneer in relations with the Palestinians, as he looks today, seated in his Tel Aviv apartment before a portrait of his Russian grandfather.

Years later, it became so obvious that you had to meet Palestinian leaders and come to terms with them. That's what Olmert is trying to do now. It's not enough, to my mind, but that's what Rabin was trying to do. But in that period, it was heresy.

Akiva Eldar   I became the diplomatic correspondent of *Ha'aretz* in 1983. I supported a Palestinian state and negotiations with the PLO. Most of my colleagues thought that I was anti-Zionist because I supported two states. Until 1993, until Oslo, the mainstream media and the Labor Party didn't believe in a Palestinian state. There are still some people who believe it was a mistake to go to Arafat and bring him back from Tunis—that we could have reached a deal with the Palestinians without having to worry about the refugees. But the PLO was very clear that we had to tackle the refugee issue.

Uri Avneri   At the time of my resignation from the Knesset in 1973, I started my contact with the PLO. After the Yom Kippur War, a high-ranking PLO officer published an article in the *Times* of London, calling for a change of Palestinian policy and practically calling for an accommodation with Israel. It could not have been written without the approval of Yasser Arafat, so I established contact with this PLO man.

I met him, and we established a secret contact that went on for about a year and a half, during which time an assassination attempt was made on me here, through the door. Afterward, Arafat called me in the hospital. His contact started a secret contact and person-to-person contact, and after about a year or so, I got an okay from their side to turn this into an institutional contact—still secret, but institutional. So I set up a Council for Israeli-Palestinian Peace, for which we got a lot of very important figures, and contact continued between the PLO and this new council. It was leaked to the press, and it became public, and this contact went on until 1982, the First Lebanon War, when, during the war, I crossed the lines in Beirut, during the siege of Beirut, and met Arafat personally for the first time.

It was the first time that Arafat met any Israeli. It was public; not only did Arafat's office announce it, post facto, but it was also televised the same day, and part of it appeared on Israeli television. On the way back to Israel that same day, I heard that four cabinet ministers demanded that I be put on trial for high treason—meeting with the enemy during the war—but I was not arrested. But the government decided to instruct the attorney general to start a criminal investigation, and the attorney general, who was a very nice person, officially decided that I had broken no law and could not be prosecuted. Since then, I was in regular contact with Yasser Arafat in Tunis—I met him there many times, which was also breaking the law, of course.

All of these contacts, by the way, were when Yitzhak Rabin was prime minister. I informed him about these contacts when they were still secret, and he gave me the okay to continue them while rejecting the whole idea. When I first informed him, he was totally against this idea of making peace with the Palestinians. But he said, "If you want to meet them, you can do so. And if you hear something that the prime minister of Israel should know, the door is open." That was so typically Rabin. And I met him many times after that, to inform him. There was a time when I became a courier, in a way, between Arafat and Rabin. But all of this with Arafat was rejected out of hand by Rabin.

Moshe Sharon   How are we going to establish a Palestinian state for the Arabs? When are we going to give them more rifles? [As a result of the Oslo Accords, fifty thousand rifles were turned over to the Palestinian Authority.] How are we going to create for them a better army? How are we going to give them more money? That's such a crazy thing! I mean, have you ever heard of a state in the world strengthening an enemy with whom it is at war? To give rifles to Mahmoud Abbas—everybody calls him "Abu Mazen," his nom de guerre—can you imagine? You court your enemy, and you give him rifles, and you know that these rifles are used against *you*, and you think that's *okay*? Do you think that Abu Mazen is your friend more than he is a friend of Hamas? You must be out of your mind! He is an Arab, and they both want the same thing. Do you think that if you give him more rifles, he's going to be *your* friend?

This has not happened before. If anybody was ever, ever caught giving *half* a rifle to an Arab, he was regarded as a traitor. And here you have a government of Israel strengthening its own enemies and telling everybody that, politically, it's a wonderful move. Why is it a wonderful move? Nobody asks that question.

Clinton Convenes a Second Camp David Conference

During the summer of 2000, Arab terror continued against Israel's civilian population. President Clinton, with an eye toward enhancing his legacy, invited Yasser Arafat and the Israeli prime minister, Ehud Barak, to Camp

David. There, Barak offered the Palestinians unprecedented concessions, including 95 percent of the West Bank, in exchange for peace.

Arafat, inexplicably, rejected Barak's offer—evidence of Israeli diplomat Abba Eban's observation that in dealing with Israel, "The Arabs never miss an opportunity to miss an opportunity."

Abraham Foxman   Clinton did, in the nice sense, what Israel wanted him to do: if he embraced Arafat, it was not because he had this vision of *Arafat*; it was because the Israelis then in power believed that one might be able to make peace with Arafat and the Palestinians. And that's what Clinton did. At a period where the Israelis thought that they had an opportunity for peace, Clinton did whatever they wanted, whatever they felt they needed, to bring this partner to the table. And I believe that Bush is ready to do that as well, but it would depend on Israel.

Moshe Sharon   Yasser Arafat was saying, "No, I don't want to!" Madeleine Albright was running after him—"Mr. Arafat? Mr. Arafat?" It was absolutely degrading. Who is he—I don't want to use bad words—but a piece of *nothing*! A little terrorist, uneducated—he never spoke good Arabic; his Arabic was *bad*—totally uneducated.

And he was a liar, first class—the world *knew* that—and still, he spoke a language that they understood very well. And that was to say, "No!" Never say "Yes." In the language of the Middle East, you say, "I'm not coming with any plan." It's very important; a leader should know that in this part of the world, you *never* come with your own plan because the minute you do, you are *finished*! The other side knows that this is a plan that is going to pull you down. And the second thing is: if the other side comes with a plan, you always say, *"No."*

Why Did Arafat Not Accept Barak's Offer?

Akiva Eldar   Barak believed that he could convince Arafat to give more. Barak looked at the history of the conflict from 1948 and said, "We are willing to give up 78 percent." Israel started from 1967 and said, "We want East Jerusalem and the Jewish neighborhoods, we want Ma'aleh Adumim; we have created facts on the ground; we didn't ask if that's okay with you; that is the price you have to pay." And Arafat wouldn't take it.

If he had agreed to make concessions beyond the 1988 declaration, he would have lost the support of the PLO. He said to Barak, "If I give you what you want, I'm a dead man." He knew his limits. He was a visionary and made mistakes, but he was very realistic. He knew what he was able and not able to do. He would have given up the right of return for the refugees. But he couldn't do *both*. And Barak wanted both.

Moshe Sharon   Look, in the bazaar when you come to buy something, if you say, "Oh, I love this shirt," before you know what's happening, this shirt is going to be ten times its price. But if you walk out, the vendor runs after you. It's very simple what happens in a Middle Eastern negotiation. It's how to deal, how to enhance.

We advance the interests of somebody else—that's what we're doing all the time. Peres goes to Davos [to international economic forums] and says, "We've got to establish a Palestinian state; that's very important." Why is it important? To destroy yourself; are you out of your mind? Why are the Arabs not saying, "What are we doing in order to establish a state of Israel?" "They [the Palestinians] are demanding: give us this; give us that!" Of course, they are demanding. What are *you* demanding? "We are demanding that the Arabs stop terror." The Arabs are laughing at you, saying, "Terror is part of our lives; what do you mean, *stop it*? Stop our *life*?"

Arie Lova Eliav   In the back of his mind, Arafat thought that maybe, with continuous fighting, the Israelis would someday, somehow, be vanquished and disappear.

The Second Intifada: Sharon's Provocative Visit to the Temple Mount

On September 20, 2000, Ariel Sharon, then in a leadership struggle with Prime Minister Benjamin Netanyahu for control of the Likud Party, visited the Temple Mount in Jerusalem, a site holy to both Jews and Muslims. The following day—whether due to Sharon's visit or according to a plan developed by Arafat after the failure of the Camp David meeting—the Second Intifada erupted, resulting in hundreds of deaths.

Raanan Gissin   He [Mr. Sharon] saw the gathering storm, the new forms of anti-Semitism, the incitement in the Arab world, the systematic effort to deny, not just the right of the Jews to go and pray on the Temple Mount, but to erase history—to deny that there ever *was* a Temple Mount. "That's Haram al Sharif," that's when it started, a thousand years after the Temple

Mount was the holiest place, accepted by over a billion people around the world, including Christians! And for the radical Islamic groups—not all of them—"Let's just erase it and start from here." It's a denial of Jewish history and, therefore, for him, this was a symbolic assertion: this is something that we, the Jews, must stand for. There are certain things that if we don't stand for them, we'll never have. We will be pushed out. And Jerusalem and the Temple Mount were to Sharon part and parcel of who we are, of the Jewish identity, and he wanted to assert that. He wanted symbolically to say, "Okay, you want peace, we'll *reach* peace. But there can't be peace without Jerusalem returning to the Jewish people." And, therefore, he was willing to take the risk.

Akiva Eldar   His visit to the Temple Mount in September 2000 was a crime. It happened less than a week after we had almost reached an agreement in Washington with Dennis Ross. The week before that, on a Saturday, there was a meeting at Barak's house—they came with their suitcases before they went to Washington—with Arafat and the Israeli and Palestinian negotiators. There was a very good atmosphere. Barak took Arafat out to the garden and told Arafat that he gave his people a full mandate to close the deal. They went to Washington and came back in order to receive instructions on how to lock down the Temple Mount issue. Then Sharon goes to the Temple Mount because he needs the attention of the public. This was the most important week in the recent history of Israel because the attorney general had decided not to indict Netanyahu. The polls were showing that Netanyahu was going to win the Likud primary. Sharon's cynical move cost us hundreds of casualties.

Raanan Gissin   Of course, he expected that there would be demonstrations and riots. But someone had to be the asserter. To give up what was clearly part of the Jewish identity, part of who we *are*, was unacceptable to him. There is a time when you have to stand up and hold the line.

Chapter 17

THE DEATH OR INCAPACITY OF POTENTIAL PEACEMAKERS

On the evening of Saturday, November 4, 1995, as Prime Minister Yitzhak Rabin turned from the podium after participating in a massive peace rally in Tel Aviv, shots rang out, hitting him. Hustled into his car and driven to Ichilov Hospital, he was rushed into surgery but died on the operating table.

In King Hussein's address during Prime Minister Rabin's funeral in Jerusalem, the Jordanian leader described Rabin as a "brother, colleague, and friend."

The Reverend Jerry Falwell I didn't know much about politics or the various parties in Israel. I just had a high regard for all the prime ministers because of their position. But I was impressed with Rabin. My last meeting with him was in the summer of 1995, a couple of months before he was assassinated. I have on my desk at home a plaque he gave me that has his name and the date engraved on it. I had no idea at the time that he'd be dead shortly thereafter. In the office that day, Duke [Westfield, an associate of Dr. Falwell's at Liberty University] and I were talking to one of Rabin's aides, and Duke commented, "You sure don't have a great deal of security here such as we encounter at the White House and other such places," and this aide said to Duke, "Well, a Jew would never kill a Jew, so we would never even think that way." That was the first thought that came into my mind when I heard the news.

Dan Pattir We didn't go to the rally. We thought we would see it on tel-

The blood-soaked paper bearing the words of the "Song of Peace," taken from the assassinated Prime Minister Yitzhak Rabin's jacket pocket following his assassination.

"There's no more of the old guard, no more of the 'old school' who were born with the State of Israel and fought, from the very first, for its existence."
—Raanan Gissin, speaking of the assassination of Prime Minister Rabin

evision. When it happened, there was no way to go to the hospital because the doors were locked. But [in the months leading up to November 4, 1995] we had a lot of youngsters coming to where the Rabins lived, two buildings across from here, to demonstrate [against the Oslo Agreement], all night, and we said to ourselves, Good will not come out of it. It was too violent, but I didn't believe that it would come to that end.

Raanan Gissin   There are only thirteen million Jews in the world, and maybe five million in the Land of Israel today, the largest Jewish community in the world. To lose two natural leaders within a decade is really a traumatic event. Leaders don't come off an assembly line of the military or the academic world. You have certain people who have these born characteristics, and historical circumstances have put them into such positions where these characteristics are brought out, and then you have a leader. It's

Jordan's then crown prince Hassan (right)—the brother of King Hussein, who as a young boy had witnessed the assassination of their grandfather King Abdullah—moves to embrace the slain prime minister's trusted, deeply grieving aide Eitan Haber, during a condolence visit on November 7, three days after the assassination.

once in a lifetime, and here *two* leaders are lost and, also, signifying that this is a generational change.

It does not incapacitate the society. That's the strength. Because it's a society that is constantly producing and rejuvenating itself, constantly producing new leaders, it can make the adjustment. It's similar to a ship that rides the high waves, with a strong bow and strong engines, but at the helm you don't have anyone to steer the ship. The ship will survive. It will bounce back and forth. But until you get someone at the helm who will steer a clear course, we're in for quite some rough seas and tumbling and rocking of the boat. And maybe some of us will even get seasick.

Eitan Haber   Arafat was not my cup of tea, of course—I hated him—but with Rabin he behaved totally differently than he did later. I can't tell you too much, but I have hundreds of pieces of evidence that because of Rabin's murder something happened. Somebody wrote yesterday [February 15, 2007] in *Ha'aretz* that the story of the Palestinians was murdered with Rabin.

Zalman Shoval   I know that this is sacrilege in Israel—and in America—but if Rabin hadn't been murdered, which was a terrible tragedy for everybody, not just for Rabin, he would not have been seen among the first rank of Israeli leaders. He was *not*. He was not terribly intelligent; he made wrong decisions. And he was not a very strong character—his bluster very often was in order to hide the fact that he himself was not sure what to do. We saw this on the eve of the Six-Day War. And after Oslo, he was once heard to say, after he had had one drink too many, "I had to adopt Oslo like someone adopts an illegitimate child."

What do you mean you *had* to? Ben-Gurion would never have said that! Begin never would have said that! You *make* history; you are not being *forced* by developments. Either you are for us or you are against us. He then went to Kissinger and said, "I'm not so sure; maybe I will continue with Oslo, maybe I won't continue." That was not a *leader*. But because of the tragedy, he has become a great leader, certainly to the Americans.

The Death of King Hussein

On February 7, 1999, the sixty-two-year-old Hussein, who had occupied the throne of the Hashemite Kingdom of Jordan for forty-six years, died in Amman. In 1994, the king had signed a peace treaty with Israel and had played a major role in attempting to bring peace between Israel and the Palestinians, becoming in that effort especially close to Prime Minister Rabin.

Dan Pattir   I saw him several times alone, and also with Rabin. I didn't go with Rabin to meet him, but once he was visiting Tel Aviv—he was staying not far from here, in the area where the Mossad is. Hussein was, apart from being nice and polite, a very, very, very slick operator. I realized more and more that he was indebted to Israel and, especially, to Rabin for guarding the life of the kingdom, the royal family itself.

In one of the last, greatest acts that he performed before he died, he had a special dinner party at the royal palace where he invited all the Mossad heads throughout the generations since 1948 who were still alive and also a contingent, a small group of youngsters, Mossadniks, who were liaison officers in the royal palace all the time, in case something happened and he needed our help. He insisted, "Don't forget to bring the youngsters, too." And he made a speech. He said, "I want to salute you people for protecting the kingdom and because I'm here myself." He was a man who knew how to do that.

The Death of Arafat

Yasser Arafat, the PLO's chairman for almost all of its bloody history, died in Paris on November 11, 2004. Brought back to the Territories from Tunis in 1993 as a result of the Oslo Accords, Arafat had been granted international status by virtue of his having become chairman of the Palestinian Authority. He had signed off on the massacre of Israeli Olympic athletes in Munich, the Entebbe hijacking, and many other terror attacks, including the slaying of U.S. diplomats and the murder of a wheelchair-bound American Jewish tourist aboard the *Achille Lauro*, and had initiated two Palestinian uprisings. Arafat was succeeded by his colleague Mahmoud Abbas, also known by his nom de guerre Abu Mazen. Abbas, who lacks Arafat's charisma and credentials of violence, was not able to hold together the Palestinian coalition. He lost control of the Palestinian Parliament to the "political wing" of Hamas, a violent terror organization committed to the destruction of Israel.

Akiva Eldar   I believed, and still believe, that Arafat was the only leader who had the charisma and the public support to make a deal with Israel. I knew him quite well. I once asked him why he and the Arab countries and the international community didn't take care of the refugees. He was not an easy man. I believe he wanted to reach an agreement with Israel. But the most important thing for him was Arab unity. He was a politician who was obsessed with power. He was also a religious person. He wouldn't give up the Temple Mount or Jerusalem. I knew his limits. I knew that he wouldn't make a deal that would not give the Palestinians full satisfaction in regard to the Palestinian National Council's 1988 declaration. This was for him the red line, which means the Temple Mount and 22 percent of Eretz Israel. He told me, "I'm not authorized to give up more."

Arie Lova Eliav   I met him many times. I thought he was too cunning. I had the feeling that deep in his heart or in the back of his mind, Arafat thought that maybe, one way or another, Israel would disappear. But outwardly—he got the Nobel Prize—he was all sweet when you met him. But he was not a man whom I would believe in.

Shabtai Shavit   Arafat, even though I hate to say it, was by far more charismatic than Abu Mazen. He was the founding father of the Palestinian people; there was no other man involved. Abu Mazen's image and the perception of his personality are that he's a softy kind of person. Arafat was much smarter than Abu Mazen, a very sneaky character.

"The difficulties started when Sharon became ill. For a year and some weeks now, he's been in this unbelievable condition."—Amira Dotan, speaking in the spring of 2007

In the last known photograph taken of Prime Minister Ariel Sharon, on January 4, 2006, only hours before he suffered a second stroke and lapsed into a long coma, he and Deputy Prime Minister Ehud Olmert confer during the ceremony at the Prime Minister's Bureau marking the sale of Bank Leumi shares to a private investment group.

The Incapacity of Israel's Warrior Prime Minister

In mid-December 2005, Israel's prime minister Ariel Sharon suffered a stroke. He had been gearing up for parliamentary elections scheduled for the following March that would establish his Kadima Party as a major force in Israeli politics. After a brief hospital stay, Sharon returned to work.

On the evening of January 4, 2006, Sharon suffered a second stroke, this one life-threatening and incapacitating, and lapsed into a coma. He was at his ranch in the Negev, more than one hour's drive from Jerusalem's Hadassah Medical Center,

When it became apparent that Sharon, despite a series of operations, was not likely to emerge from his coma, he was replaced by his deputy prime minister, Ehud Olmert, a career politician and a former mayor of Jerusalem.

Akiva Eldar   Sharon didn't imagine that he would get sick. It just happened that Olmert was there. Sharon gave Olmert the title of acting prime minister because he had given Olmert only a marginal portfolio, as minister of industry. He didn't take into consideration that something could happen to him and Olmert would find himself prime minister.

Raanan Gissin   I talked to Sharon a week before he had his stroke and slipped into the coma. We were discussing articles about him—he was about to win big in the elections. It would have changed the whole face of Israel. I'm not sure Hezbollah would have provoked [Israel with the kidnapping of Israeli soldiers during the summer of 2006] if Sharon had been in power and won that race. And, for the first time, there would have been the possibility of having that kind of political power, the possibility of putting the right people in the right places, enacting new social policies, and reforming government.

But even though he was going to win, people were always taking shots at him: Sharon, with all his maverick approach, won't be able to bring peace. So he said, "What do they write?" I said, "They're writing that you're not going to do it, but *you* know that; you never thought that you were going to bring peace." Then he asked me, impatiently, "So what do you think I can bring the people?" I said, "Not peace, but something much more important to a disillusioned people, to a people who are fighting day and night for their peace of mind." I said, "You're not giving them peace; you're giving them peace of mind; that's a much more important commodity that the Israeli people need, and the Jewish people need."

Chapter 18

A LEADERSHIP CRISIS AND NEW POLITICAL FACTS ON THE GROUND

Four recent Israeli prime ministers—Ehud Barak, Benjamin Netanyahu, Ariel Sharon, and Ehud Olmert—and an Israeli president, the late Ezer Weizman, faced corruption charges. More ominously, on January 24, 2007, Israel's president at the time, Moshe Katsav, faced indictment by Israel's attorney general on criminal charges, including rape, abuse of power, obstruction of justice, fraud, sexual harassment, and breach of trust. He was called upon to resign by Prime Minister Olmert, himself then facing an investigation concerning questionable actions connected with the privatization of Israeli banks in 2005.

Thus Israeli commentators, pundits, and intellectuals are wont to bemoan what they perceive to be a dearth of political leadership in a "post-Zionist" Jewish state—that there is no Begin and, for those who revered Ben-Gurion, no Ben-Gurion. Consequently, they wonder why such a dynamic nation is so bereft of visionaries.

Moshe Sharon   It's not that we don't have leadership; we've got the *wrong leadership*. That is because there is a goal that cannot be achieved, and the goal is called "peace." There is no such thing. Peace exists in the storage places of the Middle East; there is no such event. What we have today is what I call "accidental leadership." It never happened in history before that I remember—maybe in European history—that a *totally* accidental leadership was created in Israel. All of these people who are now leading the State of Israel—Olmert, Tzipi Livni—came because somebody had a stroke! And nobody would elect them, *nobody*. If they were to stand for election like in America, *forget about it*! Unfortunately, we don't have the American system here. With the American system, none of the Knesset members would be in the Knesset. Who would elect them? Some of them don't even know how to speak Hebrew; they haven't got the intellectual ability even to form a sentence. They are in the Knesset because of things that happened in the political life of Israel. It's like running a shtetl or a grocery shop—that's what we have today. That's why we are under attack in war.

Raanan Gissin   That does not mean that in the future we won't be able to develop leaders. This is a country, and a movement, that is based on excellence and on competing for leadership and people taking the lead. But right now, there's a gap, and definitely the lack of born leaders requires some interim arrangements, maybe good managers, for a change, maybe a collective leadership that is based on allocation of labor between the right people at the right spot so they can together get over this hump, over this tsunami wave that we're facing now, and then grow new leaders that can come out of the high-tech industry, the business community, the lower echelons of the military, places where we see excellence.

Right now, there's an imbalance in the society, not a lack of leaders. We have them, but they're in different locations. We find them in the Israeli economy, which has now been latched to the global economy. Now the question is: how do you lure them to go into politics or to use their talents in an area that today has a scarcity of leaders? And for that, you have to create incentives. One incentive would be reforms in the political system. There's no doubt that after Lebanon, there's a general feeling in Israel that you need to clean the stables and make certain that new blood can be injected into the system and new people can come forth and that you have the willingness to carry out this difficult mission.

Is There Potential for a New Class of Leadership?

Moshe Sharon   You never know. Look, everybody has got hope, which is placed on Netanyahu: he's intelligent; he's a leader; he's clever; he's educated; he knows what goes on; he has got an excellent record. But the leftist press does not like people like that; they want their *own* people, whom they can move. The press in the rest of the world is very strong, but here it's absolutely ruling the country. I never understood *why*, because nobody believes them—when there is a poll, you see that nobody believes the press—but that's the situation, and they are still moving the country. They are establishing kings in this country. They are enthroning leaders.

Kadima's Surprising Knesset Showing

Amira Dotan   I didn't decide [to enter the political arena]; I got a call from Sharon, who said, "Amira, I want you to go with the Kadima Party." At the beginning, I really thought it was a joke, that somebody was imitating being Sharon. Then he called again and said, "Amira! I want you in!" I said, "But I'm not bringing Ethiopians and Russians and not the religious." He said, "I want you in because of who *you* are." So I said, "First of all, it's a kind of a blessing, or saying good things about yourself while you are still alive, not when you are dead and everybody praises you." That was very good. And then, I couldn't say no to Sharon, who had promoted me and given me so much of what I know now.

But then I wondered: what should I do? Should I continue? Should I go home? And when Ehud Olmert, whom I didn't know at all, put me as the twenty-eighth number of Kadima, my family was very happy because they said, "Although everybody speaks of forty, it will be twenty-five. You've done your share; you'll say yes, you'll continue your life; everything will be happy." And twenty-eight was in!

In another surprising development, Rafi Eitan's Pensioners' Party won seven seats in the Knesset.

Rafi Eitan   There were a few reasons: first, a peace party or other parties that represent the aged tried to go to elections before and failed. Now, *our* success was a combination of a few factors. One of them is that Arik Sharon, who founded Kadima, was sick and was out of running his party and that created a vacuum. That, no doubt, is the major factor. Now, in this vacuum a few parties competed—Uzi Dayan's party or the Greens Party or what is left of Shinui ["Change"]—and also *our* party. Here you must add my personality—sorry that I'm proud—but many of my friends told me, "We were arguing among ourselves, whether to vote for you or for Uzi Dayan. And when we saw you on television and we saw Uzi Dayan, we started going toward *you*. And then, in the last two weeks, we were sure that you were going to cross the threshold, so we decided to vote for *you*." I told them, "Look, I'm not a politician; I'm going to do something for the elderly."

Amira Dotan   On the whole, *this* Knesset—I don't know about any other Knesset—contains very interesting, wonderful people. I have wonderful friendships that I didn't imagine—a friendship with a very ultra-right-wing professor, Ari Eldad, who is so to the right. We have nothing in common when it comes to politics and Palestinians and Islam, but we have so many things in common when in comes to the inner, complex Israeli society, and, of course, there are the Arabs and the ultra-*Haredim* whom I became very friendly with. So it's really very, very interesting. Most of the Knesset members now have real class, and the experienced ones have real intelligence.

I love what I'm doing. It's very challenging, very interesting. It's not easy at all, and we really give up a lot of our personal lives, but the challenge is really enormous. I am trying to do things as macro as I can and to continue this heritage that I feel. Sharon asked me to be there, and when I contribute, it's contributing to the macro. I hope I will be successful.

I am very happy that I made the decision. And I'm happy to continue to contribute; my generation was born some months before the country, and part of what we understand is that the country is ours, so this contribution continues and continues. And being sixty—I'll be sixty before my country— is a good feeling.

A Very Troubling Event in the Palestinian Territories: The Election of Hamas

Akiva Eldar   There were two factors. One was corruption. There is also corruption in Israel, and the left was willing to give a blind eye to Sharon's corruption because of the disengagement. If Abu Mazen could deliver the end of occupation—forget about peace—he would be forgiven Fatah's corruption. It became important because he couldn't deliver, because Sharon preferred to do it unilaterally. Once Oslo was over, Fatah had nothing to offer.

Uri Avneri   Hamas has to be brought into the fold; Hamas has to be socialized. Hamas is ready for this peace that we are talking about. And some of them are very nice people. Unfortunately, all of them are in prison. They are very normal people, and they are quite open, and you can really talk with them. I think it's a cardinal mistake for Israel—not to mention the United States—not to talk with these people.

Akiva Eldar   Give Hamas enough time, and they will become as corrupt as Fatah.

PART FIVE

Can Israel Survive?

Chapter 19

IS PEACE WITH ISRAEL'S
ENEMIES REALLY POSSIBLE?

Moshe Sharon   The Arabs will wait hundreds of years, but they want to see the State of Israel destroyed. There is no peace for the Jews; it doesn't exist in the Islamic thinking—there's no peace for the non-Muslim. So if you continue building your policy on a basis that does not exist, the whole edifice that you are trying to build collapses. And it has been collapsing for the last sixty years, nonstop: Jews have been speaking about peace, and the Arabs have been speaking about how to finish the Jews.

The Arabs know what they want, and the Jews are living in a dream world. When you live in a dream world, you have to wake up, and the Jews still haven't woken up, so our leaders are leading us in dreams and the dreams are called "peace." There is no such thing; forget about *this* word. You can talk about many things—how to strengthen our state; how to create defensible borders—but the Arabs are not going to do anything that, in *any* way, is going to help the State of Israel strengthen itself or establish itself as a defensible country. They'll do everything possible to make the country as nondefensible as possible. And for *this* we've got to sign a piece of paper? Words are very cheap in the Middle East. As the Arab saying goes: "On words you don't pay customs."

Akiva Eldar   Moshe Dayan said, "For me, Sharm el-Sheikh without peace is more important than peace without Sharm el-Sheikh." On the other hand, he opened his eyes after Sadat's visit to Jerusalem. Dayan visited Vietnam during the war and told [U.S. secretary of defense Robert] McNamara,

"There is no way you Americans can win this war." But he [Dayan] couldn't realize that we could not win the war against the Palestinians.

———————

At the core of any negotiation for the establishment of a Palestinian state are three central issues: Israel's borders; the right of return for Palestinians; and the status of Jerusalem, which most Jews—and their Christian supporters—view as the eternal, *undivided* capital of the Jewish state.

The Reverend Jerry Falwell   My first trip was after 1967. It was really an eye-opener. I had somehow thought Israel was much larger, and the smallness of the country and the vulnerability of Israel impressed me. I really wouldn't have called myself a scholar at that time, but I felt that Israel would never again fall into the hands of anyone because I considered what had happened in 1948 and then in 1967 such a miracle. And while they have had severe and very critical times since then, I have never believed for a moment that Jerusalem would ever be divided or segmented off or any portion given away. I don't think I've ever met in Israel—I'm sure there are some there—a significant Israeli who would negotiate on Jerusalem.

Assertions about the Validity of the Palestinian Claim to Be a People

Not only right-wing Israeli leaders, but staunch Laborites, including Golda Meir, have maintained that there is no such thing as a "Palestinian people."

Yossi Ben-Aharon   It's a fact: there *is* no such thing as a Palestinian people. I know from my studies and from our experience. In the Arab society around us, there are several levels of identification other than Arab, as an individual identifying himself and his background. First, he belongs to the root of Islam because he is Muslim; second, his tribal affinity—they are all tribal, some are very close to it and some looser, based on family; and third is the immediate family. These are his loyalties; there is no such thing as "state." This is very recent.

In speeches Arab representatives gave during discussions on Palestine in 1946 and '47, before the Palestinian Resolution, the Arabs—the Iraqis, the Egyptians—said, "There is no such thing as a 'Palestinian'; this is a Crusader term, a foreign term. We are all *Arabs*. This is part of the Arab nation, and what you call 'Palestine' is Southern Syria, part of Greater Syria, part of the Arab nation. And this was promised to us by the British . . . and it is now being stolen by you"—the French, the British, the Americans—"you want to steal part of our homeland and call it Palestine." And, of course, this is true: the term "Palestine" never existed in Arab literature or in their history books. It was made up, and later they used to say—although not too loud—that they invented the terms "Palestinian people" and "Palestinian state" as a counter to the peoplehood and the nationhood of the Jewish people.

Rav Shalom Gold I gave a speech in Toronto in January 1994, five months after Oslo, and I said that the mistake that was made was our modern belief that all problems are open to solutions. There are problems that *cannot* be solved; there is no solution to the Arab problem. We are the ones who, having recognized such a thing as the "Palestinian people," have made a tragic, tragic mistake. There is no such thing as a Palestinian people. I don't understand it. There are so many ethnic minorities all over the world that don't have countries, and these people [the Palestinians] have twenty-one countries to go to. Who stops them from establishing a beautiful society in Gaza? A two-state solution means the destruction of Israel. There is no solution, and we have to stand our ground.

Is the Road Map Kaput?

Matityahu "Mati" Drobles No, it's not kaput at all. You can't take it back—it's closed; Palestine is a fact you cannot stop. You can't be alone. There is no justice all over the world. There are no borders—there are no distances—everything is global, open, *huge*.

Shlomo Ariav I agree with Ehud [Olmert] that we have to find a solution with all those settlements that are important for us, with a Jewish majority. We have to give all the others away. Not give them away for free but for land exchanges; there are some sections we are unable control. We have to do what is possible. Will we be able to do it? I don't know. But we will try. We still have to have that dream with us. But there are some superpowers involved.

Moshe Sharon The Green Line became a sacred concept. Now, if Israel is stupid enough to retreat to the cease-fire line, the next demand is going to be—and it's going to be an absolutely legal, acceptable demand—that Israel should retreat to the lines that were delineated in the decision of

November 1947 by the United Nations. That's very natural because that's the only border that has been accepted internationally, not the Green Line.

Sharon's Withdrawal from Gaza

Matityahu "Mati" Drobles   I wonder if Sharon said, "Okay; if Begin withdrew [from the Sinai], why should I not withdraw from Gaza?" But you have to understand that what Begin did fit that time.

Rav Shalom Gold   [Dan] Halutz became the chief of staff because Sharon knew he was ready to implement the disengagement. The president [Moshe Katsav] could have stopped it. Then one of the people behind the disengagement, Haim Ramon, had to step down from the cabinet due to a scandal. Politically, Ehud Olmert and Shimon Peres are walking dead men. They are realizing it quickly. The process of healing has to begin with the removal of all the pus, getting rid of all the rot. There is a process of destruction that is laying the groundwork for rebuilding.

"The disengagement was a criminal one toward the settlers. If I were a settler, I would at least hope that if I give away my house, it will be for peace."
—Akiva Eldar

On August 18, 2005, residents of Kfar Darom, in the Gush Katif area, sit atop a wire barricade on their synagogue roof as security forces attempting to evacuate them wait in the container at left to storm the building.

The positive process has begun, and we may have Gush Katif [an area of Jewish settlement in Gaza]—remember that Gush Katif was clearly a blow calculated against the religious Zionist community—to thank for everything that is happening. That brought out the illness of our society. If you make a list, you see that everybody who was involved in the disengagement is getting it in the neck. Usually, you have to wait a lifetime, or ten lifetimes, until justice is done. In my lifetime, never, never before have things happened so quickly.

Zalman Shoval   Sharon's unilateral withdrawal misfired very badly, from many points of view, and probably wasn't well thought out. But at least many people who supported it at the time supported it because they said, "We are never going to have a real peace partner on the Palestinian side, a partner who is willing to compromise—not to mention those who don't want anything with regard to Israel. Therefore, we should try, with American help, to set our own borders."

But it didn't work out like that because if you look at the history of Zionism, in the past we didn't wait for the Arabs or the Palestinians to agree with us; *we* decided; *we* created facts. That was the great attitude of Ben-Gurion. But Sharon didn't have the foresight of Ben-Gurion. He didn't take into account that there might be some negative results of that.

But after what happened to Hamas [in the elections of January 2006], the feeling that we *have* to do this has disappeared, which does not mean that there is today a widespread feeling that we know what we *do* have to do. And that's worrisome. No leadership. No direction. No agenda, as Olmert himself said. And that is Israel's greatest problem right now.

Akiva Eldar   Sharon was a man of war. I don't think he wanted peace. He wanted disengagement from Gaza to stop Bush, to stop the Road Map, and to make sure that we will stay in the West Bank. The disengagement was a huge mistake.

Can Israel Really Accept a Palestinian State?

Matityahu "Mati" Drobles   It's *very, very* hard; there's a bottle [a reference to the genie's being out of the bottle] and the bottle is open. The Arabs are surrounding us. There are borders—red lines—and Jerusalem is a red line, of course. No army will take it from us. We should not be afraid. We want peace and everything that belongs to us.

But you can't have everything. We don't want people to be killed for us. We want one fact to be forever—there is no other nation in the world that has suffered so much as the Jewish people. We are asking, "Let us, the Jewish people, live quietly in our own land, the *Promised Land*."

We can't have war all the time; we can't see mothers sacrificing their sons in the war. And, of course, all the political government, the officials, don't care. But one soldier is the whole nation. I believe in peace, now or later. But for peace, one side is not enough. For war, we need one; for peace, we need *two*. We only have one. This is the best time for the Arabs because we know the Jewish mind—there is no other mind like the Jewish mind—and we can give it to them if they want to have peace with us. I believe that the time will come. I wish it to be in *my* time.

Arie Lova Eliav   Israelis must [accept a Palestinian state] because the alternative is future annihilation, continuous bloodshed, and in the end, God knows, there will be no winners if things go on the way they do. I can say one thing, that during the last decade or two, things have been coming closer to my point of view. Many, many more people in Israel now understand that a two-state solution is the only way to go. When I started, people like me were a small minority. When I left Labor and established Sheli, we were two members in the Knesset. Now, 70 percent say that the majority of the Territories should be returned to the Palestinians, with conditions of security. It's a process; there's a long way to go. But we have made good progress. On the other side, you have many extremists among the Palestinians who will not abide by it.

Yehiel Kadishai   Jabotinsky, in his article "The Iron Wall," written in 1923, begins with this:

> Some people say that I am the greatest enemy of the Arabs and I want here to declare: I have nothing against the Arabs. I treat the Arabs, and I think of them, exactly like I think of any other nation, and I love all the nations, and if they are friendly to me, I am friendly to them. And if they hate me, I hate them. And if they try to do me harm—to harm us— I won't be quiet. I'll hate them. And I'm not going to take away any rights from them. But if they disturb us from doing what we have to do here, we will disturb them from existing, as well. And in order to fulfill our aims here—a Jewish State in Eretz Israel on both sides of the Jordan—and if they will disturb us, we won't let them disturb us. And in order to be able to prevent them from disturbing us, we have to build

an Iron Wall. And it's not true that there won't be peace between us and them. Peace will start being established when they come to the conclusion that they are not able to get rid of us. Only then will they start to talk to us and we will start to talk to them about peace.

"The Iron Wall" is still as valid today as it was in 1923—the year I was born! And he was attacked for this article, by *the Jews*: how dare you speak about an "Iron Wall" near the Jordan? It is a stupid thing to say! We need weapons! And what he said in this article was "not ethical." So he wrote another article, "On the Ethics of the Iron Wall." And then he was attacked on *that* article!

Now, many people think about the "Iron Wall." Without the "Iron Wall," they wouldn't exist at all. And if you want to exist, you exist thanks to the "Iron Wall." Without *koach*, strength, we don't exist.

———————

The first time that Mr. Begin met with evangelical Christian leaders in Washington, before he went to see President Carter, one of the ministers there asked Mr. Begin at the very end of the conversation, "What can you *do*?" Responding, he said, "*Rak koach! Rak koach!*" A reporter from the *Washington Post* was there, and that's how she ended the story—"Mr. Begin told the Christians: "Only strength; only strength!"

Is Support for Israel Waning?

The Reverend Jerry Falwell   I believe that with the general public, it's waning. The media, especially CNN—just as they've done Mr. Bush in, almost in unison—have done Israel in. But there are enough people in this country who are politically committed to Israel, who may not be religious people, and enough evangelicals in this country who will stand by Israel, come hell or high water, that the U.S. government can never withdraw its support of Israel.

But while nobody has broken his back in recent times to help Israel much because of an unwillingness to stand up to the Islamic force of the twenty-first century, I believe that we've got to awaken: the war isn't something that's *going* to start; it's *already* started. But the press is frightened to death of Islam. And America is letting things happen here without retribution. America is in real trouble, and it could be a Hundred Years' War.

Ronald Godwin   I'm actually a bit concerned that young people don't have the same interest in Israel as the past generation. This secularization of America has bearing on this issue. The average evangelical Christian young person is not hearing from the pulpit and from their religious influencers the same level of enthusiastic support for Israel and its right to face the future in a safe haven. And it's not quite grounded as stridently and as strongly as it was even a generation ago in our theology. It's kind of, "Well, we're pro-Israel," and they let it go at that. It's almost a groundless positive feeling. It's not a huge erosion, but there is an erosion in that level of support. If you quiz the average Liberty University student, they will be very positive toward Israel. But if you ask them to defend *why* they are, there would be a lot of generalist babble. The religion majors would be better grounded.

It's the same thing with the pastors; there's a deficit there. That kind of teaching has fallen into neglect. In certain circles, there's a renewed enthusiasm and reminding of where we're at. The basic fear that many, many Jews have is that the only reason evangelicals were ever friendly was to warm up to Jewish people in order to evangelize them. But that's the furthest thing from the truth, and people who know their Protestant theology understand that we don't have a choice, that we have clear Old Testament teaching, as well as New Testament teaching, and that that's an obligation we have, period, end of story.

The Reverend Jerry Falwell   I believe in the premillennial, pretribulational Coming of Christ for all of His church, but I believe that statement in the Gospels where "A nation shall be saved in a day," that in the revelation about what is going to be happening during the tribulation period, I believe that God will step in ultimately for the salvation of Israel herself, and that those who maybe denied the crucifixion, burial, and resurrection of Christ will declare him to be Lord, and I believe that they will in fact inherit the new heavens and the new earth, but I believe also in the vow in the new reign of Christ, that Our Lord will settle the throne of David in Jerusalem for a thousand years. And that man will beat their swords into pruning hooks.

I believe that Perfect Peace will then come and that the Throne of David—that Jesus, a descendant of David, will be the Throne of the World for a thousand years and then new heavens and new earth and the new Jerusalem coming down from God in heaven. I don't think that God has ever written the Jews off and that Romans 9, 10, and 11 are God's reassurance that although hard times over the millennium will be experienced by all, that God will keep His word to Abraham and to David and that it's an Everlasting Kingdom.

Are the Settlements an Impediment to Peace?

Bobby Brown   The best and most recent example would be Gaza, when they withdrew the settlements—in fact, any time that we have given up territory, it has never led to peace—and the corps of people at Sderot have become the front line. If you take the communities in the Northern Gaza Strip, which had no Arabs—it was a no-man's-land—by withdrawing them and giving that to the Gaza Strip, it allowed terrorists to get three kilometers closer to Israel and, for the first time, hit Ashkelon.

The problem is not territorial in nature. The problem is that for a hundred and some odd years already, we have been the targets of people who say, "We want to throw you into the sea." They say, "The Crusaders lasted two hundred years, and then we threw them out, and we'll throw you out too." So I'm not sure that constant territorial shrinkage will make peace.

And today, if you go around the areas of Judea and Samaria, the areas where you have Jewish communities, there is probably less chance of having problems with local Arabs than there is in areas where Jews *don't* live. There are going to be Arabs living in Israel, and we have to somehow come to grips with that and learn how to live with them. There are going to be Jews living there. Jews are not the big "devils" that Arabs, by and large, *think* they are, and the Arabs are not the big "devils" that Jews think they are. They are human beings, people who want the best for their families.

In our area, there have been cases where outside leaders of Hamas or Fatah would come to the locals and say, "You're not pulling your weight. You people living today have to throw rocks." And I think that if they allowed Jews and Arabs to live together, that would be a step toward peace. I still hope that day will come. But withdrawal is not the answer. They withdrew the Israeli army from Southern Lebanon, and *they* have no peace.

Matityahu "Mati" Drobles   Judea and Samaria are settled by more than three hundred thousand Jews today, and whatever happens, there will be no leaving there. In Yamit, there were only seven thousand people. I hope that these three hundred thousand will become millions—I hope for *two million*! I want *five million*! Increasing and increasing. I will not be silent until all the Jews are living here in Israel.

Joshua Matza We believed that we could control Judea and Samaria. Without believing, we couldn't have reached what we have today. But the day comes when you see the facts, and the facts are the demographic situation. And from this demographic situation, I come full circle from Germany, the Holocaust. I know that we have to compromise because of the demographic situation, but that doesn't mean that we were wrong thirty or forty years ago. We achieved things that will never change—Ma'aleh Adumim and Ariel and other places where we know that we will stay forever. We have to find a solution with the Palestinians, so we will have disengagement. Maybe from there we will find some solution with them. Of course, we have to have a solution. With the Six-Day War—a war of defense—we gained our Territories, and now we are losing them for the *sake of peace*.

Can Israel Really Solve Its Difficulties with Hostile Arab Neighbors?

Simcha Waisman The moment that the big Arab oil companies stop giving money to the terrorist groups—Fatah, al-Qaeda, and others in the Middle East—they will be forced to sit down at the table and negotiate peace. Unless you stop the money, any time that one of those countries feels motivated, it will draw a couple of million dollars into one of the groups to stir a problem in Israel. Unless you stop the money from getting into the hands of the terrorists, you are not going to have any peace. I don't care *who* you are; the Middle East is controlled by what I call "Black Gold." And the people who have it—Iran, Kuwait, Saudi Arabia—are the biggest guns; they are the ones who are pulling [the strings], like a marionette show. But if you take the money out, what are they going to do? How are they are going to eat if they don't have the money?

Malcolm Hoenlein Do people get up in the morning and ask, "Is Israel still there?" Because there's no rational explanation for Israel surviving the way it has. What I think that many people have come to appreciate as a result of 9/11—as Mrs. Bush said in an interview with Barbara Walters when she [Walters] was getting very critical about Israel, "After 9/11, we understand what the Israelis have been going through." Israel has been the front line of the war on terrorism for fifty years, but without a fifty-nation coalition, and with not one Saddam Hussein but *twenty* Saddam Husseins.

Chapter 20

CHALLENGES TO ISRAEL
IN THE FIRST DECADE OF
THE TWENTY-FIRST CENTURY

Among the Jewish state's enduring challenges are grappling with a generally hostile media, both within the Jewish state and in the Diaspora; mounting an effective *hasbara* [information] campaign to counter negative reporting and to attract investors and tourism; stemming Israel's "brain drain"; promoting aliyah; and confronting Post-Zionism.

Hasbara

Ronald Godwin   I've always thought that Israelis and the government and their spokespeople have done an almost pathetic job of trying to understand how to find resonance with evangelicals. As poor as the grades are that I give to the current crop of evangelical Protestant ministers, I give an even poorer grade to the current crop of Israeli government officials and spokespeople and those who would call themselves representatives of the government. People need to understand how to reach their market—if you're selling widgets, you figure out how to sell them to the market that you're trying to sell them to. I'm reminded of that verse from Proverbs that says, "He who would have friends must show himself friendly." And you have to do that intelligently. I would say that Israel's representatives could do a far better job.

If I were an Israeli government official, I would reach out to Christians. What was that guy behind the desk at the Hilton Hotel trying to connote when he said to me, "Welcome home"? He knew that I belong to this evangelical group of church members who showed up at his hotel's door, so he was saying to me, a Christian, "Welcome home"—that this is your land as well as my land, and your Savior lived and died here, and you are welcomed here. Israel could go a long way toward reminding Christians of how important the Holy Land is to their theology and their history, and they're welcome in Israel as fellow sharers of a many times common history.

Abraham Foxman   Everybody agrees: *hasbara* could always be better. Certainly, to have spokesmen who don't speak the [English] language is unpardonable; it's not effective or responsible. It's also the world and its standards, values, animosity, oil, politics—all these things.

The Media

Joseph Hochstein   Israel receives media attention far out of proportion to its importance. It's odd, and you need to be outside Israel to understand how odd it is. Israelis tend to shrug off stuff like that. There has been this doctrine that it doesn't matter what the world says; it's what the Jews do. We all live in this little bubble—intellectually, militarily, in all kinds of ways.

Moshe Sharon   *Ha'aretz* represents a line that, no matter how you put it, is anti–State of Israel: the Arabs are always right and the Jews are always wrong, *full stop*. So if you understand that this is the line—like the line of Tom Friedman in the *New York Times*—you can read *Ha'aretz* in a different way. But there are many people in this country who think in another way; I am not alone. These are first-class intellectuals, great people, who know what's going on, and there are many, many others who read the Arab world well.

Stemming the Brain Drain of Israelis
Leaving for Greener Pastures

Joshua Matza   I ask myself, God! What are they doing here [in the United States] and not in Israel? We need them here now. But at the same time, the entire world is like a global village—you can come and go—so I cannot prevent Israelis from coming here for a few years, to make money.

Abraham Foxman   Now you have anywhere from a half million to a million Israelis in the United States. I have no problem with that, especially since they're now becoming involved in an emerging Jewish community, and they're sending their kids to Israel.

How Can Israel Promote Aliyah?

Joshua Matza   By being a better, more attractive Israel and being moral; we are not a moral state today. That is so in many states. But we are *Jews*; we want to be special, not like all the rest of the world. For example, after the Six-Day War, Jews from all over the world settled in Israel because they felt that the Jewish world was now in power, and with high morals and ideology.

Abraham Foxman   Israelis never understood that aliyah is not something that you can preach. There is aliyah today from the United States—the overwhelming majority of that aliyah comes from the Orthodox community. Why? Not because the prime minister or the aliyah emissary comes and gives a speech or they give you benefits; the aliyah comes from the fact that it's a Jewish tradition and you try to fulfill as many of the 613 commandments as you can. Many of the commandments you can fulfill only in Israel. For those who live a stable, positive Jewish life, to live in a majority Jewish culture is the most wonderful fulfillment of wanting to be a Jew. They want their kids to grow up without complexes, without worrying whether you wear a *kipah* [skullcap] or you don't wear a *kipah*. For secular Jews, the decision to go on aliyah is based on two things: comfort level and economics. So who comes? People who can afford second homes come.

What about Israelis Who Immigrate to Germany?

Malcolm Hoenlein   For *Israelis* to go there is only greed and avarice. But, on the other hand, I don't know that those of us who are outside have the right to criticize because the truth is that *we* should be there [in Israel]. And we find all sorts of justifications, because of the "good work" we do. But it's not an answer.

Joshua Matza   There is only one word: disgusting! More than that, regarding Poland; the Polish are not less [anti-Semitic] than the Germans. They were always anti-Semites, and they [Israelis] are going there! I don't have any explanation. We are struggling to let Jews from all over the world have a place when they need it. This is my message; this is why I came to the United States at the behest of Sharon. I wouldn't have taken this job just to come and raise money. I'm here as a Zionist, and in a few years I'll be coming back to Israel.

How Can Israel Attract More Visitors
with a View to Aliyah?

Abraham Foxman   About 6 percent of American Jews have visited Israel. Let's look at another statistic: what percentage of American Jews travel abroad? We make certain assumptions. I've probably been in Israel a hundred times by now, so I skew that statistic, whatever it is. Israel is not that important in their lives. A lot of it [interest in visiting Israel] comes from education, background, family, to an extent, there's a part of the tradition, whether it's the concept of aliyah or Zionism. If you don't implant it in a child, if it's not part of the educational environment, why *should* they go? You can go to Paris or Rome. If it's part of the essence of your Jewishness, that's it.

Akiva Eldar   If you ask Israelis how many American Jews have visited Israel, they wouldn't know. If you ask the average Israeli about the United States, he will say, "Military power; Bush; McDonald's; *Seinfeld*," maybe "Hollywood." The Diaspora would come in number ten. What is important for many Israelis is Jewish power. They appreciate Jewish leverage; they appreciate power. They admire people who have access to the White House, not because they are Jewish but because of the fact that they can pick up the phone and talk to the president—that they can influence Congress to vote in favor of Israel.

Should Visiting Israel Play a Larger Role
in Jewish Education?

Abraham Foxman   It's so expensive. When I went the first time, I couldn't afford to go—my parents didn't have the money to send me—and I went on a Jewish National Fund [JNF] scholarship. I felt then that it was not fair because the kids whom I was in school with and was in the movement with and had been to camp with, the Zionist kids to whom this would be so wonderful, couldn't afford to go. And if I had not had a scholarship from the JNF, I wouldn't have gone, either. On my second and third trips I became a counselor, which enabled me to go.

It's a very expensive trip—the hotels, whether they're full or empty, are very expensive. If you're talking about taking a family, it's very expensive. And then, too frequently, I get phone calls: "Is it *safe*? I'm taking a bar mitzvah trip; should I go? Is this a good time to go?" If you ask the State Department, they'll tell you, "Don't go," because the American government's responsibility starts with its own employees. We've had discussions with them, and we would say, "What are you doing?" And they would say, "Look, we set that standard for our employees, for whom we are responsible. If we set a different standard for everybody else, we would be accused of caring more for our employees than we care for the general public." So it is almost a catch-22. But it *is* a war zone most of the time.

There's also another issue, which we're trying to change by legislation, and that's insurance. When people find out that they can't get insurance coverage, not only for the trip, but they can't get life insurance if they've got a trip planned to Israel in the next six months, which is discriminatory and all that, all of it is cumulative. It's not a question of being afraid or not; if your government says it is not safe for you, as an American, to go, it's enough to say to a lot of people: I haven't got time.

We've sometimes challenged the Jewish community, as a sign of solidarity, to go to Israel, only because people aren't going. But we never said that part of your fulfillment as a Jew is to have the Israel experience. We're doing it more now than we did for forty years. Pilgrims went, families went, but you didn't have the synagogue missions that you have today. We're talking about forty years *plus* where it was not an issue. And today, it is part of being *Jewish*; if you are actively involved in the synagogue or an organization, it's called a "mission" and you go; there are more bar mitzvah tours; there are more family tours today than ever before.

Would "Branding" Israel Help?

Abraham Foxman   "We have to brand Israel." What does that mean? Are we selling Kellogg's? Certainly, in the United States, with all the criticism, the support for Israel continues to be overwhelming, bipartisan, in all the polls—whether they're three-to-one or four-to-one—and in the Congress. And in the fifties, it wasn't always there; we had to work for it. Israel has to work for it; we have to work for it.

Where's the failure? Sure, we always want it better. We don't want to see bad stories. But Israel can't live its life in terms of how the world is going to see it; Israel has got to live its life how it can live its life and make its decisions based on reality. The world doesn't like a winner; they like underdogs. Well, if I had my choice, I'd rather get a bad editorial and be alive than have a good editorial and be dead. Everybody becomes a maven: it's easier to be tougher here or it's easier to be nicer here. Israel has different realities to make its decisions. There's no question; it can always be better. But if it gets too good and too slick, it can also become counterproductive.

Combatting the Phenomenon of Post-Zionism

There has always been intellectual ferment in Israel, personified by the utterances of the left-leaning academic elite and literary personalities. Of late, the concept of "Post-Zionism," the moving away from the ideals of the founders and citizens of the Jewish state, enunciated by the so-called Shenkin Street intellectuals, appears to have gained currency.

Malcolm Hoenlein   The impact is there; I don't think it's a projection into the future. But we should never dismiss what happens among academics and intellectual elites. It doesn't happen overnight. It's an infection and then it spreads to campuses, to young people, and then it spreads to the masses. And it becomes fashionable because it's easier to say: we want to be like everybody else; we're not different. To talk about "Post-Zionism" doesn't mean Israel should always be a foundling state. It grows up. But we should move it into the next stage where commitment to Israel and to the ideals of Israel and to what Israel represents as a *Jewish* state should be more than the fact that you don't teach Tanakh [the collective Hebrew term for the Old Testament] in the schools—it doesn't mean they have to make it *religious*; we're talking about making them *Jews*. You know that the biggest socialists could debate Tanakh and Hummash [the first five books of the Bible] better than anybody. At least, they knew what they didn't believe in. But these kids don't even *know* what they don't believe in, let alone knowing about Israel, being able to make the case that by every criticism that you have to go back now and the revisionist history of Israel that they try to impose. And I find it very disturbing. I *do* think it has an impact.

Among the Post-Zionists' agenda items is doing away with the Law of Return, legislation enacted by the Knesset on July 5, 1950, allowing any Jew or other individual with Jewish parents or grandparents to settle in Israel and gain citizenship. Of late, the Palestinian leadership has been promoting the concept of return for Arabs who fled Israel on the establishment of the Jewish state.

Moshe Sharon   Those people who want to destroy the State of Israel want to see a complete breach between the Jews outside Israel and the Jews of Israel, first, by doing away with the Law of Return. And once you do away with the Law of Return, *anybody* can come into this country. The second stage is to establish a law of return for the Arabs because they were here before. That's an elegant way to destroy Israel. As one of my colleagues in Europe said, "Israel has to be abolished, but it's not nice to do it with blood and fire; the best thing is to abolish the Law of Return and to let the Palestinians come back, and then there will be elections, and the State of Israel will be abolished *elegantly*." The world is looking for an *elegant* way to destroy the State of Israel.

Joseph Hochstein   Some people believe that the Zionist movement achieved its success by creating the state, and, therefore, we've passed beyond the Zionist period. The notion that we are in some kind of Post-Zionist era is not a mainstream attitude. In the politics of the country, people talk about the Zionist parties and the other parties, meaning the Haredi and the Arab parties.

Bobby Brown   I don't think they're talking to themselves. There is an extreme of people in Judaism who want to make it in the world, to be accepted by the world, and who want to shed their Jewish image. We've been under attack for so long in this world that people are saying, "Like me; I'll be different," or, "*Like* me; I'm not *that* kind of Jew." And remember, most Jews came here because they had no other place to go to escape anti-Semitism.

On the other hand, I believe that there's a wide marketplace of ideology and beliefs. In the beginning, the Labor government controlled the news media, controlled the amount of information. To a large extent, they [the Post-Zionists] do cause damage, and our educational system is to blame.

Arie Lova Eliav   It's not the kind of Zionism I believe in. Essentially, the Zionist movement *won*—not many ideological movements in the world have won. *Zionism* won. That brought about the future Jewish State. We should guard this idea of Zionism and adapt it to conditions. I think that Post-Zionism is a fad, and a very shallow kind of fad. But to adapt Zionist ideas to the present conditions is our task. Zionism could, and should, fulfill all its goals in the pre-'67 borders, in Israel *proper*. Settling Jews in the Territories and Gaza was a terrible idea, *non*-Zionist, anti-Zionist. Now Zionism's great goal should be to have a just society inside Israel, achieve peace through compromise with the Palestinians, and adopt Jewish and humanitarian values. That's it. One of the goals of my kind of Zionism is more social equality in Israel. So for me, Zionism can be adapted to 2007 and 2050. But we have a long way to go.

Shabtai Shavit   It very much disappoints me, and it proves to me that the balance between the Jewish religious and traditional ingredients vis-à-vis Western liberalism and Western values and norms in the equation of the existence of Israel is somehow being distorted. Now, the Post-Zionist trend says to me that these people who represent this new thinking have become detached from the Jewish legacy, from Jewish tradition, from Jewish values and norms. Now, partly, this detachment is the result of the more radical, fundamental, ultra-rightist trends in Judaism nowadays here. I consider myself very Jewish, but at the same time, I very much oppose the ultra-right Judaism, which is being represented by various groups now in Israel, settlers, those people who call not to obey the laws of the country, those extremists who defy law and order. So in a way, we are witnessing a dangerous development in Jewish people and, especially, here in Israel. Instead of doing whatever is necessary to strengthen the connections among the various groups within the Jewish people, we are witnessing a divisive trend.

Yehuda Avner   After what has happened to us, how can these people, post-Holocaust, make sense if this experiment called "Israel" is either vaporized by Iran or is corrupted ideologically from within by the Post-Zionists? But yesterday [February 10, 2007], Shabbat, Mimi and I had around our table five grandchildren, kids who are now in the army. They are not what you would call "right-wingers." They volunteered for battle units, as did their parents, and what you hear from them is patriotism. In many ways, they are superior to my generation. In our time, it was so easy—you had the Holocaust; you had the British to fight; you had a country to build. Because of the sense of commitment of my grandchildren and their sophistication of understanding, I am fully optimistic.

Abraham Foxman   "Zionism" was made a dirty word in the U.N.—or they tried to make it so. The enemies of Israel tried to stigmatize Zionism. The Jewish community was not knowledgeable, comfortable enough, to combat it in a real sense. One way to fight anti-Zionism was to say, "I am a Zionist." Jews were not ready to wear those buttons—some were. There is still this political stigma because of ignorance about Zionism.

The Post-Zionism debate to me is nonsense—it's for people who write columns and have conferences. What does it *mean*? As long as Israel is a Jewish state, as long as it takes responsibility that it's a home for all Jews who need to come, Post-Zionism is nothing. Israel is a *Jewish* state, and that's what Zionism is all about.

Chapter 21

LOOKING TO THE FUTURE

Joshua Matza   Israel today has a 6.6 percent GDP [gross domestic product]! I pray that it will continue; I would like to see my country flourishing. At the same time, I am head of the [Israel] Bonds. We have to raise money for Israel, but with such a GDP and with such investment in Israel, I am asking myself whether they will continue to ask me to raise debt for them—it's not money; we are giving Israel more *debt*—if they don't need it anymore. And I answer, "Yes. Bonds are not only money, bonds are a message of a *bond* between Israel and the Jews all over the world, and we have to keep this message by selling bonds because Israel is very interested in Jewry all around the world. Without the help of the Jews in the Diaspora, especially those from the United States, Israel couldn't reach this level."

Zalman Shoval   One of the reasons why the economy is doing so well is that mainly as a result of Bibi's [Benjamin Netanyahu's] economic policies, it found a way to stand on its own two feet, to be less dependent on the government. And it's continuing. Even the Olmert government doesn't interfere in that.

Rafi Eitan   The whole world—I'm talking about the *free* world—is changing: we have climatic change and changing communications. For the last fifty years, I have been a businessman, and today I'm able to work very easily in America, on the one hand, and in India or China. My group does mainly agriculture projects, where we have expertise, and it's very easy for us to find areas where we can contribute, and we go there and manage things easily from one center. That was impossible fifty years ago.

Take Cuba, for example. When we started working there in 1991, there was no direct telephone from Israel to Cuba; we had to put in a special exchange in London, and we telephoned to Havana from there. And today, I can *see* the man I'm talking with! That was not possible just fifteen years ago. That's an amazing revolution.

Simcha Waisman   I go often to Israel, and there have been big changes. It has become very modern, very *Americanized*. Maybe I'm wrong, but there's nothing wrong; they're going forward. That's what the young generation wants.

Joshua Matza   When we come back to Israel and land at Lod [Ben-Gurion Airport]—it is always with my wife; we have seven grandchildren in Israel—the first thing she says to me is, "Where can we find such skies in the world?" Of course, not in New York! Look at the sky [Mr. Matza was interviewed on an overcast, muggy day in May]. And this is the summer!

And then, there are all the buildings. Of course, it is development, but my big impression—it's of Jerusalem—is that we are building *history*. After four years in New York, it's impossible for me to drive in Jerusalem because I don't recognize the roads—there is always a new one. We are building history in Jerusalem, and it's something for eternity. It is my joy to see it growing and growing and growing, and they are really special buildings.

Raanan Gissin   Israeli society has changed tremendously, from six hundred fifty thousand to close to seven million [including the Arab population]; from an economy of $50 million a year to $140 billion; from an income of about $500 per capita when the state was established to $20,000. It's amazing, an unprecedented achievement.

Of course, when you have this kind of rapid growth, in all aspects, it's like a child growing up—the legs are a little bit long, and there is a certain disharmonious development. A little boy grows up, and suddenly he's six feet tall, but his mind is still the mind of a baby. And Israel finds itself on its sixtieth anniversary in this process, so certain parts of the body grow disproportionally. But, eventually, it will all balance. Now we can help it.

Unlike the human body, which is a natural process, here it depends very much on what we do. And right now, the place where we need to concentrate most of all is really reforms in government, in our leaders and how leaders are elected and the screening of leaders—mentally, physically, morally—because somehow we developed certain aspects in our political culture that need to be corrected. I'm not despairing, like others, and I'm not pessimistic because deep down I believe that we have the capacity for change, and we're a very vigorous society.

Malcolm Hoenlein   You know, people just expect and take the many miracles for granted—the military, the security situation—because there is no rational explanation for Israel to *be* there. Look at what surrounds it! Look at the odds! Look at what they had to overcome in '48, in '56, in '73, *every time*. And people are very quick to criticize, as we saw in Lebanon [in the summer of 2006], without knowing the facts, buying into the lies and buying into the criticisms, instead of stepping back and saying, "What a privilege this is! That we're the generation that was given back the Jewish state, that saw Jerusalem reunified!" To get up in the morning and say, "What did I do to have *earned* this privilege, to have seen the miracles that my grandparents, and their grandparents, would have done anything to have seen even *one* of?"

We have seen the prophetic vision of the ingathering of the exiles in our lifetime—the Jews of Ethiopia, of Syria, of Russia, of Yemen have all come home! And the Talmud says that this is the greatest day in the creation of the world. Who realizes that we've seen a world created? Who talks about it? Neither Israelis nor Americans nor Jews anywhere do. We get so caught up if there's a scandal; man, everybody's into it, everybody talks about it. What about the *miracles*? What about the *privilege*? What about our obligation and our responsibility?

All generations to come will be judged by what we do—jeopardize it or protect it. The Torah describes two kinds of an inheritance: a *yerusha* and a *moresha*. *Yerusha* is an inheritance—it's yours to do with what you wish; a *moresha* is something given to you in trust. And the Torah says there are two things that are a *moresha*: Torah and Israel—that our job is to protect it and to assure that it will be there for future generations, to assure its security, its sanctity, its wholeness, its vitality, its vibrancy. And even if we don't *live* there, we'll be judged for that as well. But at least: what did we do to assure that it will be there for us and our children and our grandchildren?

What's going on in the world? Do European Jews and French Jews now not thank God that there's an Israel? You go into a real estate place in Tel Aviv or Jerusalem or Netanya, and they don't speak Hebrew or English: they speak French. So this is not past history; we're talking always about the future. History for us is about the *future*. And it troubles me a lot that people become complacent, and young Israelis are not taught the specialness of

Israel and the privilege of it, so why should they die for it? Why should they fight for something that's not special, that's not unique, that's not holy?

Look at [Abu Musab al-] Zarqawi: our eyes are on Jerusalem; keep the focus on Jerusalem. We don't talk with the same commitment, the same fervor, about Israel, about Jerusalem, that they do. Well, as a famous general said, "Wars in the twenty-first century will be determined by will and perception about enemies killed or troops captured." They have the will—they're proving it every day. We have to have it; we have to have a rekindled spirit and appreciation, and our young people don't have it. And, above all, they're ignorant. We can talk about the crisis in our high schools; our kids don't know, and every poll that we did, even minimalist as they are, shows that the level of ignorance is astounding: even the kids in the Jewish schools don't know. And they can't make the case because it's too late when they go to campus. If they're not inoculated and they don't know how to answer, we lose them. And then they're on the other side, and everybody says, "Oh, how could it be? Our best kids are arguing against Israel!"

Well, what did you teach them? What did you tell them? Did parents sit down with their eight- and nine-year-old kids, who saw all summer long [in 2006] the images of Lebanon, and try to explain it to them, tell them that these are the lies and show them the pictures that Reuters put out and all the other lies and distortions about what Israel's role was and how many people were killed in Qana and all the rest? They *didn't*.

Rafi Eitan   The young generation in Israel is very good, very devoted to Israel. You could feel the example during the last, short war. It was a small war, by the way. But the reservists were 100 percent; once they were called, they came, all of them. That's a good example.

We don't live quietly. I'm not afraid. I feel our strength. I know what we can do. And I am sure that we are here to stay.

Moshe Sharon   There is no possibility of normal life for Jews in this country; there is no such thing. You live in a territory that is terrorist, *bloodthirsty*, a bloodthirsty culture and a civilization that doesn't want to accept anything but the Muslim world. And they will do everything possible to destroy the State of Israel, so you'll never, ever be in a normal state. If ever we come to a position where we say we are sitting under our fig tree, then we are lost.

Our eyes must be open; the army must be prepared—I call it "cleaning the stables and preparing for war." There is no such thing that you can sit down and enjoy yourself and say that we don't have to think about war anymore, that peace has come to this world. There is no such thing. Forget about the word "peace"; forget about the word "normalcy." There is nothing normal. We Jews have never been normal people. And the State of Israel is not a normal state because we are surrounded by an Arab, Islamic world, *full stop*.

Our survival is a miracle. And the only thing that keeps us is nuclear power—if we have it; at least, they *think* we have it—that's enough. Now they understand it themselves, and they want to create nuclear power, first of all, to destroy the state—that's the easiest thing to do. For them, it's an abnormal situation: how is it that the Jews established a state, which negates all the Koran? It's a reverse of history. As far as the Muslims are concerned, the Arabs are concerned, this state cannot continue existing; it is something that is absolutely impossible to have. The State of Israel existing in this part of the world on Islamic territory, Jews ruling over Muslims? Never heard of such a thing!

This creates a situation whereby there is no hope, *ever*, for a normal state. The Jews have got to sleep with their swords at their sides. That's it! If you don't sleep with your sword at your side, you are going to find yourself with your throat slit. This is the situation, and the minute the leaders of Israel come to understand it, we will have good leadership. But we have got these politically correct "nicies" going around, talking about the Palestinian state—in effect, they are saying: we want to create the guillotine by which the heads of the Jews are going to be cut. The Palestinian state is a guillotine.

Bobby Brown   I'm optimistic that the State of Israel will continue. But we're going to have hard times, and we have to continue to be smart. Maybe if the whole world had loved the Jews from the beginning, we would have all assimilated and disappeared already. At Passover, we say, "In every generation someone comes up who wants to destroy the Jewish people." And that's what we see. We have a strange situation that we can't afford to ever lose—we did lose once, namely in the Holocaust. I don't know if the Jewish people could ever take that kind of a loss again, but I do believe that we are strong, and we will find solutions because I'm not sure that I would want to live in a world where we don't have a future. So yes, we have a difficult future, but we will succeed. And yes, we will continue to grow. We've got to live!

Yehiel Kadishai   The Jews are a strong and wise nation. We are so strong that the British, the Germans, the Americans, the Dutch, and the Danes won't be able to destroy us. Not even *the Jews* will be able to destroy this country!

INDEX

Page numbers in italics indicate illustrations.
Names in boldface indicate interviewees.